C000205830

Ove Neediness and Get the Love You Want

Jack Ito, Ph.D.

Loving Solutions Publishing · Lawrenceville, Georgia

OVERCOME NEEDINESS AND GET THE LOVE YOU WANT

by Jack Ito

Published by:
Loving Solutions Publishing
Suite 405
3350 Sweetwater Road
Lawrenceville, GA 30044 USA
orders@lovingsolutionspublishing.com

Unattributed quotations are by Jack Ito

Scripture quotations taken from The Holy Bible, *New International Version, NIV*. Copyright 1973, 1978, 1984, 2011 by Biblica, Inc. Used by permission. All rights reserved worldwide.

ISBN, print ed.   978-0-9890999-4-3

Library of Congress Control Number: 2016909174

DEDICATION

For Toshie. My wife, and girlfriend, for life.

CONTENTS

Introduction   *xi*

1 How Neediness Is Messing Up Your Life   **1**
Needy idealization—seeing other people as they really aren't
Needy behavior—controlling too much, protecting too little
Needy thinking—fears and doubts replayed over and over
Needy solutions—ineffectively getting love and attention
Needy identity—who am I without you?

2 How You Became Needy   **29**
Anxious attachment—you make me mad, don't leave me
I learned too well—the wrong things
Arrested development—I'm not finished growing yet
Partial success—I never knew I could get even more
Temporary neediness—I wasn't always this way

3 Creating the New Secure You   **41**
Stop thinking and start doing
Anxiety problem, or neediness problem?
Working with and without professional help
Learn to trust experience more than thoughts
Choosing role models—your mental guides

4 Dating Like a Secure Person   **61**
Avoiding your natural match—other needy people
Why secure partners are better
Being secure before, during, and after your date
Date many, commit to few, marry one
Following the path from dating to engaging

5 Loving and Relating Like a Secure Person   77
The eight relationship killing needy behaviors you must
eliminate from your life

6 A Secure Way to Find a Marriage Partner   109
Learn to use your heart and head at the same time
Don't shop till you know what you want
Shaping up for your ideal partner
The right and wrong reasons to marry
10 Steps to finding Mr. or Mrs. Right

7 Getting a Reluctant Partner to Commit to Marriage   121
Why love alone won't do it
Getting married is under your control
Why men marry and what that means for you
5 Requirements for getting married and staying married
Your commitment may be blocking his commitment

8 Slaying the Green Eyed Monster of Jealousy   143
Self-assessment—How jealous are you?
Jealousy is an addiction secure people don't have
Your jealousy may promote your partner's unfaithfulness
End jealousy by changing your beliefs about yourself
Jealousy is a measure of neediness—not how much you love

9 Staying Secure and Attractive in a Relationship Crisis 159
Living together while being emotionally separated
Staying emotionally connected while living apart
Seeing clearly when your relationship is over
Picking up the pieces of a broken relationship and doing better

10 Securely Managing Everyday Conflicts   171

Your partner stops saying, "I love you" • your partner starts coming home late • your partner doesn't return your texts/calls • your partner doesn't tell you where he or she is going• your partner becomes angry and withdraws • your partner is physically, emotionally, sexually, or financially abusive • your partner is blaming • your family and friends are stressing you out

11 How to Help a Needy Partner   191

(Give this chapter to your partner)
Are you needy too, or just codependent?
Scratch a partner's neediness itch, get a relationship infection
Stopping seven of your partner's worst needy behaviors
Encouraging your partner to have secure behavior

12 Living a Secure Life   215

Live without illusions, seeing clearly in the real world
Be in control of your future, design your life
Be an active participant in life—no more waiting and hoping
Multiply your successes
Live life on purpose, for a purpose
Keep your balance, many eggs—many baskets
Make new friends for a new beginning

Appendix: If You Would Like Extra Help   *237*

Glossary   *239*

About the Author   *241*

Also by Coach Jack   *243*

Index   *247*

INTRODUCTION

Every second of every day, there is some relationship being damaged or lost because of neediness. But neediness is not a disease. It is not genetic. It is not inevitable. And, it can be completely overcome. In every relationship that I help to reconcile, there is some aspect of overcoming neediness. I work with the real down and out relationships. You know, the ones where one spouse wants out or cares little for the emotional well being of the other. Most counselors believe the best thing to do in this situation is to help the couple to end their relationship—amicably or otherwise. Well, I can agree that in many aspects that is easier. But, most of the time it is not necessary.

What is necessary is that one person have the strength and the love to do something that is absolutely necessary to improve the relationship. They must stop being needy. They will have to give up trying to get their partners to love them and instead focus on being secure, being loving, and having good boundaries. None of my clients will become doormats or people who just shower their partners with love, love, love. Because, contrary to what you may have heard or read, in a bad relationship, these actions will not get you the love you want. If you have ever tried to save a relationship by showering your partner with love, you will know exactly what I mean.

If you just give in to your partner's wishes, it will just get you disrespect, while just giving love, love, love will get you rejected, rejected, rejected. And, if you are needy, when your efforts to get your partner to change his or her mind about you do not work, you will go right back to the needy behaviors that drove him or her away in the first place.

What is the way forward in these situations, without driving your partner away? A big part of it is overcoming your neediness. Needy partners vacillate between chastising their partners for not being the way they want them to be and placating their partners for fear of being rejected. The alternative is being able to see and accept your partner's positive aspects as well as limitations, and to be able to love him or her anyhow—using boundaries, as necessary, to prevent ongoing damaging behavior from your partner. Good love is tough love, but it is neither demanding nor abusive.

This book was written for people who don't know how to love this way. It is to help them make the transformation from needy to secure. It provides the same kind of instruction that my coaching clients are receiving to overcome their neediness, become more attractive partners for their mates, and to improve their relationships. Transformation means change. It means giving up holding on to something that you have now, so that you can have something even better to hold on to later. It certainly will mean giving up holding on to your fear of rejection. It will also mean giving up on making your happiness the focus of your interactions with your partner.

To get love, we must first give love. This is the opposite of what needy people do. Needy people make receiving love a higher priority than giving love, and so end up with relationships where both people are competing to get their needs met and neither is really satisfied.

One of the most important changes you will be making in becoming secure is learning to focus on the long term outcome of your actions rather than the short term. This means that "What do I do now?" is not the question to start with. The question to start with is, "What kind of future do I want to have?" The next question is, "What changes do I need to make in *myself* that will enable me to have that future?" Only when those two questions have been answered do we know what we need to do now.

The people that I work with as a relationship coach usually are stuck on the question of how to make someone else love them. The change they need to make is to ask, "How can I change from being someone who tries to make others love me to someone that others really want to love?" The answer to this question is the answer to how to become secure. The essence of becoming secure is becoming a person who others desire instead of someone others want to avoid or run away from. People all over the world are looking for someone who will truly love them; not someone with insecurities they will forever need to take care of. A secure person is the former; a needy person is the latter. Are you spending all of your effort trying to find someone to love you, or trying to find someone to love? Trying to get your partner to love you, or trying to love your partner? Which one do you think has the best chance of getting you the love you want?

If you are only a little needy, it will not take so long for you to overcome your neediness. You can probably do it on your own. If, however, you are very needy, becoming someone who can love securely will take months of rewarding, but emotionally difficult work. It will help you a lot if, in the early stages, you can work with a therapist or relationship coach. This is not because it takes months to learn what to do—learning what to do is the easy part. This book will tell you what to do. It's because in the first few months your fears will be most intense and your willpower at its lowest. You will benefit from encouragement and guidance as you make necessary changes.

Most needy people know that some of the things they are doing are extremely harmful for their relationships. Even so, they find it hard or impossible to stop doing them. Usually, they are just able to temporarily suppress their behaviors. If you can work with a professional, it will help you to stay on track long enough to have many small successes. That's very encouraging when you are trying to change. Every great success is built from many small ones.

Because relationship coaching is fairly new to most people, I would like to take a moment to point out some key differences to help you decide which is best for you, if you do decide to get extra help.

Counselors are excellent at being gentle and empathetic. They work at their client's pace with more participation by the client during the session. This allows clients to explore issues as they like, with minimal direction. The emphasis of counselors is on the health and well being of their clients. "Emotional well being," is the catchphrase to think of when you think of counseling. Because counselors are providing psychological treatment, counseling can also be billed to your insurance company. Another key difference is that counselors often do not have the skills to help someone reconcile with a partner who does not want to reconcile. In such a situation, counselors usually move the client toward acceptance and amicable divorce.

If you have limited time to make changes, perhaps because of a crisis in your relationship, you will probably want to use coaching rather than counseling. Relationship coaches often have a psychology degree (for example, I am a licensed clinical psychologist), but they are less concerned with your emotional well being than your achievement of success. The coach identifies key skills to help you to achieve your goals and teaches you to use them, whether you are emotionally ready to use them or not. There is no psychological diagnosis, and very little exploration of issues. "Learning to succeed," is the catchphrase to think of when you think of coaching. A relationship coach will make some adjustments, being gentle or tough, as needed, to fit your personality and get you further than you have gone before. A small number of coaches specialize in reconciling relationships in which one partner wants out. That is my specialty and you will see glimpses of that in this book.

I am not at all biased against counselors. Overcoming neediness is not just about learning what to do—it's learning how to manage your emotions at the same time. If you decide to work with a relationship coach, it will greatly help you if you make provision for getting emotional support from a family member, friend, or counselor. There is no reason that you can't have both a coach and a counselor, since the methods and focus of each will be different. When you combine solid instruction and practice with emotional support, your chances of becoming secure are much greater. Many of my clients also have their own counselor.

Although it is ideal to be able to work with professionals, there is much that you can do on your own. And, if you are not pressed for time, it makes sense to see how much you can do on your own before getting professional help. The methods in this book will help you to improve your relationships. If you need more help after that, you can still get it. Indeed, many relationships have been saved through relatively small changes. The trick is to know what changes to make, to make them consistently, and to never go back to the old, unsuccessful behavior.

In this book, you will quickly learn that I will hold you responsible for making changes and will not allow you to use excuses or blame your partner for your behaviors. My aim is neither to please you nor to shock you, but rather to wake you up to realities that you have never noticed. You have been living in the fantasy world of a needy person and it is time for you to learn that real life doesn't work the way that you think it does and *it's never going to.* When you learn how it really works, especially in regard to relationships, you will have far greater success with more love and romance. The end results will be worth your hard work.

I have been asked many times to write such a book and have hesitated. I know that the things that I must write in a book like this will be unpopular. Maybe you have already become uncomfortable with what I am saying and are feeling the urge to blame your partner for all of your problems. That's how I started out in my early relationships. It's not easy to face the responsibility that I am placing squarely on your shoulders. In some cases, you may wish that you never heard of this book. If you are like most people, you won't want to do the exercises included in it. They are not easy, they are not enjoyable, and they don't bring immediate results—three characteristics that are most often demanded by people today.

What I have learned over the years is that while most people do look for easy answers, there are some people who are willing to do whatever it takes. These people are successful at running their businesses, getting in shape, overcoming disabilities, and having better relationships. It is just such people who will benefit most from this book. They will not just read this book and say, "Yeah, I know that's what I should do." They actually will make the changes detailed in it. They will expect it to be hard at first, but they will also expect to have success in the end.

I encourage you to stop thinking of relationships as magical or as something that happens because of luck. The reality is that there are very straightforward principles to relationships, just as there are to getting into shape, tuning up a car, or running a successful business. It only seems like luck to people who don't know and practice these principles.

Also, you should not be guided by the percentage of people who have successful relationships. That should not be your guide to action or giving up. What really matters is that some people are successful. Focusing on what these people do, will also help you to be successful. Learn what works and do it. Don't concern yourself with all the people that don't. If you are climbing a mountain, don't pay attention to how far you can possibly fall. Pay attention to that next rock hold above you that will get you closer to the top.

As you can see, I'm not writing this book for everyone. I am writing it for people who are serious about becoming secure, who want to learn to love others without fear, and for those who are willing to take reasonable risks of abandonment and rejection in order to have relationships that will transcend any that they have had before.

It is also my hope that I may give those who don't have a relationship with God the sense of hope and security that comes from such a relationship. The God of the Bible is my model for being secure. He is very loving, yet has very strong boundaries. He does not want to be rejected, but He is not afraid of it. He does what is in our best interest without regard for whether we will approve or be angry with Him. He loves us so much, He died for us. And those who come to Him can have a relationship with Him forever. For me, there is nothing else in this world that offers a better example of love and security.

If you continue your current course, without overcoming your neediness, what do you see for your future? Will things turn out the way you want them to? Are you more or less likely to be in a close, loving relationship in the years to come? To be secure is to consider not only what is easiest for today, but what is best for tomorrow. Being secure also means taking responsibility for your life and for improving it. It means holding yourself responsible for your happiness rather than holding your partner responsible for your happiness. Are you willing to decide to be the one to improve your relationship—your life—even if your significant other makes no changes at all?

In the short term, it's always easier to blame someone else for our problems than to take responsibility for them and do something about them. This is particularly true when it comes to becoming a secure person. Most people's insecurity started in childhood. The more insecure a person is, the more readily it can be traced back to his or her family of origin. As a coach, it is not my desire to explore the depths of your insecurities or to find their roots. That's because we can't pull those roots out. They are there. But we can be like the flowers that grow over the septic tank. The depth of our pains can give depth to our empathy for others, which is the basis for truly loving rather than needing; for considering what is most kind and loving for someone else.

The aim of this book is not to help you understand yourself better or to resolve your internal conflicts. It is not a *therapeutic* book. This is a practical book about skills and actions. It follows a coaching model rather than a psychological one. I will, however, offer some advice for coping with your feelings during the process. After all, coping is a skill, too. I won't, however, be able to give you emotional support while you practice your new skills. This book is not sufficient in your quest to have a healthy relationship. You will also need to get support from a friend, a counselor, God, a family member, or a support group. You are not likely to be successful without at least one of these on your side.

Finally, and hopefully, the work you do on yourself will have an unexpected benefit for you—raising your self-esteem. *Competence increases confidence*, which is the essence of self-esteem. Even if you master even a few of the principles in this book, you will be more competent in your relationships, other people will like you more, and you will like yourself more, too. You will be able to get more of the love you want.

HOW NEEDINESS IS MESSING UP YOUR LIFE

Neediness creates emotional fireworks when relationships are new. When needy people find others who love them, all their feelings of emptiness disappear. It's like finally being able to scratch an itch that that they couldn't reach before. It is a great relief for needy people to find partners—people to love who will actually love them back. All their doubts and fears vanish and are replaced by euphoria. The initial experience of new love by needy people is like a rush that one could otherwise only get from drugs.

If being needy creates such wonderful, intense, passionate feelings of love, then what could possibly be wrong with it? This chapter spells out the numerous sacrifices that needy people make in order to have only brief periods of passion. This passion exists at the beginning of their relationships and when making up after a breakup or serious conflict. Both of these times have more to do with relief than love.

What is neediness?

There are several characteristics of needy people. Each of these characteristics tends to go unnoticed by needy people who believe that these needy characteristics are normal. After all, it is all they have ever known. Each of these characteristics causes needy people to behave in ways that make long-term, happy, healthy relationships very difficult. Because you are reading this book, you have already begun to recognize your neediness. It will help to continue to discover the differences between being needy and being secure. The more you can discover, the more you can change. The more you can change, the better your relationships will become.

Idealization—the "love is blind" phenomenon

Many of the characteristics of needy people are true for everyone who is in a relationship for the first time. That head-over-heels feeling, the desire to be with the other person all the time, and the belief that the other person is the best person in the world. For secure (non-needy) people, this initial intense feeling starts to die down and is replaced by a deeper love. This love is less intense, but no less real. In fact, it's more real. Secure people begin to see flaws in their partners, accept them and work around them. If they can't accept them, then they eventually tire of putting up with them and lose interest in their relationships. They break up before getting in even deeper and avoid commitment even though at first they may have felt intense desire for the other. People who are only somewhat needy may commit too soon, but then realize their mistake and break up. Completely needy people commit too soon, are blind to their mistakes and never break up. They persist until they are rejected and even after that.

Needy people continue to idealize and romanticize their relationships. They believe they have found their soul mates and no one is going to convince them otherwise—not even their partners. Their partners are idealized and idolized and continue to be seen as the *only* possible partners for them—partners who could never be replaced by another, because there is simply no one better in the world. Once the needy person latches on, she (or he) *can't* let go. To let go would mean risking the loss of the best thing she could ever have in life. It would mean a lifelong longing for that which she could never have again. It would mean the end of happiness as she knows it. Breakup for her means total annihilation. Breakup would make her feel like life was not worth living. While this is normal in our teen years, it is not normal or healthy in adulthood.

This idealization continues even in the face of contradictory evidence. Even when her (or his) partner no longer returns her phone calls or texts, even when he treats her badly, and even when he outright rejects her, she still believes he is the perfect mate for her. At these times, she is willing to do almost anything to prevent the loss of this "perfect" person. The mere thought of losing him becomes unbearable. To suggest to such a needy person that she could find someone else who would love her and treat her better is sacrilege. She doesn't want to hear it because she can't believe it. She believes no one could possibly make her feel the way that her partner has made her feel.

This idealization of the other person is one of the most damaging things that could ever happen to the relationship. Because the other person is not seen as he (or she) really is, he is never really loved. The needy person is in love with her *idea* or *fantasy representation* of the other person and not the actual person. In secure relationships, we see our partners clearly, warts and all, and accept both the good and the bad. We don't believe that our partners are the only ones in the world that we could ever have relationships with, or be in love with. But our partners are the ones we have chosen to have relationships with and to commit to.

When someone suggests to us that we could find someone better, we can admit the reality of that. We may choose, however, to turn down others because of our satisfaction with and commitment to the partners that we have. We don't live in fear that we could never find someone else to love or someone else to love us. It's not fear that drives us, but rather our conscious choices. The needy person, on the other hand, believes she has no choice. She is obsessed and compelled to hang on to her partner at all costs. And it is this behavior that ultimately leads to the destruction of her relationship. Destruction comes because her partner can never live up to her fantasy. She will spend a great deal of energy trying to get him to do that. Ultimately, this will make her partner feel needed, but not loved.

Controlling behavior

When needy people start to encounter differences that they don't like in their significant others, those differences become a threat. The differences don't fit with their belief that they have perfect partners. Unlike secure people who know that differences are to be expected, for needy people differences are not tolerable. For needy people any differences in values or desires mean that something is either wrong with them or their partners. Needy people don't want to accept differences, but try to eliminate them. This is tied to their fear that differences will lead to the end of their relationships.

The things that needy people don't like are not necessarily problems in healthy relationships. For example, one's partner may merely be going out for an evening with friends, something that he regularly did before starting a relationship with her. But, in the needy person's world a fearful question arises—"Why would he want to go out without me?" Although the question itself is not a bad one and could be easily answered by secure people, it is a mystifying question for the needy person. It signals "danger!" and makes her anxious.

Secure people understand other secure people. They know that it's not healthy to always be with the same person and that getting away to be with one's friends is important for maintaining social relationships, for blowing off steam, for relaxing, and for getting some space. All of these things help to maintain a healthy relationship. Rather than experiencing anxiety, secure people use this time apart to have their own rest or recreation. After which, they will have more desire to be with their partners.

In needy people's minds, however, their partners wanting to go out without them takes on sinister meanings and they cannot relax at all while their partners are gone. They will torture themselves with questions that they may later interrogate their partners with: *Is he getting tired of me? Why doesn't she want me*

4

to go with her? If I'm really important to him, then why wouldn't he want me to interact with his friends? Is her love starting to cool off? What is he talking about with his friends? What is she doing with them? Were there other women/men there? and so on. This is because needy people want to spend all of their time with their partners. They believe this is because they love their partners. So, if their partners don't want to spend all of their time with them, then maybe they are falling out of love. And, if they are falling out of love, then they may leave for someone else. This sends needy people into panic mode. All of these problems are not caused by their partners going out, but by their fear of abandonment and isolation. A fear that will cause them to do and say things that will damage their relationships.

Anything which can be construed as a risk to the relationship, whether it actually is or not, becomes grist for the mill in the mind of the needy person. And she will think about these things over and over, working herself up into a quiet desperation. That quiet desperation in itself does nothing to harm the relationship. But in her attempts to calm her fears, the needy person starts to seek reassurance and she starts to complain.

She will complain about his going out with his friends when she has to sit home with none. She will complain that he doesn't include her on his outings. She will complain that he doesn't contact her while he's gone—not sending updates on what is happening while she's at home worrying. She complains when he comes home late. She complains that he didn't used to have to go out with friends and now he does. If she does somehow manage to keep herself from making these comments when he comes home, she will manage to behave either irritable enough or sad enough throughout the week for him to ask what's wrong. Then she will tell him the same things. Either way, these complaints will come out.

The effect of all the needy person's comments, questions, and complaints results in one of two reactions in the beginning. Either her (or his) partner immediately recognizes her as needy and starts to distance himself from her, or else her partner apologizes or reassures her. Unfortunately, reassuring her will only temporarily make things better. It calms her anxieties, but only until the next time. If her partner continues to go out and see his friends, then he will have to reassure her more and more, each time dealing with increasing neediness. Eventually, he will either have to give up going out with his friends or stop caring about her. Either one of these is the beginning of the end for the relationship.

This example was only about one particular behavior—that of one's partner going out with friends. It holds true for needy men as much as it does for needy women. And, it also applies to other things partners might do such as spending time with their families, working on their careers, having solitary hobbies, or indeed anything which voluntarily takes them away from a needy person (since a job is not seen as voluntary, it does not cause the same reaction). From needy people's perspectives, if their partners really loved them, then their partners would want to spend every moment with them. In their minds, even when their partners have to be at work or with family, they should really have a longing to be with them again—not be enjoying themselves. The idea that a partner would have private thoughts or activities that he or she does not want to share is uncomfortable for the needy person..

Needy people often do not recognize their controlling behaviors until it is too late. Eventually, their controlling behaviors drive their partners out the door or into the arms of another. At this time, their partners will list all of the person's controlling behaviors and how they felt trapped and miserable in their relationships. They will talk about how they tried to make their needy partners happy, but how they never could. They talk about the impossible standards their needy partners had for them. And they will talk about how their needy partners made them feel like nothing they ever did was good enough.

More than anything else, for secure people, it is this controlling behavior which makes it difficult to have a relationship with a needy person. Rather than being an equal partner, the partner of a needy person has to become more of a parent. He or she has to continually take care of the insecurities and demands of the needy person. It's a thankless job that eventually leads to relationship burnout.

Poor boundaries

Boundaries are not what we tell other people. Boundaries are the decisions that we make about what *we* will or will not allow in our lives. For example, when we hang up on someone who is talking to us rudely, that's a boundary. If we choose to eat one piece of cake instead of two because two are not good for us, that's a boundary. In short, boundaries are the decisions that we make about *our own* behavior.

Needy people have poor boundaries. Because their main fear is losing their partners, all of their behaviors are weighed against that possibility. For example, if a needy person's partner is being disrespectful and rude, she (or he) may decide to put up with it rather than walk away. If her partner is selfish and treats her badly in other ways, possibly even physically abusing her, she will put up with it. She will allow all these things because, although she hates these things (like anyone would), she hates the possibility of losing her partner even more. In essence she fails to change her behavior to a way which would prevent her from continuing to be disrespected or abused. She is lacking necessary boundaries.

Rather than having good boundaries, needy people will complain—saying how they don't like, hate, or won't stand for, what their partners are doing. But, if their partners continue to do these things—despite their protests, they will just continue to complain. If their partners get really upset about their constant complaining, then they will back off and most likely shut up. Again this is because needy people are afraid if they complain more, then their partners will leave them. So, without boundaries and without the ability to continue to complain, needy people feel stuck, hopeless, and unhappy. But, no matter how unhappy they become, they won't start to use healthy boundaries. Being rejected by their spouses is even worse to them than being unhappy and prevents them from using boundaries.

7

Of course what needy people don't realize is that having boundaries *protects* their relationships. People with boundaries are much *less* likely to lose their relationships than people with no boundaries at all. To help clients to understand this, I tell them this story which I call *The Story of the Three Bitches.*

Once upon a time, there were three lovely ladies who each went out on a date with a man.

During the first lady's date, the man called her a "bitch" in a really nasty and mean way. But, because she did not want to make a scene in public or scare him away, she didn't say anything about it and just continued on her date.

During the second lady's date, the man called her a "bitch" in a really nasty and mean way. When he did this, she immediately spoke to him in a very stern voice and told him, "You have no right to talk to me like that. I don't want you to ever say that to me again. And, if you ever say that to me again, that will be the last time you will ever see me." Then, she carried on with her date.

During the third lady's date, the man called her a "bitch" in a really nasty and mean way. This lady didn't say anything about it, but instead, as soon as the man said that, she got up, left the building and went home by herself.

After this story, I ask my clients which of these ladies had the best boundary and which the worst. Needy people usually guess correctly that the third lady had the best boundary, although they admit that they have never done such a thing themselves. Usually needy people behave like lady number two. They complain enough to let their partner know they don't like something, but they don't actually do anything about it. In this situation, the man is likely to not call her a bitch…until they have a fight sometime later on in their relationship. Then, he will call her a "bitch" because he knows that she doesn't like it, and that she will put up with it. Her complaining has given him power and makes him more likely to repeat his bad behavior at another time.

If the third lady's date calls her or emails her and apologizes, and if she wants to give him a second chance, how likely do you think it is he will call her a bitch again? Not very likely. Not when they are getting along, and not when they have conflict. Why? Because he *knows* she will leave him if he does. This behavior never becomes a problem and does not deteriorate the relationship. People who are like lady number three rarely need relationship coaching.

What about the first lady? Although she doesn't use a boundary, neither does she empower her date by reacting. She may choose to behave like lady number three if this happens again, or she may decide that it is not that important to her and will let it go. So it is with boundaries. They must be used or not used. There is no in-between. Once used, they must be used consistently. Secure people don't use boundaries for every little thing—just for the ones they would not want to live with if they were to continue to happen.

People with good boundaries don't allow themselves to be repeatedly mistreated. After the first incident (which they can't prevent), they immediately begin to remove themselves from the relationship or at least from the immediate situation. This sets a healthy pattern for the relationship. It draws a line that their partners may not cross without risking the relationship. If at some point, their partners start to mistreat them again in any way, they can immediately remove themselves to stop the behavior from doing any more damage. The net result of this is far *less* conflict and also far more positive interaction.

It is not only connecting in a loving way, but also using good boundaries which preserves and strengthens relationships. This is true for every kind of relationship. Parents, for example, must have boundaries as well as loving behavior with their children in order to have a healthy relationship with them. Parents who allow their children to do whatever they want, whenever they want, are neither loving nor have good boundaries.

Some needy people don't use boundaries with their children, fearing that their children won't like them. And so they fail to set boundaries around bedtime, food, public behavior, self-care, homework, and the way their children talk to them. In these cases, their children don't appreciate their "patience" any more than their partners do. Instead, they turn into little monsters who stress their parents and take away their parents' joy in parenting. Such parents may find themselves wishing that they never had children at all. It's so sad because it was their own neediness that caused their children's bad behavior. It was their own neediness that ultimately led to their children rejecting them. What they feared (i.e. rejection) is what they created.

Contrast this with a secure parent who uses healthy boundaries. She (or he) has a number of rules and requirements for her children, and consistently enforces them. Her children don't continue to have temper tantrums from childhood to adulthood because such behavior simply does not manipulate a secure parent. The result of this is that her relationship to her children is better, there is more time for positive interaction, and she doesn't carry the stress of parenting into her marital relationship. Both the children and their parents enjoy the family more.

Steady, stable, and loving relationships are the things that needy people dream about. Needy people, rather than understanding that they create the instability, blame their children or their partners for their unruly behavior and feel like helpless victims. Their partners and children feel nagged and unmotivated to change. If there is to be any hope of a positive relationship for needy people, they must learn to show love and they must learn how to use boundaries. If they don't, their spouses and their children may both abandon them someday.

Focus on self

A needy person believes that almost everything that other people do relates to her (or him). It often never occurs to her that other people might have lives of their own. Such a thought is threatening. Because if her partner can have a life of his own, then it may mean that she is not necessary. And if she is not necessary, then maybe she will be dispensed with. She needs him to need her—to calm her fear of isolation and rejection. Everything that he does that demonstrates independence makes her feel threatened and so she will continually discourage him from growing. Just as needy parents can do this to their children, needy spouses can do this to each other.

It never occurs to the needy person that someone else having independent freedoms and activities may actually strengthen the relationship. That it's important for people to spend some time on their own. That doing so actually makes it more pleasant to come together again. So, when her husband wants to go out with his friends, instead of thinking how that's good for him, she will just think about how unfair it is for her to be left alone. She may intrude on his time by calling him or texting him several times while he's out with his friends. If she does restrain herself from contacting him, then she may expect that he will call her or text her. Rather than looking forward to seeing him, she will look forward to being reassured by him. For this reason, she is more likely to be accusatory when he comes home than she is to be friendly. She does not think about how he experiences her. She only thinks about how she experiences him.

Of course, just like the other behaviors of the needy person, this focus on one's self actually makes it more likely that she will end up alone. By not considering and allowing for her partner's needs, he will become more and more needy himself. But not in the same sense that she is. He will start to need space from her. He will start to need someone who is different from her. Her intrusiveness drives him away from her and toward someone else.

If you can stop focusing on your own needs and instead help your partner to get his or her needs met, then your relationship will actually become more secure. You can choose to recognize that he needs time away from you to spend with his friends, hobbies, or career. You can even encourage him to do this and give him the space to do it. Instead of becoming intrusive when

11

he's doing these activities, you can instead make it a point to welcome him back with open and loving arms. In this way, he will not only enjoy himself and find his needs met, but he will enjoy returning to you time and time again. He won't feel the need for additional space because he will have enough. By focusing on his needs, your needs for love and assurance will also be met.

In order for you to transition to this way of behaving, you have to learn to be able to take care of yourself in his absence. You need to learn how to reassure yourself instead of reaching out to him for reassurance. Stop thinking of it as his job to reassure you. Secure people don't need reassurance and continually seeking reassurance is not part of a healthy relationship. If he repeatedly reassures you, he is being codependent for your insecure behavior. He makes you temporarily feel better, but he is not helping you be better. If he can stop reassuring you, you can break your habit of seeking his reassurance. This, in turn, will help him to look forward to being with you more than before. If you can stop yourself from asking for his reassurance, you can also create this good result.

Prisoner of fear

As a needy person, you never feel completely at ease. Even in the midst of a loving relationship, you have doubts and remain vigilant to danger—to any sign of rejection. You can never be fully at ease because you don't believe that you could emotionally survive the loss of your relationship. You are sensitized to any comments that your partner makes which could be taken to mean he or she is losing interest in your relationship.

The secure person, on the other hand, can relax and go with the flow even when conditions are less than ideal. This is because she (or he) has an inner assurance that no matter what happens, her future can be good. She knows that there is an unlimited supply of love both within her and within others. She knows that relationships are to be enjoyed and that they don't always last, but even when they don't, she is confident that there is something new and maybe even better around the corner. She takes what her partner says at face value.

It is this self-assurance in the secure person which makes her relationships much more likely to be long-term. She will accept her partner on his own terms, be able to live and let live, and this will make her partner feel more comfortable with her.

A lot of work to others

If you have a regular need for reassurance, and you carefully scrutinize all the words and actions of your partner, your partner will inevitably begin to feel that you are a lot of work. He (or she) will have to keep secret things that might upset you, and will have to be careful about voicing his desires to do things which may make you feel anxious. He will need to check in with you regularly. He will need to hear your complaints about how he does things without considering how it makes you feel. And, because he actually is careful not to upset you and gets blamed anyhow, he will feel like he is in a no win situation. He will feel trapped and like a relationship with you is a lot of work. He will feel like he is in a seven-day-a-week job that he gets paid too little for.

Needy people become victims

Needy people have a healthy desire for a lot of intimacy in their relationships, but have behavior which actually creates more distance. Needy people often don't see themselves as having a problem because they become focused on their partners' behaviors. Their partners often tell them unkind things and behave in ways that make the needy person feel rather unimportant. Not only that, but their partners become progressively less affectionate as the relationship goes on. With a focus on these partner behaviors, the needy person looks, and feels, like a victim. Other people may start to advise her to get out or end her relationship. Because she can't bring herself to do this, this is the point where needy people often discover that they are really needy.

You see, people who are not needy (secure people) would end a relationship if they felt victimized and mistreated. But, a needy person wouldn't. People who have a needy partner can do *whatever* they want because, although needy people complain, they don't leave. In fact, they desperately clutch onto their relationship like it was their only source of oxygen. Because of that, they give away any kind of power they have to make changes—improvements to the relationship. The secure person does not fear losing her relationship, so does more effective things than criticize and complain. She uses boundaries to draw a line her partner may not cross.

Needy people have unrealistic expectations

Without boundaries, the power imbalance between the needy person and her partner grows as the relationship goes on. The relationship becomes vertical, with the needy person at the bottom. She (or he) may even be in a lower position than her own children, with her spouse at the top. She will know and feel that he does not consider her to be his equal. Not that the partner enjoys his position at the top. He often feels and behaves like a parent—having to both take care of and put up with the needy person's ineffective complaints and demands.

Needy people are seductively attractive at the beginning of relationships. They fall in love quickly and love intensely. They have the same intense, in-love feelings experienced by teenagers with their first crush. Their dates feel gratified to receive so much love and attention. If both of them are needy, the relationship is even more intense. They will declare each other to be "soul mates" and will shut out the rest of the world and anyone's dissenting opinions about their relationship. Warnings from others will go unheeded. There is nothing that can get between them—especially reality.

Eventually however, the needy person's partner will do something that will make the needy person feel like he is less intensely involved with her. For a secure person, this would be no big deal as she would also understand the initial intensity is giving way to a more relaxed, but deeper love. But where the secure person experiences comfort, the needy person experiences anxiety. As her partner needs time to himself, she feels hurt, or angry, or both. She will start to emotionally tug at her partner's coat to get him to stay in the bubble that they had together at the beginning of their relationship. He may give in at first, but will eventually resist. She will then become more angry with him, but desperately want his love and attention. She will appear erratic and moody. This will result in him also becoming moody and distant.

If they are both needy, they will both fight to get each other's attention and affection. Neither one will want to be the first to give it because of the fear of rejection and the obstinate belief that his or her partner should be the first to give in. This fighting can be maintained for years. Each of them being dissatisfied with the relationship, but each of them too fearful to let go of it.

If one partner is secure and the other is not, the difference in power will grow larger as the needy partner feels more and more desperate, and the secure partner feels more and more like getting away. It is a vicious cycle that can lead to constant fighting or near total withdrawal. Rather than go on indefinitely however, this battle usually ends by the secure partner having an affair or ending the relationship. When that happens, the needy partner will be contrite and devastated. The needy partner will see the error of his or her ways, but too late as far as the secure partner is concerned. The relationship is very unlikely to be rescued at this point without the right kind of professional help.

Needy people feel in love, but don't really love their partners

Because needy people are afraid of making changes that might cause them to be rejected, they don't set healthy boundaries, even if that is what their partners need. This means that they become codependent for their partners' unhealthy behaviors. Loving people will not become codependent, because of their concern for the welfare of their partners. They don't allow their partners to continue to do damaging things, even if it means risking the relationship. A person who loves his or her spouse, for example, will separate from a spouse rather than cooperate with their abusing drugs or alcohol. Whether a parent or a partner, a person who loves will not sit by while their child or partner slowly kills himself with drugs or alcohol. The same could be said for affairs and abusive behaviors.

Rather than using healthy and helpful boundaries, needy people will complain and may even threaten to leave (although they never would) until their partners in turn threaten to leave. At which point they become very nice and loving again. Both sets of behaviors, complaining and being nice, are aimed at three things—to get love, attention, and reassurance from their partners. None of needy people's behaviors are done because they actually care about the happiness and well being of their partners. Needy people *feel* in love, but they don't actually have the kind of sacrificial and mature love that cares about their partners' well being. Most needy people are surprised to find that they have never loved their partners. They have confused their feelings of love for the real thing, which puts its emphasis on the happiness of one's partner and not oneself.

Neediness can be anywhere from mild to extreme

Extremely needy people (who are extremely fearful people) may never complain, but constantly "walk on eggshells" lest they make their partners upset. Like all needy people, their deepest fear is being abandoned, and they would do anything to prevent that. Instead of focusing on loving their partners, extremely needy people become focused on not upsetting their partners. Their carefulness and anxiety take all the joy out of their relationships.

People who are only *somewhat* needy may have periods when they are very strong, even breaking up rather than allowing themselves to be further mistreated. They can't maintain their resolve, however, and soon become needy again. They decide the behavior that they detested is really not that bad after all. Rather than having gradually deteriorating relationships, these somewhat needy people have roller coaster relationships with many emotional ups and downs. Their relationships last longer because their partners get to enjoy them at least some of the time. The pattern is something like this—the needy person becomes upset and attempts to use a boundary, his or her partner withdraws, the needy person gives up his or her boundary and becomes nice again, then his or her partner reengages. This reengagement feels good for both of them. It's the only time they both feel loved in their relationship. Couples with this pattern fight frequently, but make up frequently too. This pattern can last a lifetime.

If you are willing to become secure, then you will have the hope of having a stable, happy relationship without a roller coaster ride. In order for you to become secure, you have to learn to stop complaining or being careful and instead use the same healthy boundaries that a secure person would use. In order to do this, you will have to overcome your fear of losing your partner. If you can do this, then equality will be restored in your relationship, your relationship will become stable (no more ups and downs), and your relationship can be rebuilt.

Of course, the longer you wait to work on this, the closer your partner may be to leaving you. And, rebuilding takes time. If you are like many needy people, you only started working on this after your partner has already left you. It took you that long to realize your neediness was a large part of the problem. Even in such a case, it is still very helpful to work on becoming secure since your future happiness will depend on it.

Needy people have dissatisfying long term relationships

A needy person doesn't just want to share her (or his) life with someone, she *craves* being with someone. It is a very self-focused feeling. It has very little to do with making another person feel loved and much more to do with getting love from another person. The more insecure, lonely, and unhappy she is,

OVERCOME NEEDINESS AND GET THE LOVE YOU WANT

the more she will want someone to stop her from feeling that way. She gives no thought to the fact that an insecure, lonely, and unhappy person is not what anyone needs for a partner. Her very first desire is to get someone to take care of her emotionally. It will never occur to her that giving him an emotionally unattractive person in return is a bad deal for him.

When she is able to establish a relationship, it is the reassurances from her partner, in words and/or actions, which help her to feel better—happier, hopeful, energetic, and high on life. The change in her emotions is so quick and so dramatic, that it can only be compared to taking a drug like cocaine. Her reaction to her relationship goes far beyond the reality of the situation and she won't be able to see the other person clearly. She will only see him as the answer to her prayers—her "soul mate." It is anxiety and fear which drove her neediness ("Will I ever find someone who could love me?") and it is the mere finding of such a man that relieves her anxiety. Unless he too is needy, she will emotionally attach to him long before he can attach to her. She will be quick to commit herself and give herself to him in every way.

He may at first bask in the glow of being put on a pedestal and in the spotlight. But, he will soon discover that such adoration comes at a price that is uncomfortably high to pay. His job will be to keep her "supplied" with love and reassurance so that she won't fall apart. Indeed, some women (and men) are so needy that if they are rejected, they may threaten suicide. Again, this behavior is like someone with a severe drug addiction who suddenly is unable to get any more of the drug from her supplier. She may become insanely angry and insisting that he owes it to her to love her. For her, love becomes a commodity to be not only desired, but demanded. Only a severely needy person could have a fatal attraction.

This also explains why needy people often end up with partners who are very toxic. At first, they don't see the other person's serious flaws. Love truly is blind for the needy person. Once she does find someone, even if he is entirely the wrong person, she quickly falls in love. And, later, because she is so dependent on whatever scraps of love and attention he gives her, she will even put up with verbal, physical, or financial abuse. She will want with all her heart to restore the illusion she first had of how wonderful this man was. It can't be done, because of course he was toxic all along and she just couldn't see it or did not look carefully enough to see it. She did not want to see it.

People who fall in love before they really even know their partners are almost always needy. It takes months and even years for people to get to know each other well enough that they can say they truly love their partners and not just their sketchy image of who their partners are. Often, people don't begin to discover much about their partners until after they are married. This is why the first three years of marriage are the most difficult. Both people have to adjust to how the other person really is.

For some secure people, that will be like waking up from a nice dream by a hard slap in the face. This is often the case for secure partners of needy people, who soon regret marrying the needy person. Needy people, however, will continue to idealize their partners and demand that they get back to being normal. What needy people mean by this is that their partners should return to the infatuated behaviors that they had in early courtship. Needy people are not eager for their partners to get back to normal in terms of enjoying their families, hobbies, and friends, as they had done for years before. Their lives are supposed to have begun when their needy partners first fell in love with them. Returning to anything or anyone that came before that feels like a betrayal. Needy people's partners are supposed to have traded all desires to do anything independently from their needy partners for a desire to do everything with them.

When I work with needy people, one of the things that I have to help them with is seeing their partners realistically. They must see both the good and bad characteristics of their partners if they are to have any chance of helping their partners to feel loved. Until we see people as they really are, we can't love them. We would only be loving our idea of them, which is not fair to them. For people to feel truly loved, they need to be accepted for how they truly are—the wonderful, the mundane, the beautiful and the ugly. This explains the intense love we can feel from God—who sees all of our goodness, and all of our failures, and loves us anyhow.

Needy people reject good partners and desire bad ones

Neediness is like an emotional thirst that will keep your mind on the lookout for anyone who can possibly quench it, even if he or she is entirely wrong for you. Picture yourself walking through a scorching desert with no water. The thirstier you get, the more you think about water. You might even get to the point where you would sell your soul for a cupful. And that cupful would taste like the best water you ever had. Likewise, a person who is starving will search through garbage cans for food, brushing aside the flies and maggots and the food will taste *delicious.* And a person who is lonely enough or dejected enough will be attracted to any person who shows interest in him or her. And that person will seem better than any person she (or he) has ever known. Although he may be married, or using drugs, or insensitive to her feelings, she will make excuses for him to justify her attachment—"He just has bad moods because he has a tough job," "Yeah, he's married, but his wife is awful and he's planning on getting a divorce," "He doesn't use drugs all the time. He's just a recreational user." Rationalizations make needy people's bad choices seem like good ones.

I first saw this phenomenon more than 20 years ago, when I was counseling women who did not want to make the same mistakes that they made with men in the past. I would have them write out a list of characteristics that they thought were important for the next man they had a relationship with. Then, I helped them to narrow down that list to just the bare minimum requirements. They were almost always things like, "is single," "has a job," and "isn't addicted to anything." These women insisted that they would not even consider dating men who did not meet these requirements.

In theory, when they identified any of these red flags in a man, they would immediately stop dating him. In practice however, what the women actually did was to disregard *all* of their requirements and date any men who showed interest in them. When I asked them about why they were not sticking to their standards, they would tell me that they were sticking to their standards since they weren't really trying to have a long term relationship with these men. They were just dating them until they found someone who did meet their requirements.

You can probably guess that these women did not give up these men. Because of their neediness, they were willing to make excuses both for the men and for their choices to do something they knew to be bad for them. Maybe these women really didn't intend to have long term relationships with the men when they first went out with them, but does anybody have such intentions from their first date? The difference is that secure women would not have had anything to do with men who did not meet their minimum standards. They would have been able to pass up on the quick emotional fix for someone who is really worth it. One way to identify needy women in public is to look for the men who are behaving like jerks and the women who enjoy being with them. If your boyfriend or husband is a jerk, and you want to be with him, what does that say about you?

There is another problem with being quick to date the wrong person, which is not so easy to see. When you date the wrong person, you miss out on any better person who may come along while you are with him (or her). If you are in a bad relationship for two or three years, it is a good possibility that your relationship prevented you from finding someone much better. Many women and men feel cheated out of having had a better relationship with another person after they have been in an unhappy relationship for a long time. Then, they tend to blame their partners as if it was their partners' fault that they stayed in the relationship. In many cases, the partner really didn't change much from when they first committed to each other and it is the needy person that is responsible for having spent those years with a partner he or she really did not enjoy—once they were able to clearly see their partners as they actually had been all along.

If you are single, the longer you have felt dejected and alone, the more you will excuse in a potential mate. You will be more eager to believe what he (or she) says without checking out if it is true or not. Then, after you quickly get attached to him, you are likely to stay with him even if you find out that he lied to you about some very important things. Hopefully, you will not get to the point of some needy women who will put up with severe abuse, blaming yourself for it, and making excuses for his behavior. Because, once you have been with him long enough to overcome your loneliness, you will suddenly realize you have been eating out of the dumpster.

Needy people often have self-esteem issues

If a woman has always felt like she were no good, undeserving, or just fooling people into thinking she is good, then she will put up with any kind of mistreatment as long as, *once in a while*, he is nice to her. She may crave his love and yet feel unworthy of his love at the same time. This kind of person will put up with almost anything his or her partner does or says. Even though all of a woman's friends may point out how bad her situation is, she may refuse to see it. For example, she may be very fearful of her partner cheating on her, but be practically blind to any evidence that he is cheating on her.

For very needy people, relationships have more to do with what is going on in their heads than what is actually going on between them and their partners. They don't see their partners realistically, they don't see themselves realistically, they don't see their relationships realistically, and, they are scared to take a good look at the way things really are. It's usually only after the reality of another woman showing up pregnant with her boyfriend's child, all of her money being removed from her account, her boyfriend moving out, her finding herself locked behind bars as an accessory to her boyfriend's crimes, or she loses her job because she hasn't recovered from her last beating, that she will begin to see just how sick her situation is.

Needy people are not desirable for long term relationships

Well, that is really an overstatement. There are actually many people who would be glad to have a long term relationship with a needy person. The ones who would are themselves not very desirable as partners. Often they are people who are very selfish or self-absorbed. They have often failed to have long term relationships with others. They are bottom feeders and take what they can. Usually this means needy partners.

Why don't better quality people (secure, kind, thoughtful, sociable) want to have long term relationships with needy people? At first they might, but something happens to secure people when they are in relationships with needy people. Eventually, they tire of their relationships because of the constant requirement to manage the anxiety of their needy partners. They often feel more like parents to teenagers than like partners to equals.

When a secure person has a needy partner, the needy person's behavior seems childish and the secure partner loses respect for the needy partner. After this, it is really hard to love the needy partner, no matter how submissive and accommodating the needy partner becomes. Talking to the needy partner becomes a job that the secure partner *has to do* to keep the needy partner happy. Nice people with needy partners end up being caretakers—surrogate parents for their needy spouses. They don't even have the reassurance that real parents have with their children, because needy people neither grow up nor move out.

Most secure men and women feel incredibly stuck with their needy partners and after a while find it hard to love them. Depending on how patient they are, they either consign themselves to being martyrs, leave, or have affairs. Many times, men and women have affairs not so that they can have their cake and eat it too, but because they want to find someone who loves them while they continue to take care of their unattractively needy spouse. It is not healthy or moral, and it is wrong, but it is understandable. If you treat your partner badly day after day, eventually he or she will long to leave or to be with someone else or both. This is equally true for women as for men.

Needy people's relationships end suddenly and shockingly

As explained above, needy people are loved much by their partners at first, but eventually the love fades and the needy person's partner may find himself or herself longing for another partner or just to get out of the relationship. Although the healthiest thing for the secure partner to do would be to discuss this with the needy partner, he or she could in reality *never* mention it. Mentioning such a thing would tap into the needy person's deepest fears and escalate all of his or her controlling behaviors. So when the secure person is having problems with the marriage or relationship, he (or she) has to hide them to himself until he's ready to leave—with little chance to work through the issues with his partner. Needy people are often caught by surprise when their partners end the relationship.

If you are needy, your relationship is likely to end at an unexpected time. You may find your partner leaving even when he has not complained about your relationship before. When that happens, you will want desperately to save your relationship, but it will be too late because he will have already burned out. He will have already mentally checked out of your relationship and be thinking about a more hopeful future—without you. Any reconciliation is only going to happen after you have been secure for quite some time (at least several months). And, by that time, he is likely to be with someone else. As a needy person, the best time to work on becoming secure is long before your partner burns out on your relationship.

If your partner has already left, then you can work on becoming secure in preparation for either a possible reconciliation or for a new relationship. Either way, you are going to need to do better than the last time. If you don't, you will eventually find yourself in another relationship that follows the same pattern. You will keep creating what you fear the most—abandonment.

Neediness maintains a cycle of failed relationships

Just as a drug user may dump her drugs during the peak of her willpower, swearing that she will never use drugs again, a needy person in a bad relationship may leave her partner, vowing never to take him back. He has hurt her "one too many" times. But, just like the drug user who will soon start craving the very drugs she gave up, soon the needy partner will crave the man or woman she (or he) gave up. Unless another man is available who can satisfy her cravings, she will get back together with him. Practically all he has to do is to avoid contacting her and for each passing day, her cravings will grow stronger until she no longer cares what he did before—if only he will take her back.

Even if such a needy person were to find another partner fast enough to be able to resist going back with the man (or woman) who treated her (or him) badly, she is not likely to be very careful in her new selection. Her cravings to feel loved and accepted will again make her overlook the very same kinds of warning signs that were there in her previous relationship. Rather than doing something secure, she will have traded one troubled relationship for another. Her former partner is also likely to end up with another needy person. Different faces, same problems—for both. This pattern creates a great deal of "shuffling," resulting in many needy men and women being available at all times, keeping the online dating sites quite busy. People in secure relationships do not change partners as often, resulting in more needy people being available than secure people at any given time.

Sometimes shuffling happens before breakups by cheating and affairs. Rather than leave the relationship for a period of time and then find someone else, needy people will sometimes find someone else and then breakup. This has the benefit of preventing initial heartache and cravings, but still results in the shuffling of needy people—different faces, same problems. This is because no one but a needy person, or person with poor values, would date her while she was in a committed relationship with someone else. Secure people with good values don't date people who are already in committed relationships.

If the needy person cheats, whether married or not, she is much more likely to end up with a relationship that is worse than the first one. But, when that happens—shuffle again. This pattern can repeat indefinitely, over a lifetime, unless she learns to deal with her neediness. If she doesn't, then she will start to have a crisis when she reaches her 50's and finds that it is no longer easy to find another man who wants her. That is, unless she is willing to take someone even worse than she had before. Needy men have less trouble finding partners as they get older, but still continue to have the same kinds of relationship problems.

In this way, what seems an ok way to have relationships when you are young and needy, turns out to lock you out of enjoyable relationships as you get older. The person who learns to think and behave securely when he or she is young has a great advantage as he or she will be able to select the cream of the crop as far as partners go and have a much better chance of being able to keep their partners over a lifetime.

Because needy people don't often have the resolve to leave their partners and take them back too soon when they do, *permanent* breakups are usually initiated by their secure partners. Of course if they are both needy, as is often the case, then they may break up and get together many times before it becomes a permanent condition. That will be when one of them has found someone else.

When a needy person's partner ends the relationship, it will simultaneously create feelings of anguish, anger, and desperation in the needy person. At this point, she (or he) will do almost anything to get her partner back. There will be no such thing as a friendly breakup with the possibility of being friends. Her desperate behavior will make sure of that by driving her partner even further from her. The harder she tries to get him back, the more distance he will want. It is a very pitiful situation for the needy person. Although he begs her for space, she will only be able to hold out for a short time before she is contacting him again—confirming to him that he did the right thing by leaving her. Just like earlier in her relationship, the very behavior she uses to try to salvage the relationship becomes the same behavior that ends it. This situation is no different for needy women or men.

Summary

Needy people are not bad people. They don't set out to hurt anyone and they just want to be loved—like everyone else. But, they have an excess of fear of abandonment and isolation. This results in intoxicating and intense early relationships that make them feel like they have won the lottery. However, as the initial excitement wears off for them and their partners, they become vigilant for signs the relationship is failing—seeing danger where most people would not. Then, they are compelled by their fears to have any number of controlling behaviors toward their partners. Their partners naturally don't like to be controlled and emotionally pull away. This makes the needy person even more fearful and even more controlling, creating a vicious cycle. Eventually, this results in the secure partner falling out of love.

While some people would be content to stay with a woman or man even if they were no longer in love, most people won't. Nowadays, not many people will choose to stay in a relationship solely out of obligation or for moral or religious reasons. Needy people end up being abandoned precisely because of the behaviors created by their fears of abandonment.

Being needy is not something that someone would ever choose to be. So, just how did you come to be this way? The next chapter should help you to make more sense out of you.

How we got here is not nearly as important as where we go from here.

♥2♥

HOW YOU BECAME NEEDY

Being a relationship coach, I am less concerned about the origin of neediness than I am about how to overcome it. There has been a trend in psychology away from the analysis of problems and toward the practical treatment of them. People no longer have the time or money to be in analysis several days a week, recounting the minutia of their lives. Even when they do have the time, there is very little evidence that figuring out the origin of their problems is actually helpful.

Analyzing the cause of your neediness is analogous to the following situation. Imagine you get a flat tire while driving down the highway. Suppose that after getting your flat tire, you get out of your car and call a tow truck. The tow truck operator brings two chairs to the scene of your flat tire. He sits in one chair and you sit in the other. He asks you to relax and to begin telling him about your travels thus far. You ask him about fixing your tire, but he says that he can't really help you with your flat tire until you examine why you got your flat tire. This situation makes a lot of sense if the tow truck operator is being paid by the hour. This used to be the way things were in psychology.

Things have changed. Tow truck operators are not paid by the hour and to a large extent, therapists aren't either. Health insurance companies expect therapists to treat your problem in a certain number of sessions or less. As a result, there is very little analysis of problems in psychotherapy these days. Everyone receives basically the same treatment for the same problems. It is only when that treatment fails to provide relief does further analysis occur—to find out what is different in your situation. This method actually results in more people being helped more efficiently, but also results in some problems being overlooked.

I also suggest that you don't start off by trying to figure out how you became needy. Although there may indeed be something unique about the way you developed your neediness, it is likely to be improved in much the same way that other people's neediness is improved. My recommendation then, is to try the standard methods first, and if you continue to have problems, get additional help and go more in depth in the search for the cause of your problems. For most people, it is better just to fix a flat tire than to search for the causes of the flat tire. However, if after being fixed, the tire continues to go flat, it's time to investigate further.

All this being said, however, there is some usefulness for understanding the origins of your neediness. But not because it will effect a cure. The reason is so that you will feel less crazy. If you can make sense out of how you became the way you are, you will feel more hopeful about changing. What has been programmed can be reprogrammed. One of the biggest services that psychotherapists have provided for people is helping them feel less crazy and more hopeful. Where psychotherapy often fails people is in the practical, *everyday application* of methods to overcome problems. Therapists don't go with you into your everyday lives and help you deal with the nitty gritty of what your partner said to you last night. This is where coaches come in. Good ones help people with the nitty gritty—the practical application of skills to everyday life and conversations in order to improve relationships.

Let's take a brief look at some of the reasons that people become needy in the first place. If you can find yourself in any or all of these explanations, then hopefully you will feel less crazy—less defective, and be ready to get on with the skills involved in doing things in a more secure way.

Theory of anxious attachment

Attachment is our desire to connect with at least one other human being. Infants have ways to signal that they need the care and attention of their parents. They signal their need to be fed, to be changed, and to interact socially. Parents respond to these signals and the child is satisfied—that is unless the parents respond incorrectly to the signal. For example, if a child is hungry and the parents play with the child rather than feeding him or her, the child will continue to signal his or her hunger. Most parents will then "get it" and feed their child. The same goes for all the child's other needs—the child signals and the parents respond until the need is correctly met. In this way, the child comes to trust and feel secure with the parent. Children who have such responsive parents usually form *secure attachments.*[1]

Securely attached children are thought to develop personalities in which they feel relaxed around their parents (and later, their partners), prefer to be with their partner than without, and are happy to be reunited with their partner if the partner leaves them for awhile to go do something else.

Children who are not so lucky as to have such caring, attentive parents meeting their needs, are thought to develop *anxious* styles of attachment which influence their personality development in a different way. As children who did not get their needs met consistently, they became both angry and helpless in their efforts to make their parents meet their needs. Children with such anxious attachments may be preoccupied with getting their needs met in their adult relationships. They behave in angry, controlling, and manipulative ways. They are also very fearful of losing their partners, who are thought to hold the keys to the kingdom in terms of meeting all of their needs.

---

[1] Salter Ainsworth, M., Blehar, M., Waters, E. and Wall, S. (2015). *Patterns of Attachment: A Psychological Study of the Strange Situation, Classic Edition*. New York and London: Routledge Taylor & Francis Group.

This is the prevailing psychological theory about neediness in relationships. While it makes logical sense and does add weight to the argument that parents should be responsive to the needs of their young children, I don't find it particularly helpful in terms of treatment. We cannot go back and undo what happened to you as a child. And, simply having insight into how this happened to you has limited effect. Still, it might help you to feel less responsible for becoming needy. It will not however, keep you from being responsible for becoming secure, since that is under your control. You cannot continue to blame your parents for your choices, once your choices become obvious to you

Theory of exaggeration of normal fears

You may find, if you ask other people, that most people have a fear of abandonment and not being able to make it on their own. It *is* scary to think about being rejected and having to struggle with loneliness and all the tasks of living all by ourselves.

Although fear of abandonment is normal, most people are able to put their fears in perspective. For example, most people have some fear of being in a highway accident. They don't however, *think* much about having a highway accident. They simply get in their cars and go where they need to go. When they get there, they shift their focus onto the next thing they need to deal with.

But, if there are dangerous driving conditions, such as heavy rain or snow, then people will have an increased fear of having an accident and so will be more cautions. It works this way in relationships, too. When most people have high amounts of stress in their relationships, they become more cautious and more alert. They then deal with the stressful conditions as best they can and when the crisis has passed, they get back to their other concerns.

Needy people are like other people when there is a real crisis in their relationship. But, they are unlike other people when things are going relatively well. This is because they *always* have some level of alertness about what their partners are doing and always find a way to make it relate to them. Their fear is *exaggerated*—it is beyond what the situation actually merits. This exaggerated response results in more conflict, which exacerbates the fear even more. This negative spiral can result in the end of the relationship, which acts to confirm what the needy person originally feared.

If needy people could be as relaxed as other people when there are no serious problems in their relationship, then they would not focus so much on their relationship, and as a result, would be less needy. They would behave in ways that help their partners to enjoy them—resulting in better relationships.

Theory of maladaptive response to healthy fear

Fear is not such a bad thing if you deal with it in an effective way. One way to think of neediness is simply as an ineffective way to deal with a realistic fear. That is, most people have similar fears as the needy person in regard to the possibility of being abandoned, but unlike the needy person, they actually do things which are productive. For example, they may give their partners extra attention or improve their listening and use of affirmation so that their partners will be more responsive. They may also choose to use good boundaries to prevent ongoing harm that their partners' behavior might cause if left unchecked. They would not let little problems build into big problems, and they would not contribute to the problems.

This is not so with a needy person. Needy people's responses to their fears are to complain, control, deny, or withdraw. These are their ineffective attempts to restore things to normal or to continue to see them as normal. This is ineffective because rather than improve the relationship and so reduce their fears, their reactions actually make their relationships worse, which in turn *increases* their fears. Their attempts to reduce their fears create bigger fears. Then, they complain, control, deny, or withdraw even more. This is the vicious cycle of neediness which destroys relationships and makes people even more fearful in their next relationship (with an even more intense level of neediness).

The psychotherapeutic perspective of neediness

Everyone has some amount of neediness. This is true in the same sense that is true for psychological disorders. For example, everyone feels depressed sometimes, anxious sometimes, has unwanted thoughts sometimes, and has maladaptive behaviors sometimes. No one has inherited a perfect mind or body and if you examine a person closely enough or long enough, you will be able to identify a number of imperfections.

It is not normal for someone to meet the clinical definition of depression, since it requires a number of symptoms to occur for at least a two week period. The same is true for anxiety disorders, behavioral disorders, and personality disorders. In other words, a single symptom does not make a syndrome (a diagnosable condition). Neither does a single needy behavior now and then make someone a needy person.

When someone is cured of any psychological disorder, it doesn't mean that they will never have any more symptoms of that disorder. A person who recovers from an anxiety disorder will still experience anxiety. A person who overcomes obsessive-compulsive disorder will still have unwanted thoughts, and a person who overcomes an eating disorder will still have anxiety around eating. Likewise, when you overcome being needy (when you become secure), there will still be times when you feel insecure. And there may be times when you do something needy.

So, one way to look at neediness is as normal except when there is so much of it that it results in personal distress or impairs your ability to function. When it reaches that excess, it needs to be treated because left untreated it would lead to even more personal distress and even more impaired functioning. This is the disease model which is followed by every profession which takes health insurance. The main goal of such professionals is to return you to normal functioning. If you go to counseling for help, this will be the goal of your therapist. But, if you get coaching, you will find that your coach has little interest in helping you to be normal.

The coaching perspective of neediness

Coaching, in contrast to counseling, doesn't seek to restore people to *normal* functioning. Coaching strives to help people excel—to be their best and to go beyond what most people can do without the benefit of coaching.

From a psychological perspective, if your neediness is not causing significant problems in your relationships, work/school, or enjoyment of life, it is not a problem. As a coach, I can tell you that it may not be a disorder, but it may still be a problem.

The reason that your neediness may be a problem, even if you are doing fine compared to most people, is that you might be able to do far *better* than most people if you were not needy. People who use coaches want to be the best that they can be and want to have the best that they can have. They want to maximize their potential, even if they are doing just as well as the Joneses. In my coaching, I strive to give people relationship skills that will take their relationship beyond the societal norm, which is too low of a standard. For this reason, coaching is not mental health treatment and cannot be paid for with medical insurance. It is personal excellence and not wellness that coaches are after.

Neediness as failure to reach a developmental stage

There are different psychological theories about how people grow and develop. Because most people go through predictable changes as they grow, psychologists often break our lifetimes down into a series of phases or stages. For example, all people go through a period when they have not yet learned to talk. We call that infancy. The same is true for walking, growing tall, and developing characteristics that match our gender.

In addition to these physical changes, we also undergo psychological changes as we get older. When these changes occur is a matter both of genetics and our environment. Just as we can see that some children grow up faster than others physically, some children also grow up faster than others emotionally.

It doesn't stop with childhood, though. Not everyone is relationally "grown up" when they reach legal adulthood. In fact, many people don't grow up relationally until they are in their 30's and some people never grow up relationally at all. They just stop maturing somewhere along the way.

For young children, it is natural and normal to depend on parents for survival and emotional well being. Then, as children grow, hopefully they learn many self-care skills and also learn how to make friends with others. If they are guided well, they learn to value creation as God's gift, they learn that other people are loveable and valuable, they learn to help people just for the joy of it, and they learn how to let go when someone moves away or dies.

But, not everyone learns these things. Some children learn to be careful *all* the time, lest their parents or others turn on them. Some children experience the pain of loss before they are ready to deal with it and don't get good guidance when it does happen. Some children learn to place too much importance on how their behavior affects others, and some children learn to put too little emphasis on how their behavior affects others.

Neediness, in particular, is often associated with early loss of someone very important, psychologically, to the child. Something in them goes on high alert to never let such a thing happen again. Unfortunately, they have learned the wrong lesson from the loss. Loss is not something to protect oneself from; loss is an inevitable part of life. But, by valuing and treating people with love while they are here, and trusting God with our future, we need not fear loss.

It is important not to confuse neediness with dependency. We do not become independent as we grow older. We just become more capable of doing more things by ourselves. All of us, regardless of age, depend on others for the food we eat, the home we live in, the clothes we wear, systems of government and transportation, and so forth. We may depend less on our parents as we age, but become increasingly dependent on others. Others also come to depend more on us as we become more capable and productive. It is natural and desirable to depend on our spouses as they depend on us.

Neediness as a learned characteristic

Most of what we understand about relationships we learned as very young children. Long before children enter elementary school, they are observing and absorbing the behaviors of their parents. In traditional families, boys and girls pay particular attention to the parent of the same gender as them. Little girls learn not only how to be a mom, but how to be a wife as well. Little boys learn not only how to be a dad, but how to be a husband as well.

As little boys and girls grow, they are exposed to many other people's relationships, such as their friends' parents and adult relationships they see on TV. However, they tend not to integrate the aspects of those relationships that differ from what they learned from their parents' example.

Even little girls and boys who grow up to be psychologists—experts in human behavior, will be surprised to find themselves behaving much the same way their mothers and fathers did.

Because needy people also tend to have needy partners, it is likely that if one of your parents was needy, the other one was, too. This also worked to prevent you from seeing a contrast in the behaviors of your parents—reinforcing the "neediness lessons" you learned from them.

Specifically, if you grew up in a home where people criticized, complained, argued, interrogated, and nagged, you are much more likely to do those things yourself. And, if you grew up in a home where people complimented, agreed, found the good in others, and showed interest in one another, you are not likely to be reading this book at all. And, if you grew up with certain expectations about what it means to be both a husband and wife, then when you became interested in dating other people, you were intuitively drawn to other people with matching expectations.

When people break up or divorce, they tell themselves that the next person will be different—that they will not choose the same kind of man or woman again. However, the kind of person that they are most attracted to is the person who most resembles how their former partner *initially* was, when they first dated him or her. If you choose someone who is the same way your ex was at the beginning, there is a very good chance that your partner will also become the way your ex was at the end.

For me, this behavioral model of neediness is simplest and accounts for most of the reasons that people are needy. But, it does not account for all of the reasons that people are needy. In fact, it is possible to grow up with very secure parents and yet to become insecure and needy yourself. Like most things in life, there is no single cause for our behavior or our partners' behavior.

Neediness as a Result of Trauma or Loss

In my experiences both as a psychologist and as a marriage and relationship coach, I have witnessed needy behavior resulting from other causes than problems in early childhood, The development of neediness can occur in a person of any age.

Some of the needy people I have worked with have experienced the loss of a parent, friend, pet, or other close relative in a traumatic way. As a result, they developed an extreme fear of losing their partner as well as other family members. Their minds are trying to protect them from experiencing more loss. This resulting neediness tends to be pervasive and experienced as part of the person's personality. If a person experienced trauma when young, they don't feel it is at all abnormal to be needy and have a hard time understanding why others are not that way as well. A person like this is likely to be slower to make progress using purely cognitive and behavioral techniques like the ones in this book. They are also likely to need psychotherapy to treat post traumatic stress issues. In fact, very little progress may be made until they do.

Neediness as a temporary reaction to the threat of loss

Otherwise secure people can become *temporarily* needy in the face of their spouses or partners leaving them. This situation is different because the person was, until that time, fairly secure. It is a kind of reactive neediness which results in behaviors aimed at preventing the partner from leaving (such as begging and crying). However, these temporary needy behaviors have the same affect that general neediness does—it drives the other person away more quickly. It is much easier to remedy because these temporarily needy people soon realize their "mistake" and become alarmed at their own neediness. Because of this, they can easily stop their needy behaviors.

Summary

There are different theories of how neediness develops. It is not necessary to decide which theory is correct in order to work on becoming secure. However, these explanations for how you became a needy person can help you to feel more normal. You are not crazy and your neediness is not the result of some kind of genetic defect.

Knowing that your neediness is largely a result of your earlier experiences suggests that new, corrective experiences may undo a lot of the damage that has been done. The difficulty is that people who are needy usually don't recognize the specific things that they do that are needy. Because most needy people have been that way since childhood, they have no past frame of reference to compare their behavior to. Also, because their parents may also have been needy, they can't identify their needy behaviors by comparing it to that of their parents.

Neediness may also result from trauma which occurred in late childhood or early adulthood. The earlier in life the traumatic loss occurred, the more likely the person is to become needy and to feel normal being that way. People who have been needy since childhood have to initially make changes based on faith because they don't know from experience that their lives and relationships can be better if they are more secure. Doing things based on faith always feels scary until we get a good result.

Adults can temporarily become needy. When that is the case, they can remember how they used to be when they were secure. Their recent neediness will feel uncomfortable to them and they will easily see it as a bad thing. These "more recently needy" people can more quickly become secure because they remember being secure before and they miss being that way. In essence, they already know how to be secure, but for one reason or another have stopped being that way.

Whatever the reason for your being needy, you can start becoming secure again, or for the first time, starting today.

CREATING THE NEW SECURE YOU

Needy people, like anyone else, can change. Change is never easy, and this is doubly true for needy people. Overcoming neediness is possible and many people have done it. It is a worthwhile pursuit that will enrich your life in many ways. If you are in a relationship, your neediness is likely to be part of any problems you may have. Neediness however, rarely occurs in isolation and is most often identified when there are other problems in your relationship as well. You and your partner may argue over which came first—your neediness, or your partner's behavior. Fortunately, figuring out the answer to this question is not important for taking action and making things better.

It doesn't matter if the chicken or the egg came first

It would be a mistake to overlook your neediness and see all of your relationship problems as coming from your partner. But, it also would be a mistake to see all of your relationship problems as coming from your neediness. How do you know which came first—your partner's bad behaviors or your neediness? This could turn into a real chicken and egg question—does your partner's behavior cause your neediness or does your neediness cause your partner's bad behavior? This could even turn into an argument that is replayed again and again and again in your relationship, but it doesn't have to.

The fact is, regardless of where the problem started, your best place to start is always with your own behavior. If you were to start by dealing with your partner's behavior, your partner would be able to point a finger at you and what you are doing to damage your relationship. Then, all you would get would be an argument which would increase your fear of abandonment and fuel your partner's anger. Then, you would be further apart than when you first set out to make things better. People do this all the time by the way—making their relationship worse in their attempts to make it better. No matter what kind of relationship problem you have, you will *always* have more success when you work on yourself first. I have been reconciling relationships for more than 20 years and I do it not by working with couples, but by working with just one person—the one who wants to save and improve their relationship.

Many times, just by working on yourself, you will create enough of a positive change in your relationship to turn a downward spiral (things getting progressively worse) to an upward spiral (things getting progressively better). Please note that I said *progressively.* There is no such thing as instant improvement in a relationship. You will need to change first. Then, your partner will adjust to your changes and a new pattern of relating will happen. By changing yourself, you change your relationship. It takes from one month to a few months to achieve change, depending on how many times you mess up and reset the clock. Trust is slowly earned by being consistent over a long period of time. It only takes one impulsive act to destroy trust, however.

If you are able to stop your needy behaviors and do all those nice, relationship-connecting things, and sustain them, *then* it will be time to deal with any remaining problems that your partner has—or not. If you are single, you might discover, after becoming a more secure person, that your partner is not a good match for you and you need a new partner. If you are married, then I would suggest to you that your partner can change, but it will take additional effort on your part to make that happen. This is beyond the scope of this book, but is dealt with in my book, *What to Do When He Won't Change* (written for women, but also useful for men).

You can learn from this that improving a relationship always starts with stopping your needy behaviors. Then, and only then, does it involve learning to use interventions, such as boundaries, to deal with your partner's behaviors. If you tried to do the boundaries first, before becoming secure, you would give up on your boundaries too soon or combine them with your own damaging behaviors and end up with a worse problem than when you started.

General anxiety problem, or neediness problem?

Can you hear your "inner voice" of neediness giving you "what if" messages that prevent you from being happy and prompt you to seek reassurance? "What if he has found someone else?" "What if he gets mad at me?" "What if he wants to break up?" and so on. These messages don't really do anything to protect your relationship, since they prompt you to do things which damage your relationship (such as frequently checking up on your partner, questioning, avoiding sensitive but important topics, complaining, etc.).

Because neediness is a particular kind of anxiety, people who have more general anxiety problems may also ask themselves the same kinds of questions. The difference is, the needy person will mainly be anxious about relationships and the person with general anxiety will be anxious about many other things as well. A generally anxious person will have anxious thoughts about other things such as, "What if my car breaks down on the highway?" "What if my boss doesn't like my work?" "What if I get sick?" and so on.

If you are a "what if" person in general, then you have a more general anxiety problem and you should get help for that. Taking care of your general anxiety problem may take care of your neediness problem at the same time. It is possible to have both a general anxiety problem and a neediness problem. In that case, get help with your general anxiety first. Then, if a neediness problem remains, continue to work on that. If you are generally an anxious person, simply working on being less needy will not be enough and your general anxiety will sabotage the work that you try to do on being less needy.

Trust results and not your own thinking

Overcoming neediness means having a different way of responding to these "what if" questions than by doing damaging things. How do you know if something you are doing is damaging or not? You can determine this by looking at the results your behavior produces. Does your relationship get better or worse when you: check up on your partner, criticize, interrogate, argue, complain, explain, repeatedly talk about problems, nag, or make promises to change? Take a minute to answer this question before going on. If you can honestly say that these behaviors improve your relationship, I will be very surprised. These are exactly the same behaviors that do the most damage to relationships and are the damaging behaviors most commonly found in needy partners.

You need to get away from asking yourself if your behavior makes sense or if other people do it. Everything that is done makes sense to the person who is doing it. It makes sense to people who are having affairs that they have them. It makes sense to bank robbers that they rob banks. It makes sense to abusive parents that they abuse their children. Everyone can and does make sense of their behaviors. There are always reasons that people can use to justify their behavior. But, as you can see from these examples, no matter how much something makes sense, it can still do a lot of damage. Being moral and being loving often contradicts what makes sense to most people. And, if you decide that doing what most people do is right for you, then you will also get the results that most people get. For me, those are results that I absolutely don't want to have.

Arguing, for example, makes a lot of sense and happens in the majority of relationships, but is absolutely destructive to relationships. It does make sense to think that if you can persuade your partner to think the way you do, then you will have less conflict and get along better. The reality, however, is that arguing leads to increased conflict and greater emotional distance. As I discuss in my book, *Connecting Through Yes!*, finding a way to agree with your partner will actually bring about more of the changes you want than arguing will. Agreeing connects you to your partner emotionally, which makes your partner more willing to do what you want. Agreement, like being secure, is not something that comes naturally. But, like becoming secure, it can be learned. Becoming successful is not about doing what makes sense, but rather doing what works. In the same way, do what creates good—not what feels good.

No matter what you think or feel may be a good thing to do, if it has long term damaging effects on your relationship, it is *not* a good thing to do.

Get extra help and support if you can

Getting help from a book is good; getting help from a person is even better. What you need depends on your ability level, your motivation, and your ability to persist long enough to get lasting change. Just as with any other problem, getting help will make things go a lot easier. Many people do overcome problems by themselves. They overcome addictions, depressions, lose weight, and make many changes in their lives. There are also many people who could not have made these same changes if they did not have help. I would not want to discourage you from working on overcoming neediness on your own if you truly have no one who can help you in some way. Neither do I want you to try to go it all alone if help is available. It makes sense to maximize your chances of success by taking advantage of whatever resources you have.

It won't do you much good to get help from someone who is as needy as yourself. You will need the help of someone who is secure—at least someone who is more secure than you. The ideal situation is to work with a coach (what I am) who can meet with you by telephone or Skype once a week and to whom you can write to in between sessions. The once a week meetings help you to learn new skills. The email support helps you to know how to deal with things during the week, when they come up, instead of having to wait until the next session.

The next best level of support is a therapist who you can meet with once a week. The main benefit of a therapist is keeping you focused on positive changes long enough to have some lasting improvement. Also, the therapist can certainly recognize the difference between insecure and secure behavior. If you have never been in therapy before or would like to benefit more from therapy, please see my book, *Therapy Beyond All Expectations.*

If you want help, but can't afford professional help, don't despair. If you have a friend, family member, pastor, or coworker who is more secure than you, they may be willing to be your barometer for what is needy and what is not. You might like to do a little test with them before you trust their help too much. Simply take a behavior you know to be needy and ask them if they think you are needy if you do that. If they say "no, that's not needy," then don't rely on that person as your neediness barometer. For example, if you say to them, "Is it needy to ask my boyfriend to call me or text me whenever he is out doing something with his friends?" and they say, "No, that's not needy," then don't ask them such questions again. They have too much neediness to help you with yours. You will just end up supporting each other's unhealthy behaviors.

You may find that you need to do this test with quite a few people before you find one secure enough to help you. Because needy people tend to bond with other needy people, you may have to go outside of your regular social circle (get out of your comfort zone) to find someone suitable to help you. Being secure and being successful tend to go hand in hand, so try talking to the most successful people you know. Many successful people have had to overcome their own neediness.

If you still need help, but are unable or unwilling to find such a secure helper, then you may need to save up to have at least one session with a coach every once in a while. Therapists usually frown on people who just want one session once in a while, but you won't run into that problem with coaches. You also can often get additional information on coaching websites that may be helpful to you, free of charge. (You are welcome to visit my website at coachjackito.com to read articles and download helpful information for free).

Signs of progress

Very definite signs of progress are an improved relationship, less fear about losing your partner, and seeing more faults with your partner and still being ok with that.

Needy people simply do not see their partners as they are. They think of their partners as they used to be early in the relationship, or as they want them to be—some ideal version of their partners that is not true 99% of the time. Then, they react to the difference between that image and anything their partners do that don't match that image. The bigger the difference between needy people's images of their partners and the way their partners actually are, the more upset needy people will be with those differences. We are bound to be upset whenever our expectations don't match reality.

To take an extreme example, let's imagine that you believe your partner to have no interest in any woman (or man) except you. You believe you are the only person your partner finds attractive, and the only person he (or she) thinks about. Then, if you happen to notice your partner looking at another woman or enjoying a private conversation with another woman, it will set off all kinds of alarms inside you and make you feel angry with your partner. You may confront your partner about it in an attempt to get your partner to reassure you that you are the only one for him (or her). Then, because of your distrust and confrontational behavior, your partner will become a little more distant from you.

Now, imagine instead that you have a more realistic belief about your partner. Namely, that he (or she) finds a variety of women (or men) to be attractive (particularly normal for men) and that he can have a conversation with a woman without going after her like a dog after a piece of meat. When you notice him glancing (not flirting or leering) at other women and having casual conversations with other women, you will feel more at ease. This is because it matches your expectations.

I sometimes have female clients complain to me that their husbands or boyfriends are attracted to other women. I then let them in on a well known secret—if their husbands are not attracted to other women, then they won't be attracted to their partners either! Maybe you would like to tell me that you don't find any other men (or women) attractive. Do you mean that there are no singers or actors who you find to be attractive? Would you talk to one of them if you had the chance? Does that make you unfaithful to your spouse or partner? This is just one example of an unrealistic expectation. Needy people have many unrealistic expectations about friends, doing everything together, how many times to say "I love you," and on and on.

When you see that what you thought were faults are actually normal, you will be more at ease. However, you will start to notice other faults that are not so normal. These were "hidden" from you when you were very needy, early in your relationship, because they would have been too threatening for you to see clearly. You would have been in *denial*, an involuntary ignorance of reality. After all, if you had seen his or her actual faults clearly, that may have threatened your relationship. And a needy person cannot tolerate threats to his or her relationship.

You may discover, for example, that your partner is selfish and self-absorbed. Your partner may enjoy receiving, but not giving, and may be less affectionate than most people are. Your partner may do a lousy job of managing money, keeping healthy, or being organized. Your partner may have no friends or mistreat the ones he or she does have. Your partner may not be good at his or her job or not well liked. Your partner may lie to you even when he or she doesn't *have to*, because he or she has had a habit of lying since childhood. When people begin to take their idealized partners off the pedestals that they have put them on, they often put their partners in the gutter instead and wonder how they could have become involved with such low lifes in the first place. It is a remarkable mental transformation when your Prince Charming becomes Peasant Charlie or when your Pretty Princess becomes your Petty Princess.

When you start to see these actual faults, which are not a result of your neediness, you may begin to spend a lot of effort trying to get your partner to once again fit your idealized image. Without the aid of denial, you won't be able to do it. Like it or not, every person in this world has some serious faults. Learning to live with, deal with, work around, and use boundaries with these faults is part of the work of having a relationship. This is one of the reasons that the first few years of marriage are most difficult. It's as if until that point we only saw our partners in a soft twilight and now someone has turned on a harsh spotlight and we see all the scars and blemishes we did not see before.

Non-acceptance makes both partners feel angry and is one of the biggest factors that lead to the end of relationships. We feel threatened when our partners are not just like us—even if it is only the way they hang the toilet paper roll. Growing, maturing, and being more secure means learning to let the differences go that don't really matter, while taking action (not arguing) for differences that do matter. Once again, you will need someone to guide you as to what really matters and what doesn't. Does his looking at pornography matter? Does her not going to bed at the same time as you matter? Does his keeping a password on his cell phone matter? Does her having male friends on social networks matter? These can be difficult questions to answer when you are working on becoming more secure. For secure people, though, they are much easier. Get guidance from secure people whenever you can.

It's not all about you

Probably one of the biggest surprises that you will have, as you become a secure person, is learning that most of what your partner does has nothing to do with how he or she feels about you. My clients often need a lot of help in learning to see things from their partners' perspectives, which are sometimes completely opposite from their own. Needy people find it surprising that their partners may think about them very little, because needy people are used to thinking *all the time* about their partners.

Because needy people tend to see their partners as they think they should be rather than as they actually are, they often relate all of their partners' actions to themselves. Because she puts him at the center of her world, it comes as a surprise to her that he puts *himself* at the center of his world (or he puts God or his job at the center of his world). Rather than condemning him for that, the needy person needs to move more in this direction and be able to take care of herself better, just as her partner does.

Our partners should be an important part of our lives. But, they should not be our entire lives. Contrary to what needy people believe, this actually makes the relationship stronger and closer. It's a real 180 degree turn from their normal world view. To make your partner a smaller part of your world does not mean you value him (or her) less. But, it will help you to be less afraid of losing your partner. That is essential if you are going to be able to love your partner better and strengthen your relationship.

"How will things change when I overcome neediness?"

Because you won't be afraid of your partner's answers, and because your partner will no longer need to "walk on eggshells," you will be able to talk to your partner more comfortably about many things you avoided before. Your partner can also feel more comfortable talking to you. Your partner won't have to be careful not to set off your insecure behavior. The result is that you will both be able to get to a deeper level of communication, and on a more equal level. You will learn how to take him (or her) at his word and to stop mind-reading and assuming. You will be able to tolerate and even endorse your partner wanting to do some things without you. The more success you have in handling things that you don't want to hear, the more secure you will become, and the more your partner will want to be with you.

You will learn that some independence in relationships is not dangerous and can even be enjoyable. You will also find that dealing with real things is a lot easier than dealing with imagined things. It will be become more okay for you and your partner to have differences. Your relationship will become more normal because in healthy relationships people have many differences that they learn to accept.

These changes don't happen overnight

The first few weeks of change will be the hardest. This is the time when you will most need support. Most clients who work with me on becoming more secure only need *one month* of coaching. Although they still have work to do after that month, they are better able to go the rest of the way on their own.

In the first few weeks, you will be struggling with your fears, as well as your anger, and you may find it difficult to be able to restrain your needy behaviors without support. Often, it is good just to have someone you can blow off steam with other than your partner. Needy people who are in the process of becoming more secure have urges to tell their partners off as they become more aware of how their partners really are. They also have times when they just feel like giving up because changing is hard. I don't know of any way to make this process easy. All I can do is to assure you that it will be worth it when you become secure.

Pain is a natural part of any change, and must be expected. People who believe change is difficult may hesitate to work on change, but have more progress when they finally do. People who expect change to be easy may more readily get started, but will also more easily give up. You should expect the process to be difficult, but you also need to remind yourself that the most difficult part is at the beginning and then it will become progressively easier. The successes you have will encourage you to continue and then you will have even more successes. You will believe more in yourself and your partner will be able to stop taking care of you and just enjoy you again.

If you use coaching as part of this process, you can also work with your coach to become more likeable and effective with people. The best way to increase your self-esteem is to become more competent at your job, as a parent, or as a partner. My clients typically learn social skills they have never used before, such as how to be assertive without being aggressive, how to handle criticism without being defensive, and how to express their needs without complaining or criticizing.

Whether you have a coach or not, you can choose to learn the skills you most need. The information is available in many forms in addition to this book. No longer will you depend on your partner changing in order to make you happy. You will be able to stop worrying and start living—maybe for the first time or for the first time in many years. (For more information on getting additional help, please see the appendix).

Helping others to relax with you

Needy people have often developed communication habits that prevent other people from being honest and open with them. Other people have learned to be careful about what they say to the needy person. This is because they are afraid that the needy person will overreact, becoming terribly depressed, terribly angry, or both. This is true not only of partners, but also of coworkers, friends, and family. Having to be careful makes talking less enjoyable. Needy people need to learn how to respond in a relaxed way in order to promote relationships.

Your partner may never say to you that he or she is not attracted to you anymore. But if you learn a secure way of responding to this, you will be less fearful if it happens. Therapists call this kind of preparation *stress inoculation*. For every bad thing that you imagine can go wrong, there is a good way to deal with it. Often there is more than one good way to deal with it. I often have my clients tell me the worst thing they can imagine that could happen in their relationship and then help them to come up with effective (secure) ways to deal with it. You can do the same. In this way, your fears can actually be the starting point for your increased competency and self-esteem.

The beneficial side effect of this practice and preparation is being more relaxed with other people. When you relax, others relax. It will be one of the first things they notice about you as you begin to be more secure. When people relax with you, they will share more with you, which will make your relationships closer.

Responding effectively

Every needy behavior that you do is done with the intention of changing another person's behavior or to reassure yourself. For example, when you complain (a needy behavior) about your partner not sharing his (or her) thinking with you, you are actually trying to *improve* the way he shares with you. But, because needy behaviors actually push people away, the end result is that by complaining about his not sharing, you make him even less likely to share with you. The more distant he becomes, the less he will share. If you then try even harder to get him to share, you would push him even further away and he would be even more reticent to share with you.

You might think that his not sharing in the first place caused this vicious cycle, but it did not. One behavior cannot cause a cycle. Relationship cycles are caused by responding in either effective or ineffective ways to another person's behavior. Effective responding creates a positive cycle and ineffective responding creates a negative cycle. When you criticize, your partner's behavior becomes worse, which leads to your continuing to criticize, which makes your partner's behavior become worse, and so on.

In becoming secure, your job is to replace your ineffective responding with effective responding so that your relationships will get better rather than worse. You do have the power to change your partner's behavior, but you do that by focusing on your own behavior.

For example, if he (or she) doesn't like to share with you, it is either because he has had bad experiences sharing with you before or with someone prior to you—possibly going back to his childhood. Rather than complain about his not sharing (which would make him feel not good enough for you), you must instead help him to enjoy talking to you. If a man can't talk to you about the weather, or fishing, or cars, or sports, or whatever else interests him at a more superficial level, then he is not going to take the chance of talking to you about more serious things. The same is true for women. In short, if you want your partner to share with you, you need to listen and be interested in what he or she likes to talk about.

Many people have found that men or women who will not share with their partners will often share with someone they are having an affair with. The reason for this is simple—the people they are having affairs with are interested in them, and what they are saying, without being critical. This makes them comfortable enough to talk with a new love interest. In many respects, people can learn how to behave toward their spouses by imagining how other people, who might want to have a relationship with their spouses, would behave. They are much more likely to agree and empathize than they are to complain and criticize. Whatever someone else would do to attract your partner, you can also do to attract your partner.

Find a role model for being secure

The most natural way for people to learn is by imitating other people. This is how children learn almost everything. What they learn in school by direct teaching is very limited compared to what they learn by observation and imitation. All those hours of TV, computer, and socialization teach them how they are to behave as adults. If I were to ask you what you learned in elementary or high school, how much could you actually tell me about what you learned in class? But, if I were to ask you what you learned from your parents about how married people are to behave, what would you tell me? Undoubtedly, you would be able to remember some very significant things about your parents relationship with each other.

As adults, perhaps because of our training in school, we often try to learn things by reading about them in books or on the internet. The truth is, we have to spend hundreds or even thousands of hours of time studying books or getting degrees even to do a few basic things. But, when we learn from experience and observation, we quickly learn things that we never forget. In my own case, I trained for 12 years *after* finishing high school. I have an undergraduate degree and three graduate degrees. I studied all kinds of things about human relationships—psychology, philosophy, science, theology, and so on. If I were to have a test on those things today, my scores would be pretty poor. I remember a few interesting things, but those hundreds of thousands of pages of material that I studied for thousands of hours are long gone from my memory.

The most useful things I learned in school were from observing others and from actually trying them out. I watched and listened to other people doing therapy. Then I did therapy with some "practice" clients. People observed me and gave me feedback. I kept practicing. Finally, I was ready to start seeing "real" clients. That's when my education seemed to really begin. I went through the same process again when I learned to become a relationship coach.

Fresh out of school, I found that many of the things that I needed to do with clients, I was poorly prepared to do. Real people are not the same as other students pretending to be clients. Fortunately, there was one method that I used that was very helpful to me. In fact, it even allowed me to go on to excel in my field. That same method is one that you can use to become a secure person. Everybody can use this method for changing their behavior.

The method is to choose someone, mentally, who you know to be better than you in some aspect you would like to improve about yourself. For example, when I started working with children I thought about Dr. Fred Rogers of *Mister Rogers' Neighborhood,* an award winning children's TV program. I thought that if I could be more like him, it would only improve my ability to help children. So, when I went to the waiting room to get a child, I asked myself, "How would Mr. Rogers go out and greet a child?" When I brought the child back to my office, I asked myself, "How would Mr. Rogers take a child back to his office?" And when I got to my office, I asked myself, "How would Mr. Rogers talk to a child once the child was in his office?" And so on.

Although I did not know how Mr. Rogers would actually do these things, I could make a pretty good guess. Occasionally, I was even rewarded by some parents telling me "You're just like Mr. Rogers." As I grew accustomed to working with children, my questions about what Mr. Rogers would do faded away and I had my own style. I felt like I learned it from Dr. Rogers, even though I never had any direct contact with him. Similarly my role model for working with couples was Dr. James Dobson, who I was familiar with from his *Focus on the Family* radio program that I listened to regularly. Likewise, the Rev. Billy Graham was my role model for living with integrity as a Christian. Although I never met any of these men, I feel like I owe it to them for helping me to become both caring and successful.

If you want to be secure, choose a role model who is secure. Because you are not secure now, your role model probably is not going to come from your family of origin. But, your role model or models can be anyone who is more the way you would like to be. If you don't know anyone who is secure, start paying attention to others—characters from books, TV, movies or anywhere. They don't need to be perfect and they don't need to be good in other areas of their lives. They don't even need to be real people. The only requirement is that they be better than you in some area where you want to improve.

Once you have selected your role model or role models, ask yourself "What would [role model name] do in this situation?" "What would he or she say?" Many times with my needy clients I ask the question "What would a secure person do in this situation?" Interestingly, even though they are not behaving this way themselves, they often know or have a pretty good idea of what a secure person would do. There is some part of us which knows better what to do than we actually do. And, when we can't think of what to do, it is often helpful to think of someone else who would know what to do. Just thinking of them can guide us to the right answer.

When you have a guess about what your role model would do, you need to actually follow through and do it yourself. This will not feel comfortable. It doesn't match what you are used to doing. And, you will do it poorly, compared to your role model, until you have been able to practice it many times. Then, you might actually become better at it than your role model.

A role model does not have to be someone you admire. They just have to be someone who is better than you in some attribute that you want to improve. If they are not better than you in that attribute, then they are not a suitable role model—no matter how good of a person you consider them to be. Even a person who you don't like may be a good role model for a particular skill or way of behaving.

You are learning from this book which behaviors make a secure person. Now ask yourself, which person or persons do you know who behave that way? Even if you can think of only one, use that person as your role model until you find a better one.

If you get stuck somewhere along the way

Knowing what to do does not make doing it easy. There is no easy way to become secure. The things that you need to do to change are difficult. But choosing to learn to be secure is not a difficult choice when you realize it is the only way that you will ever know true love. It is immensely significant for your life, your relationships, and your happiness. Even becoming just a little more secure can make a big difference. Set your sights on becoming more secure rather than on becoming perfectly secure.

There are not only varying degrees of neediness, people also differ in their abilities to make progress on their own. You may be able to make all the progress that you will ever need solely with the help of this book. It is also possible that you will make progress to a certain point and then not make any more. That is, you may reach a plateau on your way to becoming secure. This is normal for any person with any endeavor. Except for the naturally gifted, people will reach a plateau in whatever skill they attempt, be it baseball, playing the piano, or becoming secure.

When you reach your plateau, you will need to decide if you have become secure enough or if you want to press on to become even more secure. You don't need to become secure for security's sake. But if you are unable to have a really satisfying relationship, then you may want to get help to start making progress again. What you will need to decide is which kind of help to get.

Because neediness is so common, it is easy to recognize by most therapists and life coaches. Either one of these professionals should be able to help you with becoming more secure. The main difference between the two is that a life coach or relationship coach will be more skills focused, and a therapist will be more issues focused. There are pros and cons to working with either one.

If you would like to understand yourself better, talk about the history of your relationships, or figure out how you became needy in the first place, a therapist is a good choice for you. All of this exploration however, does come at a price. You will learn skills at a slower pace and you will not learn as many skills as you would with a coach in the same period of time.

On the other hand, with a coach you will work more directly on skills and will learn them at a quicker pace. But, you will have less exploration and also less tenderness. Sometimes, my coaching clients start out trying to spend the session crying and complaining. I remind them that my job is not to comfort them or listen to their complaining, but to help them learn the skills they need to do better. I'm not being mean to them, I'm just focusing on teaching skills rather than exploring feelings.

There are a couple of ways to determine whether you should get coaching or counseling. If you know what you need to do, but are unable to bring yourself to do it because of emotional issues, then counseling is best for you. If you have the emotional ability to make changes in your life, but you don't know what to do to have more success, then coaching is your best choice.

It will be no good for you to learn new skills in coaching if you are too emotionally unstable to use them. On the other hand, if you are pretty stable and are spending week after week in therapy without improvement, you may need to change to coaching. Sometimes, it is possible to have both. This is true when you are emotionally able to make changes, but also need extra support. You can get the support from a therapist, while you also get skills from a coach.

Summary

Needy people live in an anxious world of "What if's." they overreact to what is either normal or just small issues for most people. As a result, their partners often start to hide things from them to prevent them from getting upset. This can lead to vicious cycles of conflict and relationship deterioration. Having a secure person to talk to can help you to sort out "needy" from "secure."

By using the appropriate role models and learning to change key behaviors, you can gradually become both empowered and more attractive to others. Although people who feed off of your neediness will be put off and may not be able to continue to have a relationship with you, many others—more healthy and attractive, will enjoy their relationships with you more than before.

As you learn more and more how to make changes in yourself, you will find that other people will respond to you differently. Ironically, by demanding less from others and being more secure, you will end up getting more of what you originally wanted from others. As you make changes and grow, you will get respected, feel more important, and your partners will want to be with you more. And when they are with you, you will get more honesty and affection.

We cannot truly love someone until we accept how they truly are.

♥4♥

DATING LIKE A SECURE PERSON

Needy people and secure people don't just behave differently, they think differently, too. Needy people are far more invested in the outcome of each date than secure people are. For secure people, going on a date carries no commitment, no obligations, and no unrealistic expectations. It is simply what it is—a date. To have fun. To get to know someone.

For a needy person, there is much more at stake. Before the date, they often romanticize and fantasize about the date, building their hopes and expectations to an unrealistically high level. They are ready to commit to the person they have a date with even before they go out on the date! Because of this, needy people have to be very careful about who they date since they may be spending the next three years of their lives with the person they are going out on a date with. It takes them that long to find out they are with the wrong person. They date far fewer people and make worse choices for who they commit to.

A secure person, on the other hand, can date a great variety of people without having to worry about whether each person is right or not. Because, if they don't have a good time, or the other people are not matching them in some important way, they simply will not go out with the same people again. They will have no more than one or two dates with a person who is definitely wrong for them.

Needy people date only one person at a time. They have no one else they are dating. Because of that, the stakes are much higher. If their date does not go well, they might not have another one for a long time. They will tend to hold on to the person they date, even if they are not really a good match, because they know there is no one else who is going to be going out with them otherwise.

Secure people have other people that they are dating as well. If some new person they go out with is not a good match, it is no big deal. They have other people to date next time. If their dates are needy, they are not likely to date them again and will not continue to think about them.

The needy people's dating style results in experience with only a few people with whom they quickly become overly involved, then go through long, roller coaster type relationships, before ending their relationships in heartbreak. Each partner they think is their "soul mate," but each partner does not work out. Because of this, needy people start to think that all men or women are the same, since they have only a few relationships which all tend to be the same.

Secure people's dating style, on the other hand, results in their meeting and dating a large number of people, but only becoming serious with a few. These few have characteristics that make them stand out from the rest. Their serious relationships are more stable and end by mutual agreement. Secure people maintain other relationships and activities while dating, and never become desperate about keeping or losing a relationship. Secure people are much more likely to have long, stable relationships with mutual acceptance and respect.

As you can see, the differences between needy people and secure people reflect differences in the way they think about dating and relationships. They also reflect what they do on their dates, and what their expectations are about repeat dates with the same person. They reflect differences in levels of cautiousness, with needy people being more careful before dating, and less cautious after. To a very large extent, how and who you date today will determine how your relationships will be later on.

Needy people are (unfortunately) made for each other

Some relationships that needy people have last for a long time. Others fall apart after the first date. There are different degrees of neediness and this partially accounts for how long and how healthy a relationship can be. But there is another very important factor—the kind of people that needy people date and marry.

When two people who are both needy come together, there is a great intensity of emotion. They fall in love very quickly and see each other as ideal partners. They will consider themselves to be soul mates and will feel drawn together like moths drawn to a flame—an irresistible, insuppressible, urge. Whether they marry or not, eventually they will get past the infatuation phase of their relationship. Then, they will start to see each other clearly and to become dissatisfied with behaviors that do not make them feel loved. There will be a competition of needs. They may fight or withdraw, breakup, and makeup, many times—creating an emotional roller coaster relationship.

The emphasis of this chapter is to help you to avoid prematurely committing to the first person you date, to make sure the people you go on to have relationships with are better matches for you, and how to behave so as to attract more secure partners. All of these changes will help you to have longer, more stable, and emotionally satisfying relationships. They will be less intense at the beginning, but they will go deeper and last longer than any relationships you have had before.

Needy couples vs. secure couples

Because needy people often don't have many relationships or friendships, they are lonely people. When they fall in love with another lonely person, loneliness is instantly cured for both of them. Not only that, but there are no outside threats to the relationship because there are no other people competing for attention. When you date a needy man, he is unlikely to be dating anyone else. A pair of needy people can meet one day, be in love by the end of the day, and meet every day after that. They create a relationship bubble for themselves and everyone else is locked out of it. If you have ever experienced it, you know that it is a wonderful feeling. A pair of needy people will be able to envision a future of joy and happiness with their partners.

How does this differ from two people who are not needy getting together? Normally, when two people who are secure meet each other, they talk and do activities and gradually find common interests. They are not likely to fall in love right away and are more cautious. They realize that they don't truly know the other person, that both of them are on their best behavior, and that this is an unreal time that will be different once the relationship is established—if it is established at all.

Secure people are better able to detect and except flaws in their dates. They notice the flaws and make a determination about whether they are relationship killing issues or not. If there are big differences in values or personality, politics or religion, gender expectations or even eating habits, the relationship may end. If both are secure, they will recognize their incompatible differences and go their own ways while still being friendly. A secure person never overlooks significant differences or works to change such differences. They just move on to someone else.

When a needy person finds a secure person

Contrast this with a needy person who dates a secure person. Secure people will start to notice significant differences from the first date. Their needy dates will have an intensity of emotion which has not yet been earned. The needy dates will have a desire to connect again soon and will become anxious if there is any hesitation to do so. By the end of the date, needy people will have revealed much of their insecurity. This insecurity would be overlooked by another needy person, and taken advantage of by a player (men or women who seek partners solely for their own benefit without regard for their partners' emotional well being) .

If needy people are able to fake being secure for the duration of the date, then they may appear like secure people and make it to a second date with a secure person who is not a player. For secure people, the second date may be a week later, two weeks later, or even a month later without there being any kind of problem. For needy people, such a delay in getting to a second date is torture. Needy people will create all sorts of mental stories and continually review what happened on the first date, trying to determine what went wrong. They may even become angry because their date has not contacted them. Even from the first date they begin to impose their expectations on their dates.

Although nothing may have gone wrong, needy people think that if their dates were truly interested, then they would have been contacted soon after the first date with an overwhelming desire to go out again. Needy people may or may not contact their dates, but will most certainly want to and also will want to ask them what went wrong and why they haven't been contacted. Even at this point, after just one date, there is a controlling quality about needy people. However, needy people dare not accuse or be too harsh when asking what went wrong, lest they scare the other people away.

As their relationships go on, if they do go on, then needy people will become more and more insistent on explanations for any change in behavior such as less texting or phone calls and less frequent dating. Secure people who are experienced in dating will just see that the relationship is not working and will continue to date others. There is no need to chase after the other person and try to "fix" the relationship.

Needy people will also demand exclusivity early on. Secure people will feel controlled by this and their attraction will diminish. They will want to shake off their needy partners. This is like trying to shake off sticky gum from your shoes. But as you know, gum cannot be shaken off—it has to be scraped off. This is a difficult job for secure people. They have to become more and more intensely rejecting, and repeatedly rejecting, until the needy person gives up. All this time, needy people will be trying to rescue their relationships instead of graciously letting go of them. After all, they believe these are the only right persons— their soul mates. They get anxious and despairing at the same time. By clinging on, needy people kill any chance of romance in the future with their secure dates, who will by now just desire to get away from them.

What I have just described to you is a *hopeful* situation—a needy person and secure person identifying their incompatibility before marriage. Unfortunately, few people are one hundred percent secure. Some people have just enough neediness in them to get to the point where they make a lifetime commitment to a very needy partner. But, because they are mainly secure, they start to feel the same kinds of stress and tension in their marriages. This leads to divorces and much more messy situations than would have happened if the breakups had happened earlier in their relationships. If someone is not right for you before you marry, they won't be right for you after you marry, either. There is nothing about marriage which will fix problems in a relationship. Marriage *intensifies* any existing problems.

Changing the outcome by behaving securely

If there was nothing good about being needy, no one would have needy behaviors. One of the reasons that needy people continue to be needy is that their behavior brings immediate gratification. After all, needy people can have intense relationships even if they are short term. Compared to the initial meetings of two secure people, a needy partnering is much more exciting. It is more like a peak experience.

Unfortunately, not all peak experiences are good things. For example, a person could have a peak experience by using cocaine. Cocaine would energize them and give them a confidence that they might not otherwise have. But, is this peak experience worth the social, economic, and health costs? The answer to that is no. The reason it is not worth it to use cocaine is because repeated use is destructive. Probably you can think of some other peak experiences that would be very exciting, but would also be destructive. People are choosing every day to do these peak experiences via casual sexual encounters, risky driving, gambling, thrill seeking, and any number of other destructive activities. People are losing their lives and relationships every day in the pursuit of temporary pleasures.

Although a needy person has to be willing to give up an intense, fantasy-like early relationship, doing so will allow the needy person to have even *greater* rewards that last for a much longer period of time. She (or he) will be able to have the love that she has craved and she will be able to live without fear. Although these may not be considered to be peak experiences, their value is far greater than a few months of fleeting infatuation.

In order to make this trade of short-term infatuation for long-term love and stability, the needy person must make a transformation. It's a very difficult transformation because it takes faith. It is faith because the needy person has to make these changes without proof that behaving in a different way will actually get her more than she has had before. She will have to risk losing that which she wants to hold onto most dearly. Most needy people won't be able to do that early on. They won't be able to take such a risk until after they have had a number of failed relationships and have suffered the pain and agony of repeated loss. It is at that point that the needy person is most willing to make a change and try something new. This is more likely to be between relationships than at the beginning of a new relationship. At the beginning of a new relationship there will be a tremendous temptation to give in to the peak experience of infatuation.

I often get emails from single men and women who tell me they have been dating their current girlfriend or boyfriend for three years. They say that the relationship has been rocky practically from the beginning, but they know that they are absolutely meant to be together. They desperately want to fix their relationship and any suggestion that they need to date others is met with anger. Once committed, the heart has a hard time letting go—even when the relationship is bad. This is a major reason why you must avoid committing too soon to anyone—no matter how wonderful they seem at first. Just because people have been together for a long time does not mean that they are right for each other.

Date without committing early

Although no change is easy, a relatively easier way to start to have secure relationships is to date more than one person at a time. This is likely to be a new experience for the needy person because she (or he) is used to becoming emotionally over involved with one person very quickly and then to have no desire for anyone else. But, if she can bring herself to date several others at the same time, it will help her to avoid prematurely committing to one person. Of course, if she is going to date several men at the same time, she will need to find several men who are secure enough to allow this to happen. This is not a new fashioned idea and has been practiced for thousands of years in conservative and moral societies. Men especially, have had to prove their worthiness of obtaining the woman's hand in marriage and be approved by her parents. Do not be thinking that I am saying that you should go out and have sex with a bunch of people without regard to morality or religious values. If you go against your own values, then you will lose self-respect, your partner's respect, scare away people with the same values, and end up with a person who has differing values.

If a woman begins to date a man who insists that she date only him, it will be important for her to let him know that it is too early for commitment and that she will continue to date others until she finds the man who is right for her. Although this assertiveness is alien to her, it is actually one of the first moves towards becoming a healthy, secure woman. It also happens to be one of the best ways to find a good man. Jealous and insecure men get weeded out quickly. The same can be said of jealous and insecure women.

She needs to follow some basic rules by not talking to her dates about her other dates and also being on her best behavior with each one. She needs to have some criteria for when to stop seeing a man. When the line gets crossed by a man, she needs to stop dating him and begin dating someone else in his place. In this way, she will be using a regular system of elimination. It is important that she replaces the man that she eliminates—otherwise she will still find herself prematurely committing to one man. This is the hallmark mistake of needy women (and a frequent mistake of needy men as well).

When to commit

I have been asked many times by women when they should commit to a man. My answer to this is after the man commits to her and not before. Then the question is, "How do you know when a man has committed to you?" My answer to that is when he engages you *to be married*. A person may be faithful to you without being committed to you. This is the person who says he or she will not date others, only you. And he wants you to not date others, only him. But, he will end the relationship when it is no longer good for him. This is not commitment. It is serial monogamy.

Committing early reduces your chances for finding the right person, *especially* if you make this decision to be loyal to just one person early in the relationship. If you are not concerned about ever getting married, but want to have a steady girlfriend or boyfriend, then you can become exclusive, but it still should not happen early in the relationship. If you are going to have a boyfriend or girlfriend, have the best that you can get—not the first that you can get.

If you do get engaged (definite promise to marry), your relationship must be exclusive. The engagement is not merely a prelude to marriage; it is a time of testing and discovering what it is like to give up all others, because that is what will be required in the marriage. This is the real purpose for engagement that has been somewhat lost in modern culture. It's best then, that the first six months of engagement not include any set time for the wedding. If after six months everything is going well and the couple still want to be committed to each other—forsaking all others, then they should set a date for the wedding which is still at least six months away. This second set of six months continues to be a trial period. It is far better to call off a wedding—even an expensive one, than to marry the wrong person. But here, we are getting ahead of ourselves and I will talk more about getting married later.

On the date

When a needy person goes out on a date, she needs to show restraint. No matter how strongly she feels attracted to the other person, and no matter how strongly he is willing to attach to her, she needs to set a pace for the relationship which will slow it down. Men may be the pursuers, but women set the pace of the relationship. Men who will not respect that should not continue to be dated.

The needy person must also try to understand the perspective of a secure person on a first date. Secure people do not expect to find their marriage partners on a first date. Usually, a long-term relationship is not even on their mind. Instead, they're just focused on this one date—going out and having a good time. They don't feel like they have any commitment to the other person and no obligations to go out again, even if things go well. The date is what it is—a *one-time* event.

If the secure person has a good time, then he or she may want to go out again—or not. This is one thing which is really hard for the needy person to understand. Just because a person goes out and has a good time with you, does not mean that he (or she) wants to do it again. He or she may enjoy going out on first dates with lots of people. It doesn't mean that the date with you wasn't special if he or she doesn't want to go out with you again. It may have been a very enjoyable time.

Think of it this way. You may like to eat at fancy restaurants. You find out about a new restaurant in town and you go out and sample the menu and enjoy your meal. The next time you go out to eat, however, you may not want to go back to the same restaurant. You may wish to try a different restaurant that you have heard about or that you have enjoyed before. This is not an indication that there was anything wrong with the first restaurant you went to.

The healthy thing for needy people to do is to have the same kind of perspective as a secure person. The date is what it is. It is not a promise for the future, it is not a commitment to continue going out, and it is not a test. If you think of the first date as a test that you have to pass, then you will be setting yourself up for a problem. The problem is that if he (or she) does not want to go out with you again relatively soon, you will feel like you have failed the test. Then, you would be tempted to react the wrong way—to find out what you did wrong, to find out how you failed the test, and it will hurt your self-esteem.

If you don't get a call from the other person, an email, or text, then you will probably feel like contacting him or her and finding out what went wrong. Make sure that you don't do that, because, If nothing was wrong, as is often the case, then you will be tipping your hand that you are a needy person. The more secure the other person is, the less likely you are to be contacted again if you call with such questions.

Consider the following message:

Needy Person: (calling or texting) "Hi Jan. How are you? I had a great time on Saturday night. I really thought that you did too. I haven't heard from you for a few days so I was wondering if I upset you in some way. If I did, I'm really sorry and hope that you will forgive me. Please contact me and give me a chance to make it up to you."

Now consider this message from a secure person:

Secure Person: (calling or texting) "Hi Jan. How are you? I had a great time with you on Saturday night. Thanks again."

The secure person who receives the first message from the needy person will be able to see right away the needy person's fearfulness and self debasement. He (or she) will be put in a one up position of power over the needy person. On the one hand, he can contact the needy person and know that she will be ready, willing, and able to date him—very available, very unattractive. On the other hand, he knows that if he doesn't contact her, she will become increasingly upset with him and may even start to stalk him. He may start to become fearful. Although he may have been thinking about dating this needy woman again in the future, he will now seek to avoid her.

If he responds to her, he has to do it very carefully. He will have to both make an excuse for not having contacted her sooner as well as make an excuse to not be available in the future. The needy person who gets this call or message from the secure man will be able to see that he does not want to date her again. She may wait and keep trying, or give up, thinking that there must be something terribly wrong with her. Ironically, the problem wasn't caused by the date itself, but by her expectation that she should be called after the date and that the other person should continue to desire to go out with her. It is these "should's" that make secure people feel trapped in a relationship with a needy person.

Now consider the secure person's response to the message from the secure date. He will feel good about himself because she enjoyed the date with him, he has an opening to contact her again, but he also feels free to just accept thanks and keep her in mind for later. He is much more likely to contact her again for another date, especially if he doesn't have anyone else he wants to be with. He may just exchange a few text messages with her, with no obligation to do anything else. Both people will have profited from their time together with no obligation to continue. There is no obligation because there is no commitment. One date does not make a relationship.

The needy person will no doubt wonder at this point, "Well if I contact him and he doesn't contact me back, then how long should I keep waiting before I contact him again?" The answer to that is both simple and difficult—*don't contact him again*. If he wants to contact you, he will. You're not chasing him will make you more attractive than if you chase him. Men will *use* women who chase them, but men will only commit to women *they* have to chase. Men value most what *they* work hardest for.

What about the needy man? If men are to do the pursuing in relationships, then should a needy man behave differently? Surprisingly, the answer is no. Needy men and women need to follow essentially the same rules for successfully dating secure people.

One of the first of these rules as I said before is simply to go out and have a good time without worrying so much about whether the other person is going to like you or not. Whatever you do, remember to give and take in conversation, and to be at least as interested in the other person as he or she is interested in you.

Dates are for two purposes—having a good time and getting to know each other. Dates are not for securing a future with the other person. Most of the people you date will not be compatible with you and will not be good prospects for the future.

A date is not like trying out a new pair of shoes. When we try on shoes, we're not concerned about the shoes. When we date, we need to be concerned about the other person for at least two reasons. First, we need to be concerned because the other person is a person and can be injured or encouraged by what we do or say.

Secondly, we need to care about the other person because of the effect that caring will have on us. If we start to think only about ourselves and our needs, using other people as much as we can, then we will lose the ability to love. When we use other people, we injure them, ourselves, and our future partners.

The temptation that many needy people have when they go out on a date is to conclude the date by asking about the next date. In general, I think this is a mistake. If your time with the other person is limited—as it might be while traveling or on a cruise, then it does make sense to plan the next date even before the first one is finished. But when there is not such a time constraint, I don't recommend planning a second date or another date right away. Instead, tell the person that you had a wonderful time (if you really did). Even if you didn't, thank the other person for spending time with you. Time is something we all have in limited quantity and when someone spends time with us, we need to appreciate it. You can probably imagine an important person such as the Queen of England thanking a commoner for taking the time to come and visit the Royal Palace or some such thing. It is a courtesy. The only time not to be courteous is if the other person has treated you badly, which wastes your time.

If the other person mentions going out again at the end of the date, then generally you should be agreeable, but not commit to anything. Men like to chase and women like to be chased. Stringing dates together *ends* the chase. Because secure people are not likely to say at the end of the date that they never want to date you again, you need to be able to use the follow-up signals (post-date contact) to determine their interest in you, as I said above.

So, to get specific about this, there is a maximum of three contacts that can be made around a date. The first is the anticipation of the date. You contact the person briefly to tell him or her that you are looking forward to your time together on Saturday, for example. This conversation should be fairly brief and can be done in a text message. It helps to build anticipation and it also confirms the date. Not much should be said at this time because the real getting to know each other happens during the date. If you have too much contact prior to the first date, you may find awkward silence during the date when you have very little to talk about.

The second contact is the date itself. The third contact happens after the date—either the next day or a couple days later when you thank the other person for the date. It doesn't matter whether you are a man or a woman as the contact is the same. Even during this third contact of thanking the other person for the date, I don't recommend arranging the next date right away.

You should not only avoid giving the other person the impression that you are constantly available to be his or her date (a very needy thing indeed), but your life should actually have so many activities that another date right away would not be practical. If the other person has enjoyed the date, he or she may say something about doing it again sometime, and if you would like to do that, then you also should say yes that you would like to do that again sometime as well. Keep the conversation or the text messaging fairly short and friendly.

After this third contact, focus on getting back to work, getting back together with your friends, meeting other people, going out on a date with someone else, hobbies, traveling, shopping, and so on. A person who has many friends and activities to choose from is very unlikely to be a needy person. In contrast, someone who is always available to date the same person is highly likely to be needy. Always strive not to pretend to be secure, but to actually be secure. Put your eggs in many baskets and don't worry if a few of them get broken. It is easy to get new eggs.

What becomes evident from these kinds of guidelines is that you must have good social skills not only for dating, but also for having friends, meeting new people, and having other people to date. Learning and practicing social skills is essential for you in your quest to become secure. Without good social skills, your successes with people will be few and far between and you will be overly concerned about losing the people who do like you.

Summary

Secure people have a number of behaviors that come naturally to them. Other *secure* people are comfortable with these behaviors. If you are needy, you also have a number of behaviors which come naturally to you. Other *needy* people are comfortable with your needy behaviors. As long as you match your dates, your early relationships will go very well. However, for you to successfully date and build relationships with secure people, you must learn to do what is not natural—to think and behave like secure people. This will be difficult because the required changes will feel risky and you will fear losing your relationships. However, if you are able to make secure changes and hang in there, you will be rewarded by more secure and stable relationships. These relationships will not feel as intense at the beginning as the needy relationships you are used to, but will be far better later on than your other relationships were. The decision to become secure means giving up the short term rush that comes with needy relationships in order to have the long term stable and mature love that comes with being secure.

In the next chapter, we will look more closely at the specific changes you can make to go from being needy to being secure.

You hypocrite, first take the plank out of your own eye and then you will see clearly to remove the speck from your brother's eye.

Jesus Christ
Matthew 7:5 (NIV)

LOVING AND RELATING LIKE A SECURE PERSON

One of the main benefits of overcoming neediness is having improved relationships with other people. That doesn't happen just because you feel more secure. It will happen because you will actually be using the social skills that secure people use. You don't have to learn hundreds of social skills to do well socially. All you need are a handful of basic principles that you can apply to every situation. In this chapter, you will discover the differences between what needy people do and what secure people do. Then, you can go and practice. In moving from being needy to being secure, it's necessary to start behaving like a secure person—even though these behaviors will feel unnatural at first.

At first, no behavior feels natural beyond the basic animal instincts. Everything you have learned in life felt very unnatural when you were first learning it. Things that you can do so easily now, like reading this book, were once very difficult and unnatural. You had to learn a step at a time and keep practicing until you were good at it. So it will be with secure social skills. You will read to find out how, then you will start practicing. The more you practice, the less you will be faking it and the more you will become it. Remember—no one is born secure.

Everyone who is secure had to learn to be that way. This means that you can learn, too.

Behaviors to avoid

Criticizing

Criticizing is telling a person, directly or indirectly, what we do not like about them, what they do, what they don't do, or what they say. It is something that needy people don't do early in relationships, but it is something that needy people very often do later on in relationships.

Needy people don't criticize others early in relationships, for fear that other people will reject them, leaving them alone. They tend to have a much greater tolerance for flaws in their partners and often make excuses to themselves as to why their partners behave this way. As a result, early in relationships needy people will put up with many disrespectful behaviors from their partners. This sets the stage for a long course of disrespect. Later on however, when they are feeling more secure in their relationships, needy people start to use criticism in an effort to get their partners to take better care of their needs. Two kinds of criticism stand out: *reassurance criticism*, and *correction criticism.*

Reassurance criticism is designed to get other people to reassure and reconfirm their love. This reassurance will provide a temporary fix for needy partners. If it only happened once in a while, it might be okay, but it tends to happen again and again as in the following example:

Needy Person: "You don't love me. You just want to be with your friends and you're tired of me. You don't need me anymore."
Partner: "Of course I love you. I just want to go out with my friends once in a while. I will always love you."

You can see in this example that the needy person does get reassured. But you can also notice something else—the needy person's secure partner becomes defensive. It is not merely reassurance to the secure partner. For the secure partner, it is a job that he has to do in order to be able to go out with his friends. The more he has to defend, explain, and reassure, the more his entire relationship will feel like a job. And like all people who do their jobs seven days a week, he will eventually burn out. He will eventually come to the point where he doesn't love her anymore and where he would much rather be with his friends or anywhere except with her. This very same dynamic happens when the genders are reversed. Secure women can and do burn out on needy men.

The lesson to be learned here is do not criticize in order to get reassurance. In fact, you should not ask for reassurance *at all*. Criticizing or asking for reassurance both cause much the same problem. Instead of criticizing for reassurance, you should learn to weigh the evidence for yourself. Although your partner going out with friends (or spending time on hobbies) and leaving you alone may not feel good, does your partner have other behaviors which show that he or she does like to spend time with you? Learn to self reassure in order to be more secure.

The second kind of criticism is *correction criticism*. By pointing out flaws in others, the hope that needy people have is that others will say "Gosh, you are right. I didn't realize I was behaving that way and that it hurt you so. Thank you for pointing it out. I will be sure to get to work on changing that behavior right away." Although this is the fantasy needy people have, partners almost never respond this way. If you say to your spouse that he or she never listens to you, that he's (or she's) selfish, that he's (or she's) a slob, and that he's (or she's) lazy, your partner will not change into a caring, considerate, industrious person who makes you feel like a priority. Your partner will instead become more and more like the person you accuse him or her of being.

What do secure people do instead of correction criticism? They tell their partners what they like rather than what they don't like and they leave it at that. "I like the way you hold me when we're lying in bed" is a much better thing to say to your partner than "You spend too much time watching TV late at night." But this is something that secure people only say if their partners actually do hold them in bed. And they don't wait until their partners stop doing it before they tell them. They make their partners feel good about their behavior from early on in their relationships. It is not a "technique" that they try only after things have gotten bad.

Get in the habit of telling other people what you like about them. Not so that they will also tell you what they like about you, but just so that they will enjoy being with you more. Don't expect immediate results. And don't feel like other people owe you something just because you say something nice about them. Learning to be secure means learning to love without trying to *make* someone love you. We all hope our love will be returned, but when we love, we say and do things just because we know our partners will like it and feel good. If you only love in order to get love (or anything else), you are not truly loving—you are needing. Jesus Christ gave us an excellent example of how to love. He did not die for us so that we would love Him. He died for us because He loves us (John 3:16).

Don't complain

Complaining to people about how they are or what they do, is criticism, as covered above. In this section, I am talking about complaining about other people (not the one or ones you are talking to), situations, or things. You might complain about how you're working conditions are unfair, how you are always doing things for other people and they don't do things for you, or complaining about how the things you buy are overpriced and low quality. You might complain about how the children get on your nerves, what a lousy job the government is doing, or about the price of tea in China. Unless you are actually doing something about these situations, complaining about them to partners takes away from their energy level. It makes them tired to hear you complaining—especially if you do it often. Our complaining adds an unnecessary burden to our partners' lives.

Men who are complained to often believe that they need to somehow do something about their wives' complaints. At first, they try offering solutions and advice, but if the complaints continue, they begin to feel ineffective and powerless. Then they will start to tune out the complaining and start wishing that they didn't have to hear it at all.

Women who are complained to by needy husbands start to find their husbands less attractive. Frequent complaining is declaring yourself to be a victim of your environment rather than a master of it. Women will initially soothe and support their poor, victimized husbands, but they will eventually tire of playing nurse maid and will wish their husbands were more secure, capable, and leader-like.

For both genders, one of the major reasons for complaining is to draw attention to themselves and to get support and empathy. If you want to tell me that everyone complains sometimes, I would agree, especially when they experience an unusual event, such as being fired from a job or breaking a leg. These situations are both very stressful and also temporary. Other people often don't mind giving some temporary support, empathy, or sympathy.

However, people get tired of needing to continuously give support or sympathy. They have problems of their own. They will start to wonder why you can't manage your own problems and why you want to burden them with yours. When you do this with a significant other, it adds to the load that he or she has to carry in being in a relationship with you.

The more you criticize, complain, and demand reassurance, the heavier your partner's load, and the faster he or she will burn out on your relationship. Even if you can't stop these needy behaviors altogether, changing one or two of them can greatly reduce the load that your partner has to carry, making your relationship better and more secure. It's not that the needy person has such unusual demands, but that the needy person has *too many* demands. So, anything you can do to reduce those demands is going to help.

Instead of complaining, which is saying what you don't like, instead learn to say what you do like. You won't get sympathy or pity for that, so when you make this change you will probably feel like you're missing out on something. On the other hand, making this change will help you to have better relationships. So you actually end up getting more than you had originally. By not trying to "force" sympathy and attention out of others, you end up getting more positive attention from others, who will enjoy being with you more.

This does not mean that you can never complain again. But you need to have some way to figure out when it is good to complain and when not to. I have a rule which may help you know when to complain and when not to:

Only complain about things which you are willing to do something about.

For example, if you're going to complain that your job is no good, then you need to be willing to do something about it. You need to be willing to write a letter, go on strike, complain to the authorities, talk to your boss, or look for another job. If you are not willing to do any of these things, then don't complain.

Let's consider a relationship example. Suppose that your spouse always meets you late when you plan to go somewhere together. If you are going to complain about your partner being late, then be prepared to do something about it other than just complaining. For example, be prepared to go without your partner. If you are unwilling to do such a thing because you think it would make your partner upset and risk your relationship, then don't complain about it in the first place.

It makes perfect sense to complain about your spouse's affair, if you are preparing to leave your spouse and are giving your spouse an ultimatum. It makes no sense to complain about your spouse's affair if you are not willing to do anything about it. You cannot save a relationship by complaining any more than you can save a relationship by criticizing. Complaining creates avoidance, not attraction.

Needy people often confuse complaining about something with doing something useful or helpful. Complaining, by itself, is neither useful nor helpful and does not benefit relationships. It adds an unnecessarily negative element to what should be a positive experience—being with your partner. When I am with my wife, I focus on her and not on the irritations that I had that day.

If you are a chronic complainer, your partner will become more and more emotionally distant from you. Learn to say what you like, or to say what you don't like and then be prepared to do something about it. These are your secure choices

Arguing

Did you know that arguing is a needy behavior? That's right, secure people don't need to argue. A really secure person can listen to the opinions of others, agree or disagree, then make a decision for himself or herself. There is no need to persuade the other person. People who argue feel it is somehow necessary to persuade the other person to their point of view. They need the other person to think that they are right.

Persuading the other person that you are right, might not be such a bad thing if it didn't cause damage. After all, if the other person thought that you were right, then you both would have the same belief and that would put you both on the same side. Being on the same side, your relationship could grow and you would be living in harmony. The problem with this theory is that it doesn't work.

When you argue with someone, that person may argue back, shut down, or avoid you. Even if the other person is persuaded by your argument, he or she will not have a good feeling because of it. Your relationship will continue to deteriorate. In all my years of counseling and coaching (more than 20 at the time of this writing) I have never heard of anyone arguing their way to a better relationship. But time and time again I have heard how arguing brought people to the very brink of their relationship. Often at that point they stopped arguing and tried to mend the relationship. It's a very curious thing, that people somehow know that when you get to the brink of a relationship you shouldn't argue. They know that more arguing will send their relationship over the edge. But before getting to the brink, they continue to argue as they watch their relationship get worse and worse. If people were truly rational, they would quickly see that arguing doesn't work and stop it before things got much worse.

They would not wait until their relationship was about to collapse before they stopped doing damage to it.

When people are first in relationships, whether they are needy or secure, they quite naturally *agree* with each other. They do this repeatedly and often about little things and big things. If there are differences, they downplay them and may not pay attention to them at all. This acceptance helps to build the connection between the couple and the relationship becomes deeper. Anybody who likes to argue on first or second dates is going to find that they don't have many dates before the people they are dating lose interest in them.

The time when arguing starts to become a problem is usually after relationships become established, when people feel like they have their partners "locked in." At this point there is a shift from the chase (the early part of a relationship), to the time of adjustment. When I say time of adjustment, I don't mean adjusting oneself but I mean attempting to adjust the other person. The typical sequence is: I chase you, I catch you, I fix you to be the way I want you to be, and then I sit back and enjoy. This is the typical approach for a needy person and it doesn't work. Needy people never get to sit back and enjoy because they can't past the "I fix you" stage. Their partners never get fixed to their satisfaction.

This problem is exacerbated by the fact that needy people tend to choose partners who match them in neediness, but who are very different in other ways. Because they tend to attach quickly, whether the other person is a good match or not, they later find themselves needing to make a lot of corrections to the other person's personality and behaviors. The *secure* person avoids this by not committing to someone who is not a good match in the first place. This makes the whole adjustment phase much easier.

But what do you do if you are already in a relationship with someone who does not match you very well and you want your relationship to continue? What you need to do is to learn how to *agree* and *decide*. These are two separate things: 1) agreeing, and 2) deciding. Agreeing will help you to maintain a relationship, and deciding will help you to maintain respect.

To agree, listen to what your partner is saying. Find the part of what he or she says that you can sincerely agree with and agree with that. Say nothing about the other things that you disagree with. Then decide what you are going to do (this is actually the boundary part). For example:

Your Spouse: "I shouldn't have to come home after a full day's work and clean up your mess when you have more time than I do."

The natural and instinctual thing to do in this situation is to start explaining why you didn't clean the house. Either that, or start complaining that your spouse never offers to help out. Or try to make a point that you actually do even more than your spouse because of childcare and other things that your spouse doesn't consider. None of these responses though, would either gain you respect or build the relationship. Let's consider what would:

You: "Yes, you are a hard worker and you shouldn't need to do more than your fair share."

What do you suppose would happen after you said this kind of thing to your spouse? It's likely that he or she would agree with you. In which case, you can probably give your spouse a hug and a kiss and clean up. Your spouse might even help you. There are other, more respect-building choices, however.

You might agree with your spouse just as I said and then not clean up. You might admit to your spouse that it is hard for you to get the cleaning done. This also would be agreement, and this also would be the truth. That is obvious from the mess around you. You can then make a decision about whether you are going to work on rescheduling your time so that you can clean up better, or whether you are going to hire someone to come in and help you, or whether you are going to delegate some of your work to someone else so that you have time to clean up, or whether you can simply leave the problem with your spouse without blaming or arguing. For example:

You: "Yeah, I really left a mess here."
Your Spouse: "Well, what are you going to do about it?"

At this point, your spouse has asked you a *question*. Questions should be easy to deal with. All you need to do when you're asked a question is to give an honest answer without a long explanation. For example:

You: "I'm not sure what to do. I just don't have time to get to it many days because of the other things I have to do. I guess I could give something else up so that I could get the cleaning done. What is it you suggest I leave undone so that I have more time for cleaning?"

Your spouse is not likely to have a good answer to this, and he or she might just forget about it and drop the issue. On the other hand your spouse might give you some good suggestions that you never would have gotten if you had argued. Even if he or she gives you an idea that you should give up something that you really don't want to give up, you can still decide whether to do that or not. Hearing your spouse's idea does not obligate you to follow it. But neither do you have any obligation to argue about it. Remember, it's the arguing that does most of the damage—not the refusal to do what your spouse wants. As long as you are connecting with agreement, most of the time you will be able to be assertive, make decisions, and have good boundaries without damaging your relationship.

Needy people tend to argue so much that when they use boundaries or make decisions, it further strains the relationship. There often is not enough good connection in the relationship for them to be able to do these necessary things. It's a similar situation in parenting. If you are always arguing and fighting with your child, then when you make rules or correct your child, your child is much more likely to hate you and reject you and not simply be angry. But, if you have a basically good relationship with your child, then you will be able to correct him or her as necessary and enforce rules without damaging your relationship. Many of the same principles that apply to parenting also apply to adult relationships.

Some people say to me that they will become a doormat if they agree with their spouses. You don't become a doormat by agreeing. You only become a doormat when you agree to *do* things that you know are not right or that are harmful for the relationship. Doing what you know is right or good for the relationship will never make you a doormat. It will make you a loving person with a mind of your own.

Interrogating

Interrogating is another relationship damaging behavior tied to insecurity. Like other insecure behaviors, interrogating someone pushes them further away. I have never seen a relationship become closer because of interrogating. And yet, needy people believe that finding out the answers to their questions will in some way protect their relationships. Needy people interrogate, looking for any kind of danger or signs of rejection. If they don't find it, they are reassured, but at the expense of their partners. If they do find it, the information in no way helps them. In fact, it usually leads to arguing and even more damage.

Simply stated, *interrogation* is asking people questions that they don't want to answer. Some typical interrogation questions are:

"Where did you go?"
"What did you do?"
"Who were you with?"
"What did you talk about?"
"Why are you late?"
"Why didn't you call?"
"Why didn't you respond to my text?"
"Why did you lie to me?"

What needy people hope is that their partners' answers will reassure them that their relationship is strong. In fact, these are the only answers that needy people will be satisfied with. Their partners quickly learn that and so usually provide the desired answer, whether it is true or not. Although partners will answer such interrogation questions without much complaint early in a relationship, the questions become tiresome the longer the relationship goes on. The more partners are interrogated, the less they know they are trusted, which makes them pull even further away.

Another problem is that needy people often feel threatened even by reasonable and honest answers. Although their partners may not have done anything wrong, their answers may make needy people feel insecure. For example, in answering the question "What did you talk about?" He (or she) might say that they talked about their college days. Although that would be a common thing for people to talk about, especially if they went to college together, in the insecure person it raises further questions. She (or he) may have a line of thinking something like, "We weren't together when he was in college. He had different girlfriends at that time. If he's enjoying talking about his college days with his friends, then he must be missing being with other women." As result of this line of thinking, she may interrogate him some more, accuse him of not loving her, or be angry without explanation.

Because he said nothing wrong, and yet gets this kind of bad response from her, he will start to become more secretive or careful about how he answers when she interrogates him. Unfortunately, this will only exacerbate the problem because she will see that he is becoming more and more reluctant to answer her questions. In turn, this will make her more and more insecure and make her ever more vigilant to signs that he is losing interest in her (or gaining interest in someone else). He, in return, will become less comfortable talking to her and sharing with her the things that he does.

He will not only feel the need to be careful, he will start to feel like he has to "report" details about what he does. Reporting to someone is work. It is very different from voluntarily sharing with someone because you enjoy the conversation. This will become his job if his partner is needy. He will have to answer questions and report on his behavior and perhaps his thinking too. He will have to become good at lying—not because he's doing something wrong, but because he has to give the answers which make her satisfied.

This kind of extra work, which is required by the partner of a needy person, will eventually make the more secure partner feel burned out. He or she may spend more time at work, playing video games, using social media, watching TV, going out with friends, or even turn to alcohol to medicate feelings of being burned out on the relationship.

So, if interrogating is a needy behavior, what do secure people do? *They don't interrogate.* They don't ask people questions they don't want to answer. They trust others until it has been proven that they can't be trusted. They give others the benefit of the doubt. As a result, their partners feel comfortable to go out, have a good time, and to come back and share what they will. They look forward to seeing their partners. They don't have a dread of coming home and being questioned. They don't dread getting their partners text messages. And, they don't need to think up lies.

Secure people welcome their partners home and have the assumption that their partners love them and are not going to do things to damage their marriages. This assumption actually helps to *protect* the marriage from the damage that would otherwise be done from the mistrust and questioning.

Secure people are not naïve. They know that it is quite possible for their partners to cheat on them or to be involved with other behaviors which are damaging. They don't want that to happen any more than you do. But, instead of being ever vigilant for that, they have the self-assurance that if something like that arises, they will be able to deal with it at that time. They don't live in fear of it, because it is not something to be feared. It is just something to be dealt with if it happens.

One of the ways that you can develop this capacity in yourself is to make contingency plans. That is, you predict the thing that you fear and make a plan as to how you would deal with it in a successful way. For example, if you were afraid of your home burning down, you would make sure you have fire insurance. You could then reasonably say to yourself,

"If my house burns down, the insurance company will give me money to replace my belongings. In fact, my new home might be even better than the one I have now. Even if I lost something that was important to me, I could get other things that are important to me. I would be okay. Many people have had homes burn down and then were okay after that."

You can extend the same line of thinking to your relationship. What if your spouse did have an affair? Or what if your partner did break up with you? As a needy person, that thought becomes so intolerable you don't even want to deal with it and you may spend all of your energy protecting against that possibility. In fact you can spend years of your life being anxious. If you were to deal with this fear, it would actually raise the quality of your life by helping you to enjoy your life more.

One of the exercises that I have my needy clients do is to imagine their partner rejects them and leaves. And then to make a written plan as to what they would do three months, six months, two years, and five years after their partner abandoned them. Although this is a difficult exercise, it forces them to see that their lives would go on, that they would spend time with friends, and hobbies, and eventually date someone else. I also have them look at the possibility that the new person they date might love them as much or more than their partners who rejected them. After all, how hard can it be to find someone better than someone who rejected you? When they can see this possibility, losing their partner is still not something they desire, but something they can be a little less afraid of. By repeatedly doing this exercise, you can gradually decrease your fear of losing your partner.

In this example, we use abandonment, but you could use anything—affairs, drugs, death or any other scenario that scares you. There is a way to deal with all of these things and to still come out okay. Needy people usually stop with their fear rather than going on to the answer. They ask themselves "What if my partner leaves me?" But they don't want to answer that question and so they are stuck with their fear. They never get the chance to realize that they will eventually be fine if their partner leaves.

Secure people may consider such questions, but they are able to answer those questions and that's what helps them to go on. I have heard many secure people say "If my spouse cheats on me, I'll divorce. I don't need a partner like that." This kind of answer is satisfying, because it doesn't foster fear. And these secure people don't need to continually ask their partners about their whereabouts, thinking, or behaviors. They are free to love them and love them well. Their spouses, as a result, are much less likely to have affairs than the spouses of needy people who continuously are mistrusting, critical, and anxious.

Talking about problems

This one is going to come as the biggest surprise to readers of popular psychology self-help books. Most self-help books for relationships recommend that whenever you have a problem, you should talk about it with your partner. The idea is that if you talk about problems, you can do something about them—which is much better than letting them fester and build until they become really big problems. This theory makes sense to me too. But when theories can't withstand the test of reality, they need to be discarded—no matter how much sense they make.

What I have seen time and time again is that when people try to talk to their partners about problems in their relationships, the very act of talking about the problems creates even more problems. It takes very mature, healthy people, to sit down, rationally talk about problems, and come up with solutions. Typically, people become defensive, explanatory, and critical. And, because people continue to believe that talking about things is essential to making them better, they continue to try this strategy, again and again, without looking for more effective alternatives. The result is that every time this talking happens, the tensions get higher, the relationship gets worse, and it becomes harder and harder to talk to each other. Unless this strategy is abandoned, people may come to the point where they don't talk to each other at all.

A better strategy is to talk about a problem once, and then if there is no improvement, or if things get worse, consider alternatives to talking about problems. Ask yourself, "What can I do about this problem other than talk about it?" When you seriously ask yourself this question, your focus will shift. Your focus will change from trying to get your partner to understand and make a change, to *your* taking responsibility for making changes. It is always easier to change oneself than it is to change one's partner.

For example, if your husband retreats for days at a time in moody silence, that is obviously a problem for your relationship. If you try to talk to him about this, he will undoubtedly blame you as the reason for his withdrawal. If you try to tell him it's a problem for your relationship and that it needs to stop, he will give you a solution—your no longer doing the thing which caused him to withdraw (in his opinion). Then, you either end up having to suppress the behavior which he reacted to, or you start to explain why that behavior was necessary for you. As a result, he is likely to withdraw again or you are likely to become more and more withdrawn as you suppress your behavior more and more to avoid his withdrawal. This problem can grow to the extent that both of you become permanently withdrawn from each other.

Now let's consider, instead of talking to your husband about the problem of his withdrawal, you do not talk to him about it. Instead, you go about your routine and allow him his withdrawal. You don't go to him and apologize. You don't go to him and talk about it. You don't go to him and try to fix it. When he eventually stops being withdrawn, you're very nice to him and welcoming to him as well. You don't talk about his having been withdrawn or the problems which started it. The result of this kind of behavioral change in yourself will make him withdraw less and less. The opposite—talking to him about the problems—will cause him to withdraw more and more. It may not make intuitive sense, but taking a positive action rather than talking about problems will lead to a closer relationship.

Needy people don't feel wanted when their spouses do things like withdrawing, avoiding them, not returning messages, and so on. And it is hard for needy people to be able to emotionally tolerate those kinds of behaviors. They become impatient and confront their partners about these problems. As a result, the problems get worse and worse. What is clearly needed is a way for needy people to remain strong throughout this withdrawal or distancing behavior of their partners, so that they can once again be friendly and welcoming when they do get interaction from their spouses. This is important for encouraging interaction by their spouses rather than discouraging it.

One way to remain strong is to change what the withdrawal or avoidance means to you. Needy people say to themselves, "He's withdrawn. That is terrible. If this continues it is going to be the end of our relationship. Then I will be all alone. I have to put a stop to this now." And of course with this kind of thinking the needy person tries to intervene and actually makes it much more likely that his or her relationship will end. So, the needy person's thought processes create behaviors that turn her fears into reality. A better thought process is to think something like this:

"He's withdrawn. That's his way to reduce stress and to try to punish me for something he doesn't like. He obviously still cares about the relationship or he wouldn't do this kind of thing. He would leave instead. I can take advantage of this time by treating myself well without getting upset with him. That way, his withdrawal won't be punishment for me and he will gradually learn it's not an effective way to deal with problems. All I need to do is keep myself busy until he ends his withdrawal and then treat him well. If I do this kind of thing from now on, he will withdraw less and less and we will get along better."

In this example, we talked about withdrawal as the problem, but you could substitute almost any other kind of marriage problem or relationship problem. Repeatedly talking about problems makes them worse. *Doing something* about problems makes things better because it creates a change in the way the two of you relate. Talking doesn't do that.

Like most things in life, there is an exception to this and it is important for you to be aware of it. It *is* good to talk about a problem if your partner has the same idea of what the problem is and is also motivated to solve it. That is an excellent time to talk about a problem. For example, if you think that you and your partner do not go out enough, and your partner also thinks the same thing, then talking about this problem will help you to come up with solutions and go out more, improving your relationship.

On the other hand, if you think that you and your partner do not go out enough, but your partner does not enjoy going out with you, then talking about it will not lead to solutions and connection. It will lead to conflict and disconnection. You will actually need to help your partner to enjoy you more before you can start to talk about this problem. This is why it is not helpful to go to marriage or couple's counseling with your partner if your partner is not motivated to improve your relationship. It would just create conflict and distance. Marriage counseling or couple's counseling is most helpful when both you and your partner want help in improving your relationship.

If your partner does not want to improve your relationship, but you do, first work on helping your partner to enjoy your relationship more. Stop any damage you are doing, learn some connection skills and use them consistently, and then you will build your relationship (without ever having talked about it). That is mostly what I am doing with people in coaching and why I work with individuals rather than couples.

Does this sound like a pessimistic view to you? That you can't talk about problems with your partner? In my opinion, this is one of the most important and hopeful lessons for anyone to learn. That is, you don't need to convince or cajole someone else to change their behavior. You don't need to have stressful talks or arguments. All you need to do is to change the way you respond to the other person and the way you treat the other person. Like a pebble dropped in a pond, this will create ripples of healing in your relationships.

Elsewhere in this book, I give advice for other secure ways to deal with relationship problems. You will see that they have very little to do with talking to your partner and more to do with making changes in yourself. This is your key to success.

Giving long explanations

Explaining is a little different from arguing and the other needy behaviors. Most of the needy behaviors that I talk about are needy whenever they occur. That is, they are to be avoided at *all* times. Explaining is not like that. People who are secure also explain things. The difference is needy people explain things even when other people are not interested in their explanations.

The reason that needy people explain things is not because they truly want the other person to know something that is vitally important. Their main concern is that they not be misunderstood or attributed with the wrong motivations or be seen in a bad light. That is, the reason for the explanations is to protect themselves from being rejected if their behaviors are misinterpreted. This is not something that a secure person would normally even think about.

For example, if you ask a secure person a question such as "Did you take out the trash?" it would likely be met with an answer such as "Yes I did," or "No I didn't." There would be no thought of explaining why or why not, unless the other person asked. A needy person, on the other hand, is likely to answer a question like this in a very different way, especially if she (or he) didn't take out the trash. Her answer might be something like this:

"Well, I was going to take out the trash, but then I got a call from my sister and she was really upset. Her car has problems and she can't afford to get it fixed. But she needs it to go to work. And, because she already has a lot of debt, she's afraid of borrowing the money to fix her car because her husband might get upset. So, I helped her to figure out how to talk to her husband about it. And then,

after I got off the phone with her, you came along at that time, so I didn't have time to take the trash out."

People who give such long explanations, when they're not asked for, will not do well in their job or relationships. Other people will get tired of listening to their long explanations. Then, when others get tired of listening to their long explanations, they will tend to stop asking questions or even interacting with these needy people. The thing that needy people fear—other people rejecting them if they don't explain, actually comes about because of their explanations. Their fear of rejection prompts them to give long explanations which then result in rejection. This rejection-avoidance (attempt to avoid being rejected), rejection-result (get rejected) is a common pattern with needy people. Their behavior brings about the things they fear—distancing and loss of relationships.

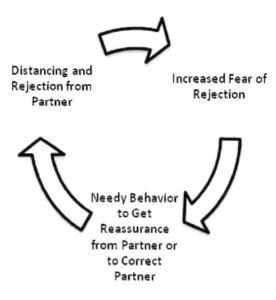

The Neediness-Rejection Cycle

You may be thinking, "But if I don't explain to him why I didn't take out the trash, he will be upset that I didn't take out the trash." And here, we can see one of the core beliefs of needy people—that upsetting or disappointing other people will cause them to be rejected. This fear of other people's anger creates the behavior of explaining and many other behaviors which may temporarily *appease* the other person, but in the long run erodes and even ends their relationships.

I don't want you to switch from one extreme to the other, however. Just as long explanations are not good, failing to provide any explanation at all also is not helpful in relationships. The secure and attractive way is to give a very brief explanation and then let your partner ask for details if he or she wants to. For example, your partner asks you if you took out the trash and you answer:

"No, I got a call from my sister and I didn't get to it."

If your partner is interested, he or she can ask you more about your sister. If not, then you just move on. If you follow this same practice with everyone, they will enjoy talking to you more. If someone asks you how your weekend was, for example, you can just say a little about what you did and let them ask you about it if they are interested. For example:

Your Friend: "How was your weekend?"
You: "Good, I saw a new movie. How was your weekend?"

After this, some people would ask you what movie you saw, but most probably would just talk about themselves. The main point is not to share as much as possible with others, but to help them to enjoy talking to you.

Sometimes, needy people get the feeling that their spouses or partners are not interested in listening to them. This is often true because the needy person gives a lot of long explanations which the other person becomes bored with. Contrary to popular belief, sharing with others does not make them want to share with you. If you want your partner to share more with you, you need to become a better listener.

With needy people, even simple conversations can be so full of explanations their partners come to avoid talking to them. They have learned that talking means meandering down this path and down that path without being able to get a word in edgewise. Especially for men, this is not a fun thing to do. If you would stay on the subject, without giving long explanations unless you're asked, your partner will enjoy listening to you much more. The result will be a strengthened relationship for both of you. You can then spend more time talking about what matters rather than what doesn't.

There is a related problem that happens with some needy people. Some needy people repeatedly explain the same things. The reason that they do this, is that they are hoping that by doing so, their spouses will come to understand their behavior. They reason that if their spouses understood the motivation for their behavior, that their spouses would no longer be upset by their behavior. But repeated explanations don't actually have that result. If your spouse does not like your behavior, repeatedly explaining why you do it will not make your behavior more acceptable to your spouse. In fact, it will just make your spouse more irritated. It is not lack of understanding that makes your behavior unacceptable to your spouse. It is lack of agreement with your reasons.

Similarly, if you explain your reasons to someone, after they have asked, and they are not satisfied, explaining again will not make them become satisfied. The secure person, if asked again, would simply say "I have already explained it. Which part do you still not understand?" That is, the secure person does not feel provoked to explain more just because the other person continues to be upset. Because of the needy person's behavior, the upset partner may repeatedly ask "Why did you do that?" in order to keep upsetting the needy person. It's something that just wouldn't work with a secure person. Secure people don't take responsibility for their partners' upset feelings or happiness. They simply love the best they can, they keep good boundaries, and if other people don't like it, it is not their problem.

Truly secure people are not afraid of their spouses' anger. They expect their partners will become angry sometimes and are okay with that. They don't try to prevent it, they are not afraid of it, and they don't feed into it. They either ignore it or deal with it. Because of this, their spouses are not rewarded for their anger and they don't become more and more angry as the relationship continues. Needy people, on the other hand, train their spouses to be angry by being reactive. It gives their spouses a lot of power and rewards them for getting angry.

Even if you don't like your partner's behavior, as much as possible don't ask your partner to explain his or her behavior. Simply deal with the behavior by using good boundaries or by deciding it's not a behavior that you need to do anything about. Asking for explanations is virtually the same thing as criticizing and leads to relationship deterioration instead of relationship improvement. You will find that even when you get explanations for your partner's behavior, that your relationship is not better off for it. It's time to take explaining and asking for explanations out of your toolbox, because they are not helpful tools.

Defending and apologizing

Your partner is very upset and blames you for something you didn't do. What is the correct response? Well, that depends on what your goal is. If you are a needy person, you may have one of two different responses. You may start defending yourself, explaining how it wasn't your fault. Or, you may start apologizing. Although these responses look different, the goal is the same—to stop your partner from being upset with you because it provokes your fear of losing the relationship. This is a goal of *self protection*.

What do secure people do when someone is very upset with them? They listen to whatever that person is saying, and admit to any truth in his or her statement. They doesn't bother to argue, to defend themselves, or to blame back. If the other person wants to be angry and go off and sulk, that's okay. If the angry person becomes irate and verbally abusive, then secure people will end the conversation and/or leave. They don't stick around to be badgered or try to convince the angry person to be more reasonable. That is not their responsibility. Their goal is to *protect the relationship* by not participating in unhealthy interaction.

So which of these approaches do you think works better for maintaining a relationship? If you are a needy person, you may be surprised to find out that the second approach, the secure one, is the one which presents the least risk to the relationship. Secure behaviors are always the ones which have better *long-term* consequences. Needy behaviors are the ones which seek to avoid short-term conflict, but lead to long-term problems. Let's discover more about this by considering both defending and apologizing, in turn.

Defending oneself is basically saying to the other person that he or she is wrong. This is the message, "You are wrong to accuse me of that and to be angry at me because (insert justifications here)." The intent of such a message is to have the other person respond by saying something like

"Oh, I'm sorry. I blamed you when it really wasn't your fault. Thank you for straightening me out. I'm going to be more careful about what I say to you in the future so that I don't hurt you again."

You will never even see this kind of response in a movie because people watching the movie just wouldn't believe it. Real people don't respond like this. The only kind of people who might actually respond like this are the ones who don't become angry and blaming in the first place.

People who get angry and blame do not respond well to correction. That is because people who blame avoid responsibility. If you correct someone who blames, then the most common response is for him or her to blame you for something else which you actually did do, even if it has nothing to do with the current situation. For example:

Your Partner: *"You didn't use that coupon I gave you for a discount on the oil change."*

You: "Yes, I did. You can check the receipt. You should check to see if you are right before you blame me for things."

Your Partner: "You are wrong so much of the time, it's not worth my time to check. Remember when you bounced that check because you weren't careful about what you were doing?"

Or, if you really do a super job of defending yourself, your partner is likely to withdraw, shutdown, or leave:

Your Partner: "Remember when you bounced that check because you weren't careful about what you were doing?
You: "Actually, I was. It bounced because you didn't deposit your paycheck when you said you were going to."
Your Partner: "I'm tired of your nagging. I'm out of here." (Withdraws to his or her room and shuts the door or leaves your home).

If you repeatedly defend yourself from your partner's accusations, then the relationship will become more and more distant. This behavior of defending oneself is an insecure one. It doesn't really promote self-esteem, because ultimately it results in rejection. It makes you feel better when you say it, but feel worse when your partner leaves you. Secure people do not need to blame others or verbally defend themselves.

Now let's take a closer look at apologizing. Apologizing is only an insecure response if you do it repeatedly or for something you didn't actually do. Let's consider a few examples to illustrate this:

Partner: "You never let me do what I want, you're always trying to control me!"
Needy You: "I'm sorry. I won't do it again. Just don't be mad at me."

What is likely to result from this is that your partner calms down, but also feels justified in treating you in an angry way. Your partner draws power from this kind of interaction. It works in your partner's favor. The next time your partner is angry or wants something, he or she will be quick to show anger and to blame you again. So, although you will immediately be rewarded by your partner's calming down if you apologize, you will also foster continuing conflict by supporting your partner's unfair and aggressive behavior.

Another apology example:

Partner: "You are always overspending our money. You think it grows on trees. I always have to be the one to bail you out."

Needy You: "I'm sorry. I guess I didn't realize how much I was spending. I'll be more careful next time."

Even if you did overspend the money, your partner is still addressing you in a disrespectful way. By apologizing like this and making promises to do better, you set yourself up for a bad outcome in two different ways. First, promises lead to broken trust because, if you later make a mistake—no matter how small—your partner can say that you promised and that you are a liar. This is a much bigger problem than if you had never promised in the first place.

The second reason why this kind of response is problematic is much like the previous example. Your partner will be rewarded for the way he or she is treating you. In the future, when your partner is upset, he or she will treat you this way again and again. Your apologies will *never* do anything to turn off that behavior, but will result in a loss of love in the relationship for both of you. You'll still be afraid of losing your partner, but you won't be in love with him or her anymore. Neither will your partner be in love with you. Apologizing is fine, but not in response to an attack.

Now, let's consider a secure person's response for both of the previous examples.:

Partner: "You never let me do what I want, you're always trying to control me!"

Secure You: "Yes, I do complain about what you do, especially when I think it's bad for our relationship."

What has happened here? Your partner has tried to push a button. Your partner has tried to emotionally strong-arm you. It didn't work. You admit the truth about your behavior without apologizing for it. Your partner doesn't win anything. He or she is not rewarded for blaming you. And, if your partner starts to become abusive, you will walk out.

If your partner asks you what you mean in saying this, then he opens himself up for more truth. It's not something he's likely to do many times because it will put him on the defensive end of the conversation. In short, this way of responding stops your partner from continuing to use this kind of blaming attack in the future. And it helps you to earn your partner's respect. You don't attack your partner and your partner doesn't blame you. You don't blame your partner either. Nor do you defend yourself. And, you don't apologize. Instead, you listen carefully, and agree with whatever you can. It's an approach that stops blamers from blaming, because their blaming no longer works for them. Blamers become powerless in the face of sincere agreement.

Let's take a look at this with a second example:

Partner: "You are always overspending our money. You think it grows on trees. I always have to be the one to bail you out."
Secure You: "Yes, I did overspend our budget."

Notice what isn't here. There are no apologies and no explanations. There is also no disagreement and no counterargument. There is no reverse blame. You simply *ignore* the part of your partner's comment that you do not agree with, while admitting to the part which is true.

By refusing to argue or cower, your buttons are not being pushed. Your partner is not rewarded with any feeling of power. You become secure, not punishing. After this, your partner is likely to come back with a follow up question such as asking you why you overspent the budget. Or, your partner may explain to you why the two of you can't afford to do such things. In the case of the question, you have simply to answer it. In the case of your partner saying that you two can't afford to overspend this way, you will again agree. By responding in this way, the discussion actually goes somewhere productive rather than deteriorating into an argument. Again, this way of responding not only prevents long-term problems in communication, but also leads to useful solutions.

The next time you are tempted to apologize and defend, or apologize and promise, agree instead.

Nagging

Nagging is probably the easiest to understand of all the needy behaviors. What is nagging? Nagging is when you ask someone more than two times, or remind someone more than two times, to do something that they have yet to do. Nagging turns you from a partner into a parent. Nagging is an attempt to control another person's behavior. Secure people don't need to do this, especially with their partners.

So why do people nag if they know nagging is bad? The main reason that people nag is because nagging works. It's like using a hammer to drive in a screw. It will do the job, but not without causing damage. Just as with the other damaging behaviors, there will be short term satisfaction that will accumulate damage to the relationship. As a needy person, you need to acknowledge the you have a choice to nag or not. When you choose to nag, you are making your immediate gratification and relief of anxiety more important than a long-term, close, secure relationship with your partner.

Let's consider how a needy woman might handle a situation where her husband has failed to make good on his promises. Her husband, a plumber, promises to fix a leak in the bathroom. He doesn't do it. She asks him again a week later. He irritably tells her that he is going to fix it. But he does not. She starts to think about how he doesn't care what she needs or wants. She attributes meaning to his behavior beyond his mere procrastination. That both scares her and angers her. It scares her, because it means the relationship might be in danger. It angers her because she does lots of things for him and feels like he owes it to her. She may alternately treat him badly to punish him for not reciprocating her love, and be extra loving to try to restore the relationship. Her unpredictable, roller coaster type behavior makes him tired. He goes to work all day and comes home not knowing what to expect from her. Maybe she'll be in a good mood, maybe she'll be in a bad mood. This behavior erodes the relationship.

Just like the other behaviors, there are healthy and unhealthy alternatives to this needy behavior. An unhealthy alternative would be to just suppress your anger and do nothing. While causing less conflict, that is also a needy behavior because it is ineffective in resolving the problem. Once again, you need to learn what secure people do and to start doing what they do.

Secure people have two choices when others are not following through. They either take responsibility for handling the problem themselves, or they forget about the thing that they want done. Let me give you an example of a secure woman in the same situation:

Suppose a secure woman is married to a plumber. She has a leak in the bathroom. Her husband has promised to fix it, but he hasn't done it. So, she asks him again. Again, he promises to do it but doesn't. She does not ask a third time. Instead, she hires another plumber to come do the job and fix the faucet. When her husband discovers that she has hired someone else to do the job, he becomes angry. But, because she is a secure woman, she does not argue with him or defend herself. She agrees with whatever he says that is true. He goes off to be grumpy for a while. She lets him be grumpy as long as he wants. When he comes back out of his shell or man cave, she welcomes him with open arms and is glad to see him again. Their life goes back to normal. There is no ongoing problem. What could have become a long, drawn out power struggle has become only a bump in the relationship and that bump has passed.

I have heard needy women tell me many times that they could never do such a thing as to take care of the problem themselves if it were to make their husbands upset. The reason—

not concern for their husbands' happiness for sure, but rather their fear that it will damage their relationships. The only recourse open to such women is to "forget" the problem and not mention it anymore. Maybe that's not so hard if the problem is just a leaky faucet. But, it's never just a leaky faucet. It's the faucet, it's the clutter in the garage, it's his staying up to watch TV instead of going to bed with her, it's his showing up late for dinner, it's his coming home late from work without telling her, it's his lack of attention to her when she wants to share something, and it's many other things, too. After a while, needy women get filled up with these things that they're holding down inside. And when they get filled up, they explode. This collection of behaviors from their partners makes them feel so unloved that they try to force love and attention from their partners. Of course that doesn't work—it just increases the problems.

When you consider these two approaches, needy and secure, hopefully you can start to see how the secure woman's response of taking care of the problem herself is the much better one— even if it makes her husband angry for a day. And, because the other six days of the week she'll be very loving with her husband, he will know what to expect from her, and he will know what he is coming home to. Although he won't admit to it, there will be some part of him that knows she was right to hire the plumber. He doesn't have to admit it though, and she's not going to bring it up again.

Whether man or woman, husband or wife, the secure way of handling things left undone is the same.

Summary

Becoming a secure person isn't easy. It is not merely a few behaviors that need to be changed. It is a *mindset* that needs to be changed. It is a fundamental shift away from living in fear to loving despite fear. It entails a leap of faith that by making changes in behavior something good will actually come about instead of abandonment and isolation.

In this chapter I have helped you to look at several behaviors that are characteristic of needy people. And, as you have probably surmised, many of these behaviors are characteristic of people in general. We are an insecure species and that makes us become very self focused, protective, defensive, and yes, even aggressive.

By starting to change the behaviors that I talked about in this chapter we have the best hope of fostering love in our relationships. There is no guarantee of that, no matter what we do. But, we are guaranteed to have worse relationships if we don't make these changes. We need to trade in short term self protection for long term relationship protection. We have become addicted to short term relief and need to break the addiction cycle.

You can start to break your addiction to short term anxiety relief by changing *one* of the behaviors that I talked about in this chapter. If you can change just one needy behavior that you have, you will begin to be a secure person. It will feel risky at first and you will have the urge to do the needy behavior. But, if you can maintain this secure change, you will most likely be rewarded by a corresponding positive change in your partner. And that will encourage you to change yet another behavior, and another. Many people have completely improved their relationships simply by putting an end to the needy behaviors discussed in this chapter.

The beauty of becoming secure is that you can improve all of your relationships without struggling to change the way other people treat you. Change yourself and this will naturally create a change in the way people treat you. You can get more love from others by being less needy and more loving first.

If your partner does have some severe behaviors, you can also change those by making a change in yourself. You can use healthy boundaries—deciding what you will and will not do, without ever having to try to control your partner. Secure behavior, good boundaries, and rapidly returning to loving behavior after there has been conflict, will keep your relationship strong and your partner close.

If you are catching the wrong fish, you are probably using the wrong bait.

♥6♥

A SECURE WAY TO FIND A MARRIAGE PARTNER

Would you like to find a lifetime "partner" in every sense of the word? The kind of person who never makes you doubt that you are with the wrong person even after many years of marriage? The kind of person who loves you for who you truly are so that you are comfortable being yourself? Whether people desire a prince, a princess, or a poet—it's my goal as their coach for them never to have to "settle" for anyone. If you use the methods in this chapter, you won't have to settle for anyone, ever again.

Finding the right partner will be much easier as a secure person, because people who were previously out of your league will desire you. And, if you continue to be both loving and secure, they will want to continue their relationship with you.

Don't get the wrong idea—this is not a chapter for hooking up with a hot partner for a hot date. It is about being an obviously valuable choice for the kind of partner you are interested in. It would do you no good to be able to find great potential mates if they would find you undesirable or would soon lose their attraction to you.

Before I start telling you how to find a marriage partner, I want to remind you of what we are trying to stop. Needy people find one person who is available to date them, begin to fantasize about that person, become overly involved from the first date, then commit as soon as possible—trying to "lock in" their partner so as not to lose their relationships. As a result, they often end up infatuated and committed to someone who is not a good prospect for a long term relationship. They lack a good basis of comparison and fail to see this until after they are married, when they are no longer infatuated and see all of their partner's flaws they could not see before. Then, they spend the rest of their relationship years trying to change their partners back into the way they first imagined them to be. Their partners feel unaccepted and eventually leave the relationship. This does not have to be you!

The emphasis of this chapter is to help you to avoid these needy behaviors by having corrective behaviors that will make you more secure. Although not exactly the way naturally secure people do things, the methods in this chapter will help you to overcorrect for neediness. There is some margin for error built in because no one does all of these things perfectly. Just do your best and keep at it. Plan to do all of your becoming secure before you get married, so that your marriage will be off to a good start later on.

Your head and heart must work together

You need to find the best potential mates that you can find before putting yourself in a situation where you might fall in love. Just as an alcoholic needs to stay away from bars in order to recover, so you have to stay away from needy people if you are to recover from your own neediness. Never count on your willpower to be able to resist needy people. Needy people are going to be the most irresistible for you and so you must avoid even putting yourself in the situation of meeting one.

Getting a partner is not like getting a car. If you fall in love with a junk car, you can fix it up. But, you will never be able to fix up a junk partner. You can't rescue, or fix someone, by having a relationship with him or her. With a needy partner, the ecstasy you feel at the beginning of the relationship will be matched by the agony you will feel at the end of it. Marriage is for life. You need to find someone who can go the distance. And, if you cannot find such a person, then you should not get married. When getting married, consolation prizes turn out to be booby prizes and not worth the effort.

Needy people usually follow their hearts from the very beginning, even if their heads are telling them they are making a mistake. Part of being secure means to follow your heart *only* when it is in sync with your head. A bad choice at the beginning will lead to valuable time lost with the wrong person when you could have been with someone else. The good news is that there is no single one person who is the best. The idea of "soul mates" is romantic, but not Biblical and not supported by any scientific evidence. Many of today's soul mates will be in tomorrow's divorce courts. There are in fact many possible right partners for you and even more wrong partners. It *does* matter who you select to date, and who you choose to continue dating.

It absolutely would not work for you to find a partner who makes you feel great but is a poor candidate for marriage. If you did, you would need to shape him or her into the kind of person that is necessary for you to have the kind of marriage you want. Needy people do exactly this. Before marriage, they hope that marriage will somehow change their fiancés in the direction they want. When that doesn't happen, they get about trying to shape their spouses. For years they keep trying to shape their spouses, still going after the kind of relationship they have always wanted. Eventually, their spouses get tired of being shaped and the relationship ends.

If you are wanting to get married, you need to date people who don't require shaping. Use your head to not put yourself in a position to fall in love with a bad prospect for marriage.

Find a match for the kind of marriage you want to have

The best jobs are not advertised in the newspaper, the best clothes are not on sale at the department store, and the best partners are not hanging out at the local bar. Sometimes they happen to be people you are overlooking in your daily life. Sometimes you need to go where you don't usually go. And sometimes they can be found on the internet. There are all kinds of people on the internet—good and bad, but it is a tool that has to be used wisely, especially if you are looking for a marriage partner. Sites that find you matches are better than sites where you find your own matches, provided they use good match algorithms and the people who submit the information are honest.

Simply trying to think where available people are and going there is one of the worst ways to find a mate. To get the partner you want, you must:

1. Know what kind of *relationship* you want to have,
2. Know where to find a partner who would enjoy that kind of relationship on a long term basis,
3. Know how to get such a partner, and
4. Be able to do what it takes to get such a partner.

If you know what you want in a relationship, but not where to find a person who would work well for that kind of relationship, you can't get such a person. If you know what kind of relationship you want and where to find such a partner, but don't know how to attract such a partner, you can't get such a partner. If you know what kind of relationship you want, where to find such a partner, how to get one, but are unwilling to do what it takes to get one, then you are not going to get one.

The only way to get a partner who will work with you to have the kind of marriage that you want to have is to know what kind of relationship you want, where to find such a matching person, how to attract such a person, and be willing to do what it takes to get one. Most people who do not have success with *anything,* whether a person or a project, are missing one or more of these vital qualifications: knowing what they want, knowing how to get what they want, and doing what it takes to get what they want.

Everybody is perfect for some kind of relationship. You shouldn't simply look for someone who has the qualities that you think are generally good in a partner. Also, you shouldn't look for a person with qualities that other people say you should look for. If you did that, you would be looking for a partner who was right for somebody else. Think about the kind of relationship you would like to have for 50 to 70 years and then seek people who would match that lifestyle.

No matter who you pick, at first they are going to be enjoyable. For example, if you are a real extrovert and you date a real introvert, he or she is going to have fun going out with you and meeting all of your friends and doing things. However, that person will eventually tire of that and settle back into a routine that is more stay at home, quiet activity, and one on one. And, if you are a conservative person, you may find someone who has a history of being rather wild, but is willing to attend church with you, trade the bar for the museum, and make other lifestyle changes. However, most of the time, such people will eventually tire of that and go back to what they enjoyed before. Differences are exciting at first, but differences cause problems later.

The best places to meet people for relationships turn out to be in the places that you most enjoy being. If you are an avid outdoors person, the best place to meet people is doing outdoor activities. If you love your job, the best place to meet someone is at your job (provided they love their job, too), if you are a fine arts person, then the best place to meet people is at fine arts gatherings. People who already have the same interests you have share enough in common with you to warrant at least going out with them for coffee. And, getting such a small date is not hard to accomplish when you already share a common interest.

Prepare yourself for success with your ideal partner

Once you have determined where the best partners (for you) are actually to be found, you must have the ability to get at least one when you are there. If you are shopping for a diamond ring and find a quality store with a beautiful selection, you must then have the means to get one or you will be out of luck. Likewise, you must have the qualities that your choice partners want, or you will not be able to get even one—no matter how many you meet. If you become the kind of person they would desire, then all you need is a chance to show that to them. If they are turned off by you, you would start to look in places where plenty of people with low standards are available. That might get you a fixer upper, but as I said before, trying to fix someone up will just get you rejected in the end.

To catch the right kind of fish, you need the right kind of bait. This means that the more you become the ideal person you want to be, the more you will attract the ideal person for you. The better you are able to become *relationally attractive*, the more success you will have with people who value close relationships.

Finding a match before you pursue a relationship makes a lot of sense. It's much better than finding someone, getting in a relationship with them, and then trying to figure out how well you match each other. By that time, you are likely to be emotionally committed to the relationship whether you are a good match or not. But, don't go to that matchmaking site yet!

Bad relationships, like good relationships, also happen with people who match us. Let's take an extreme example. If you are an alcoholic, then you are likely to get in a relationship with other addicts or codependent types. But, if you get sober first (before pursuing relationships), you will match an entirely different group of people. You will be less likely to revert to alcoholism and your relationships will be healthier. A good match is one who matches how you ideally want to be. But, in order to attract that person, you must first become like your ideal. How good of a spouse would you be for the kind of marriage partner you want to have? Would a potential mate be able to see those qualities in you now? What do you need to change about yourself first?

Don't find a partner to end your loneliness

If you have no friends, another lonely person will match you well. You will feel "made for each other." This makes short term relationships great, but presents problems in long term relationships. If one of you makes friends with other people during your relationship, the other won't feel so special or important any more. And that will be a source of conflict. Fear and jealousy will be provoked, one of you will become controlling and the other resentful.

If you make friends before pursuing romance, you will attract an entirely different (and healthier and wealthier) group of people. You will both have friends during your relationship and this will help in many ways. Your relationship will be on more solid ground. Similar examples can be made about any area of your life where it's difficult for you to stand on your own two feet or to be happy.

Don't get in a relationship in order to be happy

If you are unhappy, your relationships will tend to be "fixes" that make you feel better temporarily, before you crash and burn and start desiring a different one. This bears repeating—because of neediness in some area, people get into relationships that seem like emotional wonder drugs. But just as with most stimulants, when the emotional high is over, you will be lower than you were originally. Spouses are good for sharing happiness, but when you start needing them so you can be happy, your behaviors will begin to drive them away.

You can avoid emotional roller coaster relationships by improving your life *before* seeking out a life partner. Get a job, make friends, and live an active life that you don't want to mess up. Then, you are much less likely to get into a relationship with someone who would mess it up. If you got into a relationship with a needy person for example, you would soon have to give up many of your activities and friends. The better you make your life before seeking a partner, the more careful you will be about who you commit to.

To the extent that you solve your own problems before finding a partner, the better match you will find and the more secure your relationships will be. This puts the happiness of your relationships and the quality of the people you date under your control. This doesn't mean you need to be rich or gorgeous. It means you enhance all areas of your life where you are needy until you are not needy any longer. Then, you will have created the perfect conditions for finding a secure partner to share your happiness with.

Ten practical steps for finding a good life partner

To enhance your life so that you are attracted to the right people and so they are attracted to you, follow these steps:

1. IDENTIFY areas where you are needy or overly dependent. Examples are lack of friends, no job or income, lack of fun activities, no hobbies, lacking in social skills, and so forth.

2. GET these needs met *before* pursuing a relationship. This may require making friends, learning job skills, practicing new hobbies, learning social skills, and so forth.

3. LIST additional desires (not needs) you have for your ideal future. Examples are traveling, having children, living in the country or city, having an active party lifestyle, being a homebody, and so forth.

4. DEFINE exactly the kind of man or woman who is likely to match your desires for the future. An intense connection with a person who later has different desires than you would spell disaster for your marriage.

5. BECOME the kind of person that would be a good match for your ideal partner. You won't marry someone you don't match because that person would have no interest in committing to you.

6. MEET as many prospective partners as your time and resources allow. Date, evaluate, and eliminate. Try to have

casual meeting dates (going out for coffee, taking a walk, seeing a show, etc.) with at least 50 people over the years before you marry, just considering them one time encounters. This investment of time and energy at the start will save a lot of pain and heartache later on. We are talking about someone you will spend your entire life with. If you start dating at 18 and get married at 25, this only amounts to dating seven people per year.

7. DON'T COMMIT EARLY. Committing too soon is one of the hallmarks of needy people. They commit before they really know their partners because they feel in love. If a relationship is really right, you don't have to commit early to prevent losing it. If a potential mate will be lost quickly if you don't make a commitment, he or she is needy and you should not continue to date that person.

8. STOP DATING THE WRONG PEOPLE. Continuing to date someone who is not right for your future takes away other opportunities and is more likely to result in another failed relationship. You cannot fix someone up for marriage. Qualities like different desires and values, lying, jealousy, and verbal abuse will only get worse with marriage.

9. DATE SEVERAL PEOPLE AT THE SAME TIME. One way to prevent yourself from prematurely committing to someone who is wrong for you is to be dating several good candidates *at the same time*. This has been the traditional way to find a mate for thousands of years. Committing quickly and having a few serious relationships, one after the other, without any casual dating intensifies neediness. Date many. Hold to your values. Commit to one. For life.

10. MAKE SURE that you also have time for other activities and people in your life. Remember, secure people don't give up their lives in order to have a relationship—they have a relationship in order to share their great lives with others who also have great lives.

If these steps seem unnatural to you, remember that doing what comes naturally will just maintain your needy behavior.

If you are needy, there are a lot of people looking for you

If you are needy, there will be a lot of other people looking for you—to take advantage of you and to sell you things that won't really benefit you. There will also be a lot of people wanting to find you for short term relationships. For a lot of men, needy women are fun to fish for, but they are not the kind of fish they want to keep. This is even more true when it comes to women. What woman really wants to have a long term relationship with a needy man? Whether men or women, they know they just need to dangle the bait right and the needy fish will school around and swallow the hook. Are you in that school?

Keep in mind that predators are not just interested in sex. Some are interested in getting your money, getting married, having babies, getting a green card, making their boyfriend or husband jealous, and so on. When people can't get what they want, they get what they can. If you are a needy person, you are more likely to become someone's consolation prize than their treasure. Become secure and become someone's prize!

If you are *not* needy, there are also a lot of people looking for you

Happy and secure people, who have their lives together, will be attractive to most everyone. Not only will they attract needy people and predators, they will also attract other secure and happy people. They attract the kind of partners that most people can't have. Secure people stand out from others and are very valuable. They are alpha. They won't have anything to do with needy partners or predators, and the good partners who find them won't want to let them go.

Bad bait will only attract bad fish. Good bait will attract both bad and good fish. When you are secure, you will attract both secure and insecure people. But, you will need to quickly reject the insecure ones. Never count on your ability to resist falling for the wrong person.

If this sounds too hard for you

You may not need any extra help. You may be ready to start making all the changes you read about in this book. But, if you find that you are so needy that making the changes suggested in this chapter are too hard for you, then you just need to get a little extra help. If that is the case, please see the section at this end of this book on getting more help. Don't give up. Just get help.

Others are doing this, you can too

The worlds of needy and secure people are very different. No matter how foreign all of this sounds to you, you need to be aware that secure people are *routinely* doing this. They are enjoying their lives and relationships. They were not born secure. They learned to be that way. Some from their families, and some the way you are learning right now. You know from your past experiences whether your way of doing things, no matter how comfortable they are for you, is really getting you what want you want in life.

In changing to a secure way of finding a mate, your beliefs will be challenged. You are learning the inconvenient truth that *good relationships cannot happen naturally for needy people.* You are also learning the disappointing truth that feeling in love is not enough of a reason to commit to someone. And, you are learning the anxiety relieving truth that there is no one right person that you must safeguard against losing. In fact, that truth is one of the most important for becoming secure and having healthy relationships.

When it comes to finding a marriage partner, you can either passively wait for someone to come along or you can create in yourself a desirable person and then refuse to commit yourself to anyone but the best from among your many candidates. Most people put more care and effort into the car they choose than into the partner they choose. Unless you want to trade in your spouse for a new one every five years, you need to put in the planning and effort it takes to have a truly great partner. And, you can have fun doing it!

♥7♥

GETTING A RELUCTANT PARTNER TO COMMIT TO MARRIAGE

Needy people often become involved in relationships that have affection, but lack lifetime commitment. Some needy people have been with their partners for years, with a hollow and fearful feeling in their gut because their partners don't seem to want to marry them. If you have been in this situation for a long time and do not want it to go on indefinitely, becoming secure will help. If you are having difficulty getting your boyfriend[2] to commit to marry you, it is either because you are going about it in an ineffective way (remember, *needy* means ineffective), or he has a good reason not to marry you. This chapter will help you to become more effective in getting him to commit, by your becoming more secure, and it will help you to respect his wishes, which is also part of being secure.

Before I start telling you how to get your boyfriend to marry you, I want to remind you of what we are trying to stop. Needy people are quick to commit in relationships, see their fiancés

---

[2] Because men and women commit to relationships for different reasons, I could not make this chapter apply equally to both men and women. However, if you are a man and you are more stereotypically female while your girlfriend is more stereotypically male, then this chapter will apply to you as well.

unrealistically, get married, and then spend the rest of their relationships trying to change their spouses to become just like them. Their spouses feel unaccepted and eventually reject them—ending the relationship.

The emphasis of this chapter will be on helping you to make sure you have not committed yourself too quickly and are seeing your partner realistically. It will emphasize putting a lot of time and care into who you marry, because once you marry, you will need to accept and love your spouse as he or she is. The more needy you are, the more uncomfortable you will feel with my ideas. But, it will make the difference between you setting yourself up for a happy marriage or a troubled one.

Taking responsibility for your decisions

The first thing you need to realize is that you are not at the mercy of your boyfriend's desires or choices. He cannot prevent you from being married, he cannot prevent you from finding a good partner, and he cannot prevent you from having a long and happy marriage. He is not keeping you stuck and he can't put you on hold. The only thing he can do is to stop you from marrying *him*. Every other decision is being made by you. Part of being secure is taking responsibility for everything that is under your control. So, if you are secretly or outwardly blaming your boyfriend because you are not getting married, it is time to stop that right now. He is just making what he thinks are the best choices for him. You must do the same.

It's possible that after doing everything you can to become secure and attract him, that he may still not want to marry you. This does not mean that you need to break up with him. You can choose to continue your relationship with him. You will need to decide if marriage and having a family, or keeping your boyfriend for a while longer, is more important to you. It is a value decision that no one else can make for you. A large part of being secure is knowing what you want and making good choices for you. You can even decide not to decide, or to put your decisions on hold until a certain day in your future. To be secure, it does not matter what choice you make, as long as you realize the choice is yours. Being secure is liberating and empowering. And, because you will be more sure of yourself and not blaming others, you will be more attractive, too.

Success factors

Like everything in life, there are three principles to getting what you want:

1. You have to know what you want.
2. You have to know how to get what you want.
3. You must be willing to do what it takes to get what you want.

The lack of success that many people have is due to their missing one or more of these three principles. This does not change when your goals have to do with relationships. Getting married or having a good marriage also depends on these three principles. It is not reasonable for us to expect love and commitment from others if we are not willing to do what it takes to create in them a desire to love and commit to us. This is true before marriage, and it is true after marriage as well. If you have been in your relationship a long time and your boyfriend is not asking you to marry him, you will need to admit to yourself that what you are doing is not effective in getting him to propose. That may be because you don't know what to do, because you fear what he will do if you do what's necessary, or because he would never propose to you no matter what you did. Doing nothing certainly lowers the risk of being rejected, but if getting married is really important to you, then you will need to learn what to do and take a chance on doing it.

Needy people often want to get what they want without doing what's necessary. They become so scared of doing what's necessary, that they settle for what they don't want. Then, they blame others or "bad luck" for not doing better. Their fear of loss and rejection creates for them a life of loss and rejection. I'm all for wishing and visualization, but we can't stop there if we want to have success. We have to follow *The Law of Action.* Effective actions bring effective results, ineffective actions bring bad results, partial results, or no results at all. The universe does provide, but it requires that we work for what we get.

Needy people have a habit of repeatedly trying the same, ineffective strategies, hoping that they will eventually result in their getting what they want. Sometimes they do that because it is easier than doing what is required. Other times, it is because they don't know what to do. When you read this chapter, you will know what to do if you want to be married and you are running into resistance or lack of interest from your boyfriend. There are always internal and external forces at work to stop us from becoming healthy and improving ourselves. Just as an alcoholic may lose her alcoholic friends when she gives up drinking, a woman may lose her needy boyfriend when she becomes more secure. If your boyfriend is secure, you have nothing to fear. A secure man will not reject you when you become more secure. He will feel closer to you. You will be more attractive to him. He will be more willing to commit to you.

If your boyfriend is using you, he may prefer to have a needy woman. In my experience, many needy women prefer to stay in an unhealthy relationship, even with a man who is using her. She is willing to be used, abused, or cheated on if it means she can have more time with him. She clings to her unrealistic notion that she is going to transform this man into a man who truly loves her. If this is you, then there is no point to your finishing this chapter, but do hold onto it. You will need it one day when your amount of hurt starts to overpower your feelings of love for your boyfriend.

If, on the other hand, you do what it takes to get married, even with the possibility that you may lose your boyfriend, then you will have less delay before you get married, are more likely to marry a person who turns out to be a good match for you, and a higher likelihood that your marriage will last. Secure women know that the strength of their love is *not* a good test of the quality of a man. They are prepared to walk away from any man who is not good for them. They know they will be sad temporarily, but they also know that all will be forgotten when they find men who truly love them and want to be with them for the rest of their lives.

Love is not enough

Needy women believe that the strength of their love *is* a measure of the quality of their partners and a good predictor for how successful their marriages will be. The fact is that the strength of your love now is *not* related to the success you will have in your marriage. Most people who get married are strongly in love and feel like their partners are their soul mates, yet half of these marriages end in divorce and an even higher percentage experience affairs and loss of love. Your success in marriage is most related to:

1. How secure you are.
2. How you deal with conflicts.
3. Your willingness to maintain your spouse's attraction to you after you are married (yes, how attractive you are depends on what you do).

Secure people do a much better job of maintaining their partners' attraction throughout their relationships. They do not expect their spouses to stay attracted to them merely because they are married. They put the same loving effort into their marriages as they did into their relationships before they were married. When people say that a marriage takes work, this is the work they are referring to.

How you need to be if you want him to marry you

If your relationship has not grown closer for at least the past two months, you are at a relational plateau. Carrying on as usual will not improve your relationship, but will gradually decrease your closeness. You may be able to carry on your relationship like this for years, and there is nothing wrong with that if you are happy with what you have. If, on the other hand, you want your boyfriend to marry you, you can greatly improve your chances of marrying him if:

1. You eliminate all needy behaviors on your part,
2. You give him a good reason to marry you, and
3. You are *not* willing to wait indefinitely for him to decide what he wants.

Elimination of all needy behaviors will mean that you are less work. Loving men are happy to go out of their way to win the favor of the women they love. They don't, however. want to be pressured to do these things. If for example, he texts you because he enjoys it, he will look forward to his future with you. If he texts you because he has to, in order to avoid upsetting you, then he will be able to read the writing on the wall—"This is a woman who will never be satisfied, no matter what I do." Although a man will be willing to have a relationship with a woman like this on a temporary basis, he will be ready to trade up when the opportunity comes along.

In order to give your boyfriend a good reason to marry you, you need to learn why men get married in the first place.

Why most men marry

Imagine you have been in a relationship with a man for a long time. Perhaps even years. He says that he loves you, you talk about your future together, you drop little hints and "accidentally" find yourselves looking at the engagement ring display in the mall jewelry store. But still he makes no move toward marriage. Does he not want to marry you? Is he waiting for something else? Is there something more you should do? Is he afraid to marry you? What does he want?

There are some men who marry for sex, money, social status, or to become a resident of a different country. This is particularly true if they have had difficulty finding sexual partners or if their girlfriends are wealthy, famous, or are citizens of a more desirable country than theirs. These men are to be avoided even though they will make you feel very loved early on in your relationship. Often these men are very charming, very attentive, and want to commit very soon. If you have what they want, you will have no problem getting them to marry you—if all you want is to be married. However, I would recommend that you look for people who marry for entirely different reasons if you are actually interested in a long term *relationship*.

There are some men who marry because of cultural and/or religious expectations. If you have the same cultural or religious beliefs, such a man might be a good match for you, even if it is an arranged marriage. If you don't happen to share the same culture or religion though, I don't recommend you marry a person who has strong cultural or religious beliefs. This is because eventually his expectations of how the marriage should be will clash with your expectations of how the marriage should be. and the difficulties will be hard to resolve. I am not talking about race or ethnicity. I happen to be Caucasian and from the USA and my wife is an Asian from Japan. But, we share the same religion and both like the Western style of marriage. Otherwise our marriage would fail. You must never marry so quickly that you are not fully aware of your partner's major beliefs, values, and expectations. *If there are differences, they must change and the changes be sustained before marrying.* The greater the initial differences, the longer your engagement should be.

There are two common reasons men would want to take the next step from a romantic girlfriend-boyfriend relationship to a husband-wife relationship.

The first are men who dream of having a family. Although families are a wonderful thing to create, men who are family oriented may need to be slowed down from committing too early in a relationship. They often idealize their partners and overlook significant differences and potential problems in their rush to be married. Beware of any man who says he loves everything about you. They may have many assumptions about your expectations for how to be as a couple and how to raise children after you are married. In essence, these men are in love with their idea about how wonderful marriage is or what it can do for them. Often, after they marry, they have little or no romantic interaction with their spouses as they focus on their next goal, which is usually their careers. It won't be hard to get commitment from such people unless you are doing or have done something which drastically interferes with their marriage dream. If you marry such a man, be prepared to be very independent and to have little one on one contact with him after you start having children.

Usually what happens is that such couples will focus all of their energy on raising the kids, earning the money, and taking care of the house. Sound good? What's missing in this scenario? What's missing is the relationship between the husband and wife. There will be little dating, little intimate talking, and more individuation. Couples in this situation are often resentful and unhappy. If they don't have affairs, the relationship generally ends when the children are teens. It just becomes too hard to make the transition from focusing on the children to focusing on each other. Desiring to have a family is good, but it is *not enough* for marriage. This is a major change from the reasons that people in our parents' generation got married. What worked well in that generation does not work so well today. Today's couples are much less willing to sacrifice romance to maintain a home.

If you have followed the advice given earlier in this book—of dating several people at the same time (I don't mean having several boyfriends at the same time), you are less likely to have prematurely committed to this type of partner. You would have been going out on casual dates with several nice, eligible men. Your current boyfriend would have been one of them and as you got to know him, you would have found him better suited to you than the other men you were dating.

In the dating process, he will have had time to get through the infatuation phase and to see that you have faults—many in fact. After going through the ups and downs of dealing with your faults and his, you will have come to see him more clearly and he will have come to see you more clearly. You will be loving each other more than before because you see each other more clearly and love each other anyway. Puppy love (infatuation) must go through the fire of acceptance of real differences before you can get to mature love. Some people's marriages end early because the couple marry while still infatuated and shockingly come face to face with major differences which they cannot accept after they are married.

The lesson to learn here is to not commit to marry during the infatuation phase of your relationship. Such an emotional high cannot be sustained throughout your marriage, so you need to make sure you really are a good match once the infatuation is over. There is no way to tell that while you both are still infatuated with each other.

You don't want to get into marriage the same way teens commit to their first loves, only to be emotionally devastated a few months later. One reason that engagements are traditionally one year long is to make sure that you are past the infatuation phase when you get married. You take a huge risk when you marry a man quickly. If you do, your chances of having a successful marriage with him are not much better than random chance.

The second common reason men marry is because they simply don't want to lose the partners they have. That is a good reason as long as everything else signals a good match:

1. You both have enough dating experience to know that you each have the best person you can,
2. You both are aware of each other's faults and can live with them for a lifetime (never marry a man who has a fault you cannot live with),
3. You both are past the infatuation phase,
4. You both love each other, and
5. You both trust each other.

If you meet these criteria, an engagement is your next best step. Does this sound too cautious to you? If so, how careful do you believe someone should be if they are truly going to commit the entire rest of their lives to living with someone and never have another romantic relationship with anyone else? If you understand the seriousness of the marriage commitment, you will understand why you need each of these factors to be true for both of you before you marry. Resolve any doubt before you get married. After you get married, it will be too late. When all of these conditions line up, however, it is really great.

Some delays are good

A man can truly love you and still not want to marry you now, especially if he thinks it would not be in your best interest to do so. For example, he may wisely want to get a good job first, or to become more ready for marriage—for your benefit as well as his. He may also recognize some differences that make him think that he would not be a good husband for you. Just as it is possible for a man who does not love you to want to marry you, it is also possible for a man to love you and still not want to marry you.

If a man does not believe he would be a good husband for you, you need to respect that. An analogy might be that some people love children, but because of personal ambitions realize that they would not be good parents and so choose not to have children, or at least not at this time. If such people are pressured to have children and give up their ambitions, they often become resentful later on. The same is true for a man who believes that he is not ready to be a good husband. The younger the man, the more likely it is that he is not ready to make a lifetime commitment.

Don't marry in order to rescue or be rescued

There is also a kind of loving man who will marry you in order to help you. He is a rescuer. If you marry a rescuer because you don't have your life together, you live in a boring town, you don't have good job prospects, or you want to escape your family, and you see him as a good way to escape, be prepared for him to leave you when you do learn to stand on your own two feet. At that time, he is likely to be rescuing one of his employees, coworkers, or even some "poor" woman he met online. You should already be standing on your own two feet when you get married, with a life you already enjoy. If you can match a man under those conditions, you will still match him under those conditions after you get married. The same must be true of the man, by the way. A man may appreciate it if you rescue him (such as paying his way through college), but he is likely to later leave you when he no longer needs to be rescued (gets his first successful job after graduating). This is a common story.

What "dating experience" means

Before you decide to marry your boyfriend, ask yourself if you both have had enough dating experience to not doubt your choice after 10 or 20 years of marriage. Many affairs happen every year not only because of marital conflicts, but also because some married people wonder and doubt if they married the best person for them. Often because they prematurely committed or had too little experience dating others, they married not knowing if they really had the best person. I have worked with many wonderful women who had husbands who left them, thinking that the grass is probably greener where another woman is standing. This is a particularly common story for people who marry very young. Women are also not immune from these doubts.

Again, I want to emphasize that I am not advocating promiscuity or that you or your boyfriend sleep around with a lot of people. I am advocating shopping around, *not* sleeping around. This is to make sure you really do have the best man you can get and are sure of that. Dating for me means going to lunch, having coffee, playing mini golf (one of my favorite dates), going to the theater or a movie, going dancing, and other such activities. These are safe things that you can do with male classmates or coworkers, a guy you meet at the mall, or even guys you meet online. I think it is entirely reasonable for a man or woman to have had an average of one such encounter per month in the years before they get married. So, if you get married when you are 25, that works out to about 84 different men you have dated since age 18! It sounds like a whole lot, but most of them will have just been one time dates, many just a few dates, a few who became boyfriends, and finally one you marry. Now, I don't think it is actually necessary to have dated 84 people, but there is very little excuse for having had just a few dates.

A person who has had only a few dates is much more likely to be a needy person, since needy people commit very quickly to the people they are dating and also are the most likely to end up with problem marriages. Personally, I dated around 50 women before choosing my wife. Most of them I just went out with one time. I had several women who wanted to marry me, but knew because of my dating experience that they were not the one. When I married my wife I had *certainty* that she was the one for me. That feeling has never wavered. Marriage means committing to be with the same person and having no other romantic relationships until you are dead. Depending on how long you both live, that may mean 50 to 70 years. You need to have no doubt that you have found the best person when you get married and even 50 years after that.

"Are you saying that I should be unfaithful to my boyfriend in order to get him to marry me?"

Absolutely not! I am saying that you should not be committed to him in the first place unless you have both discovered that you have the best partners possible. It simply would not make sense to commit to each other otherwise. If your relationship remains exclusive and uncommitted, it means that you both are still unsure if you have the best partner possible. Or, it means that at least one of you is not ready to marry. In either case, it does not make sense that you have an exclusive relationship for an extended period of time—unless that is all you want. It certainly is not a good plan for becoming married.

As your relationship becomes closer, you can become more exclusive than early on, resulting in a boyfriend-girlfriend relationship. But, you should not continue this for long if your relationship has hit a plateau and you want to marry some day. Many women who have chosen to live with their boyfriends have also found this out the hard way. Living with a man *decreases* his motivation to marry because he will have nothing to gain by marrying and he will have less fear of losing you. Living with you will make him feel like you are "locked in" to the relationship. You will become less of a priority, and he will have less motivation to marry you. If you want to marry a man, don't live with him first.

Becoming secure is your first step to getting him to commit

Women who have the best luck getting men to commit to them are women who are *not* quick to commit to men. They are secure, know what they want for their future, and they don't put up with controlling, evasive, or deceitful behavior from their boyfriends. They are not afraid of losing a man who is not good for them and they do not imagine that they can transform an unsuitable man into a wonderful husband. They enjoy their feelings as much as any woman, but they don't make their decisions based solely on their feelings.

Because secure women don't waste their time with men who are not right for them, they spend a much higher proportion of their time with quality men than their needy female counterparts. A needy woman will often spend months or even years in a relationship with a man who cheats on her or treats her badly. Her fear of being without him prevents her from breaking up and seeking a better man. She clings to the idea that he will change or that she will be able to reform him. As a result, she ends up eventually losing the relationship as well as valuable time from her life. Time she could have used to find a better partner. Such needy women have cheated themselves more than their boyfriends have cheated them.

Why would men commit to a *secure* woman?

Compliance and emotional intensity are the benefits of dating a needy woman, so why are men more likely to commit to a secure woman? There are multiple reasons for this. First, because she is secure, she does not tolerate bad behavior from him. She has his respect *from day one* and he must earn her trust and respect before she will consider any kind of commitment to him. This makes her a challenge, makes her special, and it keeps him in love with her. She is not high maintenance and if he stops seeing her, she is not going to text him every day asking what is wrong. He knows that if he messes up, she is going to be gone—with some other guy. And he knows that she would be the one he would miss the most, because she had the most to offer him. If he loses her and ends up with someone not so good, she will be remembered as the one he let slip away, no matter how many women he has dated since his relationship with her.

Commitment works *naturally* with secure women

If a secure woman has been dating a man *for a while*, she will get more serious. At which time she will stop dating others. She and her boyfriend will make the decision to see each other exclusively. This is an appropriate step toward commitment that should *not* be present early in the relationship and should not go on too long if engagement is not forthcoming. Committing to a man before you know him well or expecting him to commit to you before he knows you well, is not a realistic expectation. There are even some good reasons not to commit to a man (become exclusive with him) until he asks you to marry him and this is the way it has been in many world cultures for thousands of years. A man with competition is far more likely to commit than a man without any. A woman who is admired by other men is more of a catch as well.

Commitment is a choice

You have a man who won't commit. That's why you are reading this chapter. You may tell yourself that he is committed, and that you don't need marriage to prove that, but you know in your heart that a man who will not marry you is a man who is not committed to you. He fears losing something if he commits to you. A man who will not marry is a man who is not willing to risk his freedom, his money, or any other thing, because he is not prepared to stay with you if things do get worse. He has not made you a priority. That's why marriage still matters, no matter what your religious beliefs are.

Men who won't commit need to be put in the position of having to make a choice. Either they commit, or you will stop being committed to them. You will continue to (or start to) date other men. He does not have to commit to you, but if you become committed to another man, then the door will be closed to him. There will be no more chances for him with you after that. What is the result? If he loves you, he will ask you to marry him because he won't want to lose you. If he does not love you, it does not matter what he does or how he feels about it. Your objective should not be to please him, but to get what is important to you in life. As a secure woman who wants to marry, your priority is to find a good man to have a loving relationship with and to eliminate *all* the rest.

When you put men in the position where they have to either choose you or lose you, you are being as helpful to them as you are to yourself. This is because men can also hang onto relationships which are not really good for them and sometimes they need a nudge to let go. But, sometimes, they need a nudge to make the commitment.

"Isn't this manipulation?"

One thing to understand is that this is not a ploy or manipulation. If you are afraid of losing him, then he will not fear losing you. Not that he should be fearful of losing you in the sense that he would be miserable without you. The way he should feel about you is something like him finding the best car on the lot. Although he knows that he could be perfectly fine without that car, he imagines his life would be so much better with it and other cars would pale in comparison. When I married my wife, I already had a lot of dating experience. Because of this, I was able to recognize her qualities as being exceptional. I knew she was a "keeper" and that I was unlikely to be able to find a better woman for me. I also knew that if I did not commit to her, but simply tried to continue to be her boyfriend, that she would eventually commit to someone else. She was not about to commit to a man who would not commit to her, and she had proven this by leaving a long string of suitors.

If you are currently committed and clinging to a man who will not commit to you, then you need to become more secure. Then he will either commit to you or leave you so that you can find a better man who will commit to you. If you believe that he is the best man for you, but he will not commit, you can be assured that you are hanging on to him out of neediness rather than love. A man who will not commit to you is not really that much of a prize.

How to communicate this to him

I have said that you shouldn't commit to a man before he commits to you. But what if he is not committing to you and you want to commit to him? Do you just keep dating him and keep waiting? Do you stop dating him? If you have committed yourself to him without his asking, thinking that will make your relationship deeper, this action may have been what made your relationship stop growing. Men don't appreciate what they haven't had to work for. Also, they are usually at their best before getting commitment and when they get it, they usually stop working on the relationship. Many women think that they need to break up when they get stuck in this situation, but it is not so. It is possible for you to keep your relationship growing by shifting back to an uncommitted level. It is at this level that he will again work for commitment.

If your relationship has hit a plateau because of your premature commitment, and you want more from your relationship, then the first thing you need to do is to communicate this to him. Communication often does not create change, but it is almost always a good first step, because it makes sense of the actions that you take after that. If you simply started dating other men, then you might make him jealous, and he might start more actively pursuing you again. But, he also might misinterpret your actions as rejecting him and as being untrustworthy. You can read lots of bad advice on the internet about making your boyfriend or husband jealous in order to get his affection or commitment. But, what they don't tell you is that this behavior damages the trust in your relationship *forever*, and he is much more likely to cheat on you in the future and justify that by pointing to how you were unfaithful to him.

The way you communicate with him your desire to marry depends on whether you are currently dating other men or not. If you have followed my advice and are currently dating other men as well, you can say something to him like the following:

"Roger, as you know our relationship is not exclusive and I am dating other men as well as you. I really have a feeling that we could have a great future together. But, if we just keep going as we are, we may never have more than we have now. I would like you to think seriously about whether you might like to marry me one day. If you would, it would make me very happy and I'm sure I would say "yes." But, if you don't want that, or are not ready for that, then I will continue to date other men and we may lose this opportunity. I don't want you to feel pressured to do anything and I'm not about to stop dating you now. I just wanted to share with you how I feel."

After you say this, it is quite natural that he will need some time to think about it. You are essentially proposing to him, but you are still not committed to him. *Never* commit to a man until he commits to you. The alternative to this approach is to continue to date him and to continue to wait for him to pop the question to you. If you choose that route, you should continue to date other men or else you may end up spending years of your life with someone who never commits to you. Or, if you have decided that getting married is not a priority to you, you may continue to be committed and dating him exclusively. What you must realize, however, is that your relationship is very unlikely to be permanent without marriage. Although the divorce rate for marriages is around 50%, almost nobody stays a lifetime with someone they are not married to. How many people do you know who have done that? Whichever way you decide to do things is up to you, because it is your life, but don't be shortsighted. Do not do anything that is going to cause you to have regrets later on.

Now, let's consider the situation where you have been dating your boyfriend for a long time, are not dating other men, and being married is important to you. This is what you can say to him to promote commitment:

"Roger, we've been together for quite some time and our relationship doesn't seem to be going to the next level— marriage. I am not pushing you to marry me, because I know you are not ready for that. So, I have decided that I will also date other men. I don't know what will happen or if there is someone who could possibly be better for me than you. But, if I find such a man, then the door will be closed to you."

Is this the big kiss-off for Roger? Not in any way. You are not ending your relationship—you are just taking the exclusivity out of it. And, if he gets jealous or controlling, then you would see how little he cares about your desire for commitment from him. If Roger really is a good man for you, then he will think a little and you should get a proposal soon. Or, if he is waiting for something specific, such as reaching a certain level of income, he may ask you to wait longer. It really is up to you whether you do that or not. You don't owe it to him to wait. You owe it to yourself to do what is best for you.

Have you committed yourself too soon?

Have you already committed yourself to a man who has not committed to you? I often work with women who have a habit of committing too soon to men who are not committed to them. They are on the road to getting older and eventually getting dumped. Some are giving up their childbearing years hoping the man they are with is going to commit to them eventually. If that is you, then try to think about whether you will regret just maintaining your relationship indefinitely if he doesn't commit to you. If you are satisfied with what you have, then by all means don't rock the boat. But, if you want more, don't just wait for it to happen. Trade your fear of losing him for a fear of losing out on marriage or having children if you stay with him.

"Are you saying that by not committing to a man I will get commitment from a man more quickly?"

Yes, that is exactly what I'm saying. Men are goal oriented in relationships as with everything else. They pursue you most at the beginning of your relationship because they are working on getting to a certain level of relationship with you. If you just give a man that level of relationship, before marriage, and before engagement to be married, you will have taken away his incentive to pursue you more. In committing to him, you will have given to him everything, so that he will have nothing to gain by further committing himself to you. It used to be that a man would marry a woman in order to have a sexual partner who would also take care of the home and children. Nowadays, with sex widely available to single men, sex is less of an incentive for commitment. You are unlikely to get a man to marry you by withholding sex from him and telling him he can have sex with you when you are married. You can, however, motivate him to marry you in another way.

Because of their very nature, men are loath to give up something they already have, whether it is their favorite video game or their girlfriend. They are territorial, and although more than before they are fighting their urge to control women, they still feel in many ways like they own the women they have. When a man is faced with the possibility of losing you if he doesn't commit to you, he is much more likely to commit to you. If you want commitment, you need to leave men with this feeling: "She's a wonderful woman and if I don't put a ring on her finger, someone else will and I will lose my chance." You help men to feel this way by being wonderful to them, and by also not committing to them. Secure women get multiple proposals this way.

"Shouldn't I commit to him on a trial basis to see if a marriage would work out?"

While this idea makes *rational* sense, in reality it doesn't work. In a review of the research on couples who live together before marriage, it has been found that people in such relationships are less committed, are more unfaithful, and have more conflict if they do marry.[3] In my experiences both as a marriage counselor and as a relationship coach, I have repeatedly heard from people who have lived with their spouses before marriage, that the happiest time in their relationships was before marriage and that after they got married things got worse. This is in contrast with people who did not live together before they were married. Such people most often say that the best part of their relationship was after they got married. It's as if people who live together before they are married *give up* something by

---

[3] Stanton, G. (2011). *The ring makes all the difference: The hidden consequences of cohabitation and the strong benefits of marriage.* Chicago: Moody Publishers.

getting married. And people who don't live together before they are married *gain* something when they get married.

Summary

No matter where you are in your relationship right now, you can begin to behave in more secure ways and move your relationship toward commitment. If your relationship has hit a plateau, the only one keeping you stuck is you. It is your decision whether to maintain the status quo and hope your boyfriend will someday ask you to marry, or to take a chance by being willing to date other men if he won't marry. There is no right or wrong in terms of the choice you make. It is only important that you be true to your goals and not to make decisions out of fear. You have one life and you need to have courage (be secure enough) to make the decisions that will help you get what you want. Once you realize this, you must stop blaming your boyfriend for not marrying you and instead take responsibility either for your choice to be with him or to date others.

If you want to marry, it is important that you understand that men pursue a certain level of relationship, and then just seek to maintain the relationship unless it is threatened. When the man believes that he will lose you if he does not propose to you, it brings him face to face with the decision to marry you or not. Secure women naturally create this feeling in the men they date, because those men know that she will not commit to them otherwise. She may have several proposals for marriage in her lifetime, but will be careful to choose the man who is truly best for her. She will not be afraid of losing a good man because she knows that any man who won't commit to her is not such a good man, and she knows that there are other good men out there. She never "settles" for less than she knows she can have and she ends up with the best.

Love is patient, love is kind. It does not envy, it does not boast, it is not proud. It does not dishonor others, it is not self-seeking, it is not easily angered, it keeps no record of wrongs. Love does not delight in evil but rejoices with the truth. It always protects, always trusts, always hopes, always perseveres.

The Apostle Paul
1 Corinthians 13:4-7 (NIV)

♥8♥

SLAYING THE GREEN EYED MONSTER OF JEALOUSY

For a needy person, jealousy always feels like it is being caused by what a significant other is doing. Because of that, a great deal of anger is generated both toward one's partner as well as the other person or people involved. When this anger is unleashed, it can do more harm to the relationship than anything that the partner was actually doing. And, when jealousy is merely suppressed, it eventually causes an explosive behavior in the needy person that may lead to breakup or divorce. If you are a jealous person, it is in your best interest to learn how to take responsibility for your jealousy and deal with it in a way that will not harm your relationship.

Rather than being caused by others, jealousy is a result of our own internal fears. It may surprise you to find out that not all people get jealous. Very secure people don't get jealous at all—not because they believe their partners would never leave them for someone else, but because they don't fear that happening. Of course, they don't want that to happen any more than you do.

A brief analogy may help you to understand this better. Some people fear that their houses will burn down. They are extra careful to make sure no electric appliances are plugged in when they leave their homes or when they go to bed. They occasionally use candles, but it always makes them somewhat nervous because candles have caused many house fires. They take other precautions as well, and remain on the alert because you just never know. Other people have no concern about house fires. They aren't extra careful and they don't think about it much. Of course, they don't want their houses to burn down any more than the people who are very careful and anxious. Which people do you think actually enjoy their homes more— the anxious ones, or the ones who are not anxious? Jesus asked, "Who of you by worrying can add a single hour to your life? (Luke 12:25, NIV)." Worrying won't help our lives, or relationships, be better. Quite the reverse is true—we lose many valuable hours from our lives by worrying and we make our relationships worse.

Jealousy is a fear—a worry—about what might happen to one's relationship. This worry adds stress to relationships and makes it more likely that the relationship will end. It serves no useful purpose. If, on the other hand, jealousy was actually helpful to relationships and helped to prevent unfaithfulness, I would be all for it. Then, it would not be a needy behavior, but would be an effective behavior. But unfortunately, relationships are lost by jealousy and not saved by jealousy. Jealousy is a feeling that leads to needy, destructive behavior.

How jealous are you?

As with other needy behaviors, there is a range of severity for this problem. Most people are probably somewhere in the middle. They feel some jealousy at times, but are able to keep themselves from mentally, verbally, or physically getting out of control.

How many symptoms of jealousy do you have? Go through the following list and see how many fit you. Also, try to identify the underlying fear that drives each item you endorse.

☐   I am concerned that I am losing my partner's affection and that it is being given, or will be given to someone else.

☐ I am alert to any indications that my partner may be attracted to others or is cheating on me.

☐ I often think that my partner is flirting with others when I am not around.

☐ I try to reduce the possibility that my partner could cheat on me by trying to be included in everything, calling or texting, limiting my partner's financial ability to cheat, or demanding that my partner stay home.

☐ I react to my thinking about what my partner may be doing by becoming upset with him or her.

☐ I tell my partner "I love you" mainly because I want to hear him or her say it to me.

☐ I fear my partner leaving me, rejecting me, or abandoning me.

☐ I have had problems in previous relationships due to my suspicions.

☐ My expectations are that my partner should want to do everything with me.

☐ I have a hard time feeling relaxed and enjoying myself when I am not with my partner.

If you identify with these behaviors, you may think that explaining (another needy behavior) how you feel and why you feel this way to your partner will make your partner sympathetic to you. In actuality though, your partner will not become sympathetic. This is because, although your feelings make sense to you, they don't make sense to your partner. No amount of explaining will make them make sense to him or her. It might help you to consider what is likely to go on in your partner's mind with each of the above behaviors:

- "She/He doesn't trust me and no matter how much love I show her/him, she/he is never satisfied.

- "Although it's natural to be attracted to other people, I have to pretend that I am not and be very careful not to glance in another woman's/man's direction or even look at an advertisement with a woman/man on it. I have to be so careful that I can't relax.

- "I always have to account for my whereabouts. I don't have any freedom to do things on my own without having to 'report in.' Sometimes she/he makes me feel smothered.

- "I'm not allowed to be friendly with a woman/man, even when I have no other intentions. I feel controlled.

- "I have to lie to her/him just to be able to go out with a friend or spend some time alone. I don't want to lie, but it's better than being cooped up 24 hours a day with her/him. Can't she/he understand that I would look forward to seeing her/him more if I could have some time without her/him?

- "Sometimes she/he gets upset with me for no reason. I'm not responsible for her/his obsessive thinking. I don't know how much more of this I can take.

- "I feel like I have to tell her/him that I love her/him in order to pass some kind of test. If I didn't say it, there would be hell to pay. I think I would want to say it more if I didn't *have* to.

- "No amount of reassurance ever lasts for long. I have to keep spending energy putting out her/his emotional fires.

- "Just because she/he had problems with past partners doesn't mean that I'm not trustworthy. I am sick and tired of being mistrusted because of what someone else did to her/him. It's not fair.

- "Why can't she/he understand that I don't want to do everything with her/him? If she/he would make some friends of her/his own, maybe she/he could understand that.

- "I don't look forward to going home to her/him. I know that I'm going to be questioned or blamed or have to lie about what I was doing just because I wanted to have a little time to myself."

As you can see from the way other people respond to jealous behavior, they feel like victims. They feel controlled and like they have lost the freedom just to be themselves. As a result, they don't feel like they can ever satisfy their jealous partners. Eventually, they conclude that they are not good enough for their jealous partners and will want to find others who do consider them to be good enough. In this way, jealous people create in their partners the outcome they fear most—their partners wanting to be with someone else.

Jealousy is a kind of addiction

When you feel jealous, you look for evidence that you are justified in feeling jealous. But, you don't really want to find such evidence. What you really want is to be reassured that there is no reason to feel jealous. When you get it, this reassurance feels good, makes you relax, makes you feel loved, and needed. But, such reassurances are temporary and the jealous feelings gradually come back. Then, you need to get that reassurance again so that you can again feel better. Do you see the addiction cycle here? Your need for reassurance drives your jealousy—not your partner's behavior.

Because reassurance makes you feel better, you may begin to see it as your partner's obligation to reassure you. And, if he or she doesn't, it might make you feel angry, just like an alcoholic might feel angry if his or her partner hid the booze. What you will need to learn as a person with a reassurance addiction, is that it is not your partner's job to feed that addiction. People who feed addictions of others are called *codependent*. A secure partner will stop reassuring you in order to help you overcome

OVERCOME NEEDINESS AND GET THE LOVE YOU WANT

your reassurance addiction. It will be a difficult transition for you to go through, but an important one.

Why is reassurance seeking so bad? It is bad because it attempts to force from your partner something that he or she should be able to give freely. And, it also shows how you doubt his or her love and faithfulness to you. Asking for reassurance is like saying, "I am doubting that you love me or really care about me." When a person hears this enough times, he or she will start to doubt it too. Fears make us do things and say things that, in turn, make our fears come true. People without these fears are able to have relationships with more fun and less stress. Although their relationships also sometimes go bad, it happens far less frequently.

Where your jealousy comes from

Jealousy is connected to a fear of being unable to thrive without one's partner. "If my partner ever left me, all I see is a big, black hole." Many needy people think that this feeling is part of love, but it is not. Love is a profound caring and concern for the *other* person. Jealousy is a profound concern for *oneself.* When you don't want your partner looking at or talking to other men or women, it is not your partner that you are concerned about. And, when you want your partner to spend all of his or her time with you, it is not for your partner's benefit.

Because needy people think they would be devastated and unable to carry on without their partners, they make controlling their partners a priority over loving their partners. In actuality, the most protective thing for a relationship is to love your partner and the most damaging thing is to attempt to control your partner. Jealousy is like grasping a butterfly tightly so it can't fly away. When you do finally loosen your grip, you won't like what you see. The gentle, loving spirit you committed to may be crushed and broken.

One question I sometimes ask people during the course of their coaching is, "If your partner left you, would you still want him or her to be happy?" You might try asking yourself this question right now. The answer will tell you much about whether you really love your partner or whether you just want him or her to love you.

Jealous people often find it hard to think that their partners are actually entitled to be happy without them. They lack empathy and personalize their partners' behaviors. They think that everything their partners do is related to them.

It may come as a big surprise, but your partner lived a long time before you came along and did many things and met many people that had nothing to do with you. And, that continues to be true now, even though you are in a relationship with your partner. Your partner may have promised to be faithful to you, but that does not negate his or her need to continue to socialize and be involved in activities that have little or nothing to do with you.

Do you recognize this line of thinking—"If my partner is happy doing things without me, that means he doesn't need me. And, if he doesn't need me, that means he is going to leave me. And, if he leaves me, my life will be horrible. I will be alone and miserable forever. Life won't be worth living"? Jealous people can think these things so many times that the thought is more like a flash of feeling. You see him laughing and talking with someone else (or imagine him to be) and then you get a knot in your stomach followed by intense anger after that. That is jealousy, which comes not from what he is doing, but from your fear of abandonment and isolation. Rather than controlling his behavior, overcoming your fear is the key to killing this green eyed monster.

Jealousy looks like mood swings

Did you know that jealousy looks like mood swings to partners? This is especially true for very needy people. The reason for this is that when people are jealous, they become questioning and controlling. They may become angry. But, needy people will not maintain such behavior when they start getting rejected for it.

As long as needy people's partners continue to answer questions and reassure, needy people can afford to be angry, suspicious and controlling. But, eventually, their partners become angry back or avoid them all the more. After all, who likes to be questioned all the time or to continually reassure an insecure partner? When this backlash starts to happen, needy people become apologetic and back down. They may go out of their way to be nice. They may even encourage their partners to go out with friends or to do the kinds of things that made them jealous before. This happens because now, instead of fearing that their partners no longer love them anymore, they fear that they are driving their partners away (which triggers the same kind of fear behind jealousy). This extreme swing from angry and controlling to nice and appeasing appears kind of crazy to others. It seems like mood swings and it is hard to predict. It makes even secure partners start to become anxious—not knowing what to expect when they get home or wake up in the morning. Far from the relationship being an adventure, it becomes an unstable stressor. It becomes just one more thing that tires out secure partners and leads them closer to burning out on their relationships.

The solution to this is not to be consistently angry and controlling so as to create a stable, negative, environment, but rather to become more stable and positive. To give up the fears and to focus on loving. A positive, loving environment, is more conducive to long term relationships.

Jealousy is always damaging

Needy people often confuse feeling better with doing better. Most good results are in fact hard to achieve. And, very often what makes us feel good is not actually good for us. In the case of jealousy, being reassured will make you feel better, but it will also damage your relationship. In the effort to become secure, you need to rely less on your feelings and more on the consequences of your actions. No matter how good something feels, if it harms your relationship, you must stop or you will eventually lose your relationship.

Needy people's jealous behaviors actually make their partners have to be *careful* around them. Even when they are not with their jealous partners, they have to think about the amount of time they are spending somewhere, and how they will have to address questions about where they were, what they were doing, who else was there, and whether they enjoyed themselves or not. The "wrong" answer to any of these questions can make life more difficult because of the requirement to reassure their partners. Stress builds and it becomes harder and harder to relax.

Secure partners of jealous people eventually come to the point where they must choose between taking care of the feelings of their needy partners, or taking care of their own needs to be accepted, trusted, and loved. If they can't get this from their jealous partners, eventually they are likely to become attracted to someone else. If *secure* people can learn, before this happens, to not reassure their needy partners, and to use good boundaries to get their own needs met, the relationship may be saved. Although people can learn this from a coach or therapist, most don't and the relationship ends. That's why you, as a needy person, must give up your jealousy and need for reassurance.

"But, if I am not careful, then my partner will feel free to cheat on me."

This is a false belief that needy people have. Men or women with *secure* partners feel free to enjoy their lives and pursue their interests, but they know that if they cheat on their partners, they risk losing their relationships. Secure people won't put up with cheating partners. People in secure relationships have an internal reason to be faithful—they don't want to lose their partners, who are valuable to them. They don't need their partners to behave like police officers to keep them on the straight and narrow.

A person with a jealous partner becomes *less and less* concerned about the results of cheating, because a jealous partner is not a very valuable one. No one wants to feel monitored, distrusted, and like it is their "job" to constantly reassure their partner. The man or woman who has to say "I love you," a certain number of times to avoid triggering an alarm in his or her partner is not a man or woman who is going *to feel* like saying "I love you." Jealous people also pick up on this reluctance and it feeds into their fears—creating a downward spiral of jealousy and loss of love. The more jealous you are, the more love you lose; the more love you lose, the more jealous you become, and so on.

"So, if I am jealous, it means that my partner is more likely to cheat on me?"

Yes, that's right. But, this is not what will happen in most cases. In most cases, it will lead to your partner finding excuses to avoid you, which will create more emotional distance between the both of you, then you will want even more reassurance that your relationship is ok, but you will be less likely to get it because your partner will become less concerned about your relationship.

In essence, your jealous behavior will lead to your partner falling out of love with you. At that point, some partners will work on the relationship, but most will start thinking about ending it. Cheating would be kind of a symptom of this. Many people though, will break up before seeking another partner. Cheating always has to be dealt with, but it needs to be seen for what it is—an indication that your relationship had severe problems even before the cheating.

"So, what can I do about it? Am I doomed to lose my partner because of my jealousy?"

Well, if you don't do anything about it, you will lose your partner physically, emotionally, or both. But, if you work on yourself, your partner can feel more at ease with you, and enjoy your relationship rather than feel trapped by it.

"How do I work on overcoming my jealousy?"

Since your fear of losing your partner is what is really behind all of your jealousy, this is the most productive place to focus. If you can come to see your relationship as something that you *desire*, but not something that you *need*, you will be making good progress. Basically, your <u>unspoken</u> belief about your partner should be:

"I am with you because I love who you are and who I am when I am with you. I am not here to change you or be changed by you, but to share this life together. You are an important part of my life."

Relationships between secure people are not all-consuming. People have many aspects of their lives that do not involve their partners. Although they reserve their most intimate selves (physically and emotionally) for each other, they share the rest of themselves with the world. That may sound really alien to you, but consider the jealous person's position:

"I am with you because I need you to make me feel secure and loved. I don't feel happy on my own and my life is nothing without you. You need to consider how everything you do affects me and whether I would approve or not. And, if I'm not happy, then you shouldn't be either."

Although jealous people wouldn't actually say that, it is the implicit message that their partners would receive. And, it makes their partners feel needed, but not loved. Spouses of jealous people have to be careful and don't feel free to be themselves. They feel kept—trapped—and eventually seek to escape.

Change your focus

Jealous people are usually focused on what their partners are doing with other people rather than on what their partners are doing with them. This sets off a chain of thinking that leads to insecurity, anger, and the desire to control their partner's behavior. It's as if their partners are perceived to have a limited quantity of life and love that must be reserved for the jealous partner's use. While it is true that you need to draw a line when it comes to *intimate* behavior, there is no reason your partner's friendships and social activities should be threatening to you, especially if your partner is loving and treating you well.

Focus on what your partner does with you rather than on what he (or she) does with other people. If there is a problem, deal with that rather than trying to control your partner. Does he treat you well? Does she tell you she loves you and touch you like she loves you? Is he enjoying talking with you and spending time with you? Does she make future plans with you? These things are much more important indicators of your partner's love than whether he or she does things with other people.

If these things are not going well, then trying to get your partner to not spend any time with other people is not going to make these things improve with you. It would actually make these things worse with you. This is what you need to realize—*your partner's relationship with you has to do with his or her interactions with you and not with his or her interactions with other people.*

I do not care if my wife is out having a good time with her friends. I do care if she never wants to go out and have a good time with me.

Have your own social life

How does it feel to go out with a friend without asking your spouse or significant other to come along? Does it feel natural and healthy? Or, does it feel like kind of a betrayal? As a needy person, you will naturally assume that your partner will want to be included in your activities—*all* of your activities. But, unless you have a needy partner, this won't actually be the case. Instead, he (or she) will be glad that you have your own friends and will be hoping that you will have a good time with them. He will hope that, so that you can understand how he can have a good time with his friends without it damaging your relationship.

But what if you don't have friends? You might think that the answer to that is for your partner to include you in all his or her activities, and to be responsible for all your social needs. But the real answer to that question is for you to make your own friends. A person who says, "The only friend I need is my partner," is a needy person. No one person can meet all of our social needs. And you can't meet all of your partner's social needs either.

Going out on your own with a friend or friends may take some getting used to. It may require you to reconnect with some old friends or to make some new friends. It probably means you will need to get out of your comfort zone. If you have a hard time making friends, it may be easier for you to begin by joining an activity with people who have similar interests to yourself. You might try taking an exercise class or some kind of educational or art class at the local community college.

One way that I increased my socialization was by practicing martial arts. I made friends and earned a black belt at the same time. Another way that I make friends is by attending adult Sunday School at my church and by joining in church activities. Such activities are stepping stones to getting together one on one or as a couple. Don't think that just because someone is married, you can't do one on one activities with that person. Other married people also need to get out without their spouses sometimes.

Now be forewarned, having a hobby is not the same thing as being social. Hobbies that you do entirely by yourself or without interacting with other people do not count as social activities. They will not help to round you out socially and will not help you to understand your partner's enjoyment of socializing without you. While it's good to have a hobby, make sure you don't use your hobby as an excuse not to socialize. When it comes to choosing one or the other, socializing should be a higher priority for you—especially since you need to become a more secure person. And becoming a secure person means that you don't rely on any one person to meet all of your social needs.

"Isn't needing someone part of love?"

It certainly is in Hollywood movies, but not in real life. Let me give you an example from my own life. My wife and I are both successful and competent people. We love each other deeply. But, I know that if something happened to me, she would be fine after an initial grieving period. And, she knows it too.

What this means is that she can listen to most anything I have to say without becoming threatened by it. Nor is she threatened if I do activities without her or talk to other women. If I were to cheat on her, she would divorce me without a doubt, but it's not something she needs to worry about or try to prevent. I feel free to be myself and to pursue my dreams, but I do know where the limits are and the consequences if I overstep them. The same is true for her.

We don't need to spy on each other, go through pockets, or monitor each other's online activity. I love it that we can share our thoughts with each other without worrying about triggering insecurities. Also, she helps me pursue my interests and I help her with hers. We are a team. We have more together than we could ever have separately. That's what makes us want to be together and faithful to each other—not any kind of control we have over each other.

Marriage should bring the best parts of each person together to make something greater than either of us could be separately, or without being committed to each other. Living together, without marriage, cannot achieve this because it is lacking in the kind of commitment necessary to become united.

Needy, insecure people have to be taken care of. Secure people can share and help, and be cheerleaders for their partner. I think my chances of finding a woman more valuable to me than my wife is about zero. It is what I call a *oneness marriage*. I can't say that I'm not attracted to other women, but I can say that I would not want to jeopardize the love and freedom that I have with my wife to be with another woman. If my wife were to start to become insecure, needing regular reassurance and interrogating me about my activities, it would do serious harm to our relationship. We wouldn't have a oneness relationship anymore. All of that would be jeopardized by her insecure behavior. The same would be true if I became insecure. Part of my job as a good husband is to do what I need to do to remain secure and attractive. I have no responsibility to make sure my wife loves me, but I do have a responsibility to love her and to be faithful to her. That is what I promised her when I married her, and that is what God expects of me.

Summary

Jealousy lends no value to your marriage or relationship. It prevents a closeness that you might otherwise have. It wears away the bond between you and your partner. If you continue to be jealous, eventually that bond will break. Jealousy is not caused by what your significant other does. Although you may have to deal with your spouse if he or she is unfaithful, jealousy in no way prevents unfaithfulness and in fact makes it much more likely to happen. By becoming a secure person, giving up your jealousies and control, you become easier to love and more desirable. If you are currently a jealous and controlling person, ending your jealousy will do more to improve your relationship than *any* other change you could make.

Don't be concerned with how people treat you. Be concerned with how you treat them.

♥9♥

STAYING SECURE AND ATTRACTIVE IN A RELATIONSHIP CRISIS

It's one thing to work on being a secure person when you are dating, another thing to work on being secure when you are married or in a committed relationship, and still quite another to work on being secure when your partner is rejecting you and wants to separate, break up, or divorce. This kind of relationship crisis is the most difficult time to be secure and the most important time to be secure. Being needy in a relationship crisis will just make your partner run from you faster.

Most of the people I work with as a relationship coach come to me in the midst of a crisis. They are usually near the end of their relationship and their spouses have already told them that they can no longer tolerate their behavior, are not in love anymore, and are leaving the marriage. After profusely apologizing, begging, pleading, and crying, all without good effect, needy people are often ready to try something else. It is sad that they were not able to see this coming and to resolve to change before getting to this point. However, it usually takes severe problems for people to give up severe behaviors. Even then, they will need to learn not only how to change their behavior, but how to re-attract someone who has lost all hope of their changing.

Sometimes, it really is too late to save the relationship because partners have already committed to someone else or because they will no longer have any contact. These two things signal the end of a relationship no matter how much one wishes it to be otherwise. In other cases, partners have someone else but are not committed, or are merely interested in finding someone else. These situations do not spell the end. There is still a window of opportunity for reconciliation.

A crisis without separation

If your partner is not in the process of leaving you, and you have a lot of conflict, you will be tempted to convince your partner of your way of seeing things. After all, your fear of your partner leaving is not as strongly activated as your desire for your partner to make you feel loved. Working to convince your partner, however, is not the right approach to resolving a crisis. This is because the more you try to convince your partner, the more conflict you will have. That would eventually lead to either separation or your (or your partner) shutting down and withdrawing. Each person can only tolerate so much conflict and eventually this will result in separation.

Even when people don't physically separate, they often separate emotionally. Breaking up and divorcing follow later. Rarely do relationships end without emotional distancing being a clear warning sign. I have had many people tell me, "If only my partner had told me how unhappy he/she was, I would have done something sooner to save my relationship." Talking to them usually reveals that their partner's behavior had spoken quite clearly even if their words did not. A lack of verbal complaints from your partner does not mean that your partner is satisfied with your relationship.

Satisfaction is best sensed in the way your partner looks at you, talks to you, and touches you. If you don't feel love in these things, then there is a good chance that your partner does not feel in love with you. If it's a temporary phenomenon because of fatigue or stress, it is quite understandable. No one feels in love all the time. But when love is consistently missing from these three things, you can assume that you are losing an emotional connection with your partner.

When you become aware of severe conflict in your relationship or loss of connection, the ideal solution is to apologize for any needy behaviors and to make a sudden change to secure behaviors. This means both being more loving and using boundaries. Making a sudden change like this is as unlikely as a leopard changing its spots to stripes. Nevertheless, you must make a new beginning—something that will give your partner hope other than your just trying to convince him or her that you are right or the right partner.

Tell your partner that you don't expect him or her to want to stay with you as you are now. That regardless of what your partner has done, you have not been a good partner. Don't promise that you will change. Promises will only make things worse. This is because even if you make a 99% improvement and slip up just one time in a hundred, if it breaks your promise, your partner will use it to say how you haven't changed. Then all of your progress will be disregarded.

If he (or she) asks you what he should do, tell him that is entirely up to him, and that you will support him no matter what because you love him. This is the beginning of starting to love your partner in a secure way. If you are a very needy person, saying this to him (or her) will come as quite a surprise. He may decide to leave you, in which case you can follow one of the sections later on in this chapter. But, it is more likely that he won't and you will have some time to begin making changes. Don't be afraid that by saying what your partner does is up to him or her, you will be hastening your partner's departure. People don't separate until they are ready, unless they are kicked out. You are not kicking him out, you are not asking him to leave, you are just loosening your grip on him.

Without promising to change, identify where you are having the most conflict. If you are not having conflict, but your partner is emotionally disconnected with you, then identify your behaviors that are most likely causing the disconnect. Undoubtedly the problem behaviors will come from one of the needy behaviors described earlier in this book. If not, then the problem is not caused by your neediness. Is the conflict coming from your criticizing, complaining, arguing, interrogating, talking about relationship problems, explaining, nagging or repeated apologies and promises? Although you may be tempted to say that the problems are being caused by your partner, it is not possible for your partner to have conflict without your participation. Although he (or she) may be doing some things which are legitimately wrong, your responding with any of those needy behaviors only adds fuel to the fire and does nothing to heal your relationship, attract him to you, or make him feel like giving up his damaging behaviors. If you are to have any success with your partner, you need to strengthen your relationship so that your partner cares about it, so that your partner cares about you, and so that your partner wants to be with you.

Identify the place where you are doing the most damage and then resolve to change that behavior with *everyone.* Don't just work on changing it with your partner. You need to have a personality change, a self-upgrade. If you just try to make it a temporary change in order to win your partner's favor, it will only have temporary results and the next time you go to make this change it will be even harder to win your partner's trust.

For example, if you are criticizing him—telling him what you don't like about him, this behavior needs to stop with *everyone.* You need to stop criticizing your parents, your friends, his friends, your children, your coworkers, and everyone else. You don't make this change merely by shutting your mouth. You make this change by saying nice things about people. By saying nice things about your partner, your parents, your friends, his friends, your children, your coworkers, and everyone else. You do a 180 degree turn.

If you are fortunate enough to have a personal relationship with the Lord, I recommend that you also pray a lot at this time. I don't recommend that you pray for your significant other to forgive you, take you back, treat you well, or any other thing directed toward you from your partner. Instead, I recommend you pray that you can better love your partner and other people. And I recommend that you pray that you will trust God to take care of you no matter what happens. Acknowledge that you love

Him and trust Him. Then, determine that you are going to love other people rather than focusing on getting other people to love you..

What is most needed in your relationship is the conversion from your needing your spouse to your loving your spouse. That has to happen if you are to have any hope of your partner loving you. I know it's not the way you would like things to be. You would like him (or her) to prove his love to you before you show love to him. If you wait for that to happen, or you try to make that happen, you will both struggle to get love either from each other or someone else. When you love your spouse first, then he or she doesn't need to struggle to get love for himself or herself. This makes it much easier for your partner to love you back (although that is not guaranteed). None of us have guarantees. We only have the hope that our love will be returned. Sometimes it will be, and sometimes it won't. But there is no better investment for getting love than giving love.

It's quite natural that when you make these changes, your partner won't respond to them right away. He (or she) will expect you to revert back to the way you were and it's a pretty reasonable expectation. If you expect that you will change quickly, things will be much worse for you as you are likely to stumble many times in your process of changing. Better for him to believe that you want to change, and to be surprised by any actual changes, than for him to believe that you will change and be disappointed by your mistakes.

When needy people hire me in the midst of a crisis (as they almost always are), I tell them that they first have to stop the damage that they are doing to their relationships. Only after that can we get to the point where we are helping their spouses to stop damaging their relationships. When the needy person can make these changes, sometimes the work is done. Sometimes that alone is enough to cause a corresponding positive change in their partners. At other times, even after the needy behavior stops, more changes are needed—like having good boundaries. But boundaries are not the place to start. Boundaries must always be balanced out with loving behavior. If there is no loving behavior, then your boundaries won't matter at all to your partner. Love comes before boundaries, except when you are being verbally, financially, sexually, or physically abused.

A crisis with separation

This is not a book about reconciling, so you won't find everything you need here in order to reconcile your relationship. But, I can help you to have a healthy start with that. So often what happens when a needy person's partner wants to leave the relationship is the needy person immediately starts to beg, cry, whine, plead, and promise.

These are all desperate attempts to get the other person to change his or her mind. They do not work. In fact, the more you do these kinds of behaviors, the more it will convince your partner that the right thing to do is to leave you. That's because these behaviors are very self focused. They show that your concern is mainly for yourself and not for your partner.

If, after your partner leaves, you continue to contact your partner and beg and plead and whine and promise, it is not going to endear your partner to you. It will make him (or her) want to escape from you all the more. He may do this by being extra harsh with you in an attempt to shut you up, stop these behaviors, and convince you to let him go. Or, he may simply refuse to answer the phone or return your messages. Needy behavior on your part is a large reason why he is leaving. Doing more needy behavior is not going to convince him to come back or stay with you.

So, what is the alternative? The alternative is to take a moment and think about *your partner*. What is it that *he or she* wants? Is it really so unreasonable? If your partner is a man, he is interested in finding another woman whom he can have more of a partnership with and not feel controlled by. He wants someone who admires him and makes him feel important. That is a very reasonable thing to want, especially if he has just spent the last few years of his life feeling controlled by you.

If your partner is a woman, she may also be looking for another man, but there is a good chance that she just wants to feel free to be herself and to be relaxed. That is also a very reasonable thing to want if she has felt trapped, suffocated, neglected, or burned out in her relationship with you.

Now the question is, what should you want for *your partner* if you really love your partner? Should you just want your partner to return to you even though that stresses him or her out? Probably you do. That is the needy part of you. "I just want him to come back to me whether he is happy or not," is the thought of the needy person. The loving person thinks something more like, "Although I would really like him to come back to me, I don't want him to continue to feel hurt or trapped. I don't want to be the person he remembers as having ruined his life."

In a marriage, we make a vow to love our spouses for better or for worse. We don't make a vow to keep our spouses in our marriage at all costs. In fact, there's nothing in the marriage vows about trying to convince, cajole, or control our spouses. It is a promise to love our spouse no matter what. This is what "for better or for worse," means. There is a lot of wisdom in those vows because that is your best course of action.

When your partner wants to get out of your relationship, you don't need to apologize and you don't need to make promises. You need to *listen* to the reasons why he or she wants to leave. You need to *admit* to the truth in them, and you need to ask what you can do to *help*. If you can do this, it will go a long ways towards a peaceful breakup. Although that word breakup may make you cry, people breakup and get together again all the time.

One of the biggest factors determining whether you will get together again is how you handle the breakup. With a peaceful and cooperative breakup, you are much more likely to get together again. The idea is to remain cooperative with your partner. You don't need to agree that you would like to breakup, too. That would be unbelievable. Your basic message should be, "Breaking up/separating is not really what I want to do because I love you. But, if it's what you need to be happy, then I will help you the best that I can."

When people work with me as a relationship coach, I help them to customize this message to their particular situation, but the message is pretty much the same. You are never going to be able to pressure your significant other to come back to you. And, you are never going to make your significant other feel guilty or sorry for you enough that he or she is going to rush back to rescue you. Your only hope in this situation lies with your being able to connect with him or her and to avoid those needy behaviors which will just remind your partner of why he or she left in the first place.

If you can maintain your new secure and loving behavior, you have a good chance of reconciling with your partner even if he (or she) is dating someone else. Unless he or she has committed to the other person in some way then most likely his relationship with her will stop being magical at some point. At that point, either he will be more attracted to you and realize what a valuable thing he has thrown away, or he will find yet another woman to replace his present girlfriend. Who he chooses will have a lot to do with how you have behaved through the breakup and after.

What to do when it's too late for your relationship

One of the things I commonly get asked as a relationship coach is "When is it too late to save a relationship?" This is a very important question because the wrong answer can either cause you to give up too soon or too late. My answer for this question is, it's too late when your partner will no longer have contact with you or when your partner is in a committed relationship with someone else. By commitment, I don't mean just dating or having sex. Commitment means an intention to be with a person long-term. Evidence of commitment is an engagement ring or living together. Although it's not really evidence for commitment, I recommend that you also don't try to reconcile with your significant other if there is a new child involved. As I was taught in seminary a long time ago, there is no way to unscramble an egg.

What happens if you try to reconcile with a man or woman who has committed to someone else? Well, there are two possible outcomes. The first is that he or she won't take you back. The second is that he or she will. That second outcome may sound appealing to you, but people who leave a committed relationship to return to partners they were previously committed to, will again leave to be with someone else. This is the same problem that occurs for men and women who date married people. Although married people will sometimes leave their spouses for someone else, when that relationship becomes stale, they will again leave for someone else. If you marry a cheater, he or she will eventually cheat on you. Secure women and men do not involve themselves with people who are already in committed relationships.

The reason for not reconciling when there is no more contact is that it's not possible. There is no way to use telepathy to build a relationship. If your partner won't have contact with you and you try to force contact, all you will get is rejection and then more rejection on top of that. You won't actually improve things, but will prolong your pain while continuing to stress your partner. I will not work with men or women who want to save their relationships if they don't have regular contact with their partners. This is because I will not participate in their needy behaviors, which are only going to prolong their pain.

So, what do you do when it's too late for your relationship because there is no contact or because your partner has committed to someone else? Well, the thing *not* to do is to immediately go out and start dating others. Although your friends will probably recommend you do that and it will make you feel better, you are very likely to get into another relationship that repeats the same kinds of problems you had in the previous one. Instead of dating, now is the time to work on becoming a more happy, fulfilled person, so that you don't connect with someone out of need or desperation. Remember that for secure people, relationships are about *sharing* happiness rather than *achieving* happiness. That's an important distinction. If you seek out a partner while you are unhappy, you will feel happier when you find a partner. But you will expect your partner to continue to make you feel happy. And, when you start to feel unhappy, you will blame your partner. Your needy behaviors will come out again and you will push yet another person out of your life.

So, work on becoming a happy person before you seek out someone else. While you may not be able to be sexually fulfilled without a partner, it is quite possible to be happy without one, and this should be your goal before dating again. You need to strengthen your relationship with your friends, make sure your career is going well, take care of your health, exercise regularly, and have hobbies that you enjoy. It will also be beneficial to strengthen your relationship with God, get out of debt, and be earning enough money to be able to save for the future. There are few things less secure than a man or woman who cannot financially make it without a partner. Also, this may be an excellent time to get into counseling to deal with any unresolved issues which affect your happiness. It also may be an ideal time to get into coaching to work on skills that prevent you from doing well at work or from connecting socially and making friends.

Think of it this way—if you were the opposite sex, would you be more attracted to an unhappy person who is out of shape emotionally, physically, and financially, or would you be more attracted to a person who was in shape mentally, physically, socially, and financially? Which one would be more fun? Which one is likely to be more stable? Which one is likely to be more work? Which one is likely to be easier to shake loose if things go badly? People don't want to step in gum. Likewise, they don't want to have a relationship with a needy person who won't let go. As attractive as you think it might be to stick to someone like gum, it is something which scares secure people away. Needy people, on the other hand, will like it. As I said earlier, two needy people coming together is intense, but like a firework, the sparks will eventually go out and leave the relationship cold.

Summary

Needy people tend to see a relationship crisis as an excuse for becoming even more needy. And then, after becoming extremely needy and further damaging the relationship, they become regretful for their needy behavior. In actuality, there never is a good time for needy behavior and there never is an acceptable excuse to do such damage to your relationship. This is true for all needy behaviors. There is *never* a justifiable time to become jealous, controlling, critical, argumentative, or a nag.

Instead of such a needy response to a relationship crisis, you must get as much help as possible in the form of emotional support from others. You must also learn to behave securely, getting professional help if you are unable to make changes on your own. The most important thing to do when there is a crisis is actually the same thing to do when there is no crisis—to have a loving response to your partner. A loving response is one which takes into account the needs and desires of your partner. Married people promise during the marriage ceremony to love each other "for better and for worse," but I don't think this only applies to marriages. I think it applies to any relationship which is important to you. And certainly, from a Christian perspective, it applies to *all* people in our lives.

The most important thing for you to learn is that loving your partner is not just an intense feeling that you have inside you. Loving your partner means caring enough to be willing to sacrifice for his or her happiness. This is not the same as allowing your partner to harm you. But, what you must learn is that your partner trying to take care of himself or herself and to find love and happiness is not abuse. You must not justify revenge when your partner's desire is to be happy or to separate. Don't do something that makes you feel powerful for the moment and makes you have regrets for a lifetime.

If you can't bring yourself to be loving and supportive, then get into counseling and let your partner go. It is not fair to keep a partner who you are not willing or able to love. Loving and supporting your partner this way does not contradict your marriage vows. It is one way of fulfilling them. If the loving thing is to help your partner go, then that is what you must do. Anything else would be selfish and also would make it less likely that you will reconcile with your partner.

If you can control the urge to be needy and can do the loving thing by siding with your partner rather than against him or her, then you will have a chance of reconciling and making your relationship a truly good one. You let your partner walk out the door and even lovingly help with that so that you can have continued contact, without stress, and be able to start to rebuild your relationship.

♥10♥

SECURELY MANAGING EVERYDAY CONFLICTS

A *conflict* is merely a mismatch—a difference of opinions, values, or ideas. Because no two people are the same, conflicts are inevitable. Conflicts only become problematic when someone feels the need to persuade the other person to change their idea, belief, or value. It is the method used to persuade that actually causes the damage, and not the conflict itself. Needy people in particular try to persuade by arguing, withdrawing, getting revenge, begging, and exerting pressure. Rather than persuade, this actually just increases the emotional distance. A relationship can only tolerate a certain amount of distance before it breaks, like a rubber band stretched too tight.

Conflicts do not need to be avoided, because conflicts alone do not cause damage. It is not necessary to feel, think, and do exactly as your partner does. Nor is it important to get your partner to feel, think, and do just like you. Needy people often fear conflict because for them, differences are seen as dangerous signals that they and their partners are growing apart. What the needy person would be better off fearing is not differences, but rather their need to be the same. The need to be the same, think the same, feel the same, do the same, is what leads to the needy persuasive behaviors that do the damage.

Conflict can be dealt with in positive ways that actually help, rather than harm, your relationship. I have devoted two other books to this subject. In *What to Do When He Won't Change*, I teach women how to improve their relationships with husbands who have no interest in working on their relationships. In *Connecting through "Yes!"* I teach people how to take situations that damage most relationships, such as affairs, addictions, parenting conflicts, and financial conflicts, and turn them into opportunities for connecting and creating a closer relationship.

Although I can't devote two books worth of space to that here, I can teach you the basics of responding securely. This will be a place for you to get your feet wet before you dive into more difficult things. You can rest assured though, that you are getting the most important help now—help with day to day interactions. It is the day to day interactions we have that determine how long our relationships will last and how close we will be. If you manage the day to day well, you will be able to avoid many of the big crises that derail and often destroy relationships.

When your partner stops saying "I love you"

Let's start off with what *not* to do in this situation. The main thing is not to pressure your partner to reassure you of his (or her) love with words or actions. Although you will feel better if he reassures you, the way you behave to get him to do it does damage to your relationship. Seeking reassurance is kind of like lighting a match to see if it works. You are relieved to see that it does, but then wish that you had saved it for another time. In other words reassurance gives you satisfaction, but is then followed by regret.

A common ploy is for needy people to say "I love you" to their partners *in order to* get their partners to say it to them. This is manipulative. Although your partner may love you, your partner may resist telling you simply because he or she does not like to be manipulated this way. Tell your partner you love him or her when he or she really wants to hear it. Telling him you love him because you want him to say it is not a loving thing. It is a needy thing.

Instead of getting your partner's reassurance, you need to be able to reassure yourself by looking at the evidence. Your partner may or may not love you. I'm not going to assume he or she does and you don't have to either. Instead, ask yourself some questions like "How does he treat me?" "Does she spend time with me?" "Does he show interest in me?" "Does she talk nicely to me?" "Does he treat me better than he treats others?" "Are there times when she puts my needs ahead of her own?" "Does he intentionally do things to try to hurt me emotionally, financially, or physically?" By considering these types of questions, you should be able to determine if your partner loves you or not.

Although it is normal to want to be loved and to want to hear expressions of love, we must never try to manipulate our partners into saying this to us. Manipulating others to say expressions of love toward you is needy. And, if you are successful at getting someone to say they love you, that still does not mean that they do. Be less concerned with the words and more concerned with the behavior which tells you whether your partner loves you or not.

When your partner comes home late

Just so you understand me, I don't think it is good if your partner routinely stays out late and neglects you or other family members. But, understand also that you are not your partner's parent. It is neither desirable, nor your obligation to punish your partner for this kind of behavior. If you choose to punish by withdrawing, complaining, arguing, or otherwise treating your partner poorly, you will create a power struggle and you will lose respect because your behavior will not *effectively* change your situation. Whenever you attempt to do something that does not effectively change your situation, you lose respect.

Before you decide to do anything about your partner's behavior, ask yourself, "Is this a relationship breaking issue? Would I rather break up than let this behavior continue?" Be very honest about the answer to this question. The answer informs you of what you need to do.

If you would *not* want to break up over this issue, and your partner has ignored two requests to come home earlier, contact you, or whatever would make it better for you, then don't ask again. Instead, work around it. Have your own activities when your partner goes out or enjoy a quiet night in. Pamper yourself. Don't torture yourself while your partner is having a good time and then torture him (or her) after he comes home. Instead, don't wait up for your partner. If you happen to be up, then greet him in a nice way. Make your partner feel welcome.

If you behave this way, your partner will look forward to coming home and it will help your relationship. If you complain, it will be ineffective, you will lose respect, your partner won't want to come home and have to deal with you, and so the result will be that your partner stays out later and later, more and more often.

Now, if this is a relationship breaking issue for you, then prepare to separate or breakup (depending on whether you are married or single). Then wait until you are having a *good* time together and tell your partner that if that behavior does not change soon, you will no longer participate in it and you will leave (or he or she can). This is what a secure person does. She (or he) doesn't argue, discuss, or beg. And, she never threatens something she won't actually do. A secure person may get dumped, but she will never lose her partner's respect. A needy person will get disrespected for a long time and then eventually be dumped.

Use the same method for dealing with all relationship breaking issues. Wait until things are calm and going well. Tell your partner what you will or won't accept, without arguing, and then initiate separation or breakup if the behavior continues.

When your partner doesn't return your text messages or emails

The worst thing you can do about this is to criticize your partner. That would only accomplish three negative things: 1) you would push your partner a little further away from you, 2) your partner would come to feel like the reason to respond to you is to keep you quiet rather than because he or she really wants to respond to you, and 3) it will eventually create a power struggle. Criticizing your partner will *never* make your partner more attracted to you, criticizing will *never* make your partner want to contact you more, and criticizing will *never* make your partner glad that he or she chose you as a partner. So, you have to ask yourself, "Is it really worth it to get forced compliance from my partner on this issue if it's going to damage our relationship?"

Instead, you will need to get used to the fact that you have a relationship with an adult who is free to respond to you or not. Also, your partner is an adult who is quite capable of taking care of himself or herself and did so long before you came along. Also, it is not your partner's job to reassure you of his or her love or his or her safety. It is your job to examine the evidence for your partner's love—by yourself, and it is your job to trust your partner and those around your partner to be able to handle any emergencies that may happen while your partner is away from you.

Those things are your job because it is part of the work that keeps your relationship healthy and positive. If you are married, then you probably heard someone tell you that marriage is work. Now, you are learning what that work really is. The work is to continue to be like your spouse's girlfriend or boyfriend rather than like your spouse's mother or father, no matter how long you have been married.

Perhaps you want to tell yourself that if your partner doesn't answer your text messages that he (or she) doesn't really love you because if he loved you he would answer your text messages. That is circular reasoning and you could use that for everything your spouse does or doesn't do that you don't like (e.g., "If he really loved me, he would chew with his mouth closed because he knows how much that bothers me," "If he really loved me, he would treat my parents well because he knows how important they are to me," and so on). Well, guess what? Your partner is going to do many things that you don't like—whether he loves you or not.

That's right—you can't use what you like or don't like as a guide to whether your partner loves you or not. A child who is made to go to bed at 9:00 p.m. or who is not allowed to watch TV before doing his homework might *feel* like his parents don't love him. That does not mean that they don't. In fact, if his parents let him do whatever he wanted, he might *feel* loved, but in fact not be loved at all. As a needy person, your feelings are a lousy guide as to who loves you and who doesn't. This is where you have to examine what your partner does for you and with you. And, if you are still not sure whether your partner loves you, ask that secure friend that I told you to line up for just such purposes.

So, am I saying that your partner doesn't need to answer your texts or emails? Yes, unless it is a genuine emergency. No partner is going to give you every single thing that you want. He or she does have to do enough so that the relationship is valuable for you. And, if your partner doesn't, then it is still not time for criticizing. It is time for using boundaries and being prepared to end your relationship. That is not a decision to make lightly.

When your partner doesn't tell you where he or she is going

Once again, your partner is not a child and you are not his (or her) mom. And, just because you tell him where you are going (which you don't have to), that doesn't obligate him to tell you. It is, however, important that he tell you the approximate time he will be returning and that you have a way to contact him, particularly if you have children together. When emergencies happen with children, one parent should be able to reach the other, since they are a shared concern and responsibility. This is also true for divorced couples.

If you believe that your partner should have to tell you where he is going, then I would ask you to figure out where you learned that rule. As a Christian, I learn most everything about relationships from the Bible. I can tell you the Bible doesn't put such an obligation on partners.

If you think you should *be able* to ask your partner where he (or she) is going, I agree with that. You should be able to ask him many things. But, that doesn't obligate him to tell you. If you believe that his secrecy makes him more likely to cheat on you, you are wrong. People who cheat on their spouses simply lie about what they are doing. Asking partners where they are going or what they are doing is not a safeguard against infidelity. It may be much more important to allow your partner the freedom to come and go, as long as you are receiving sufficient value from the relationship, as I've said before.

The exception to this would be if your partner has already broken your trust and is working on re-earning it. In that case, your partner does need to be accountable to you in any way that is necessary for you, until that trust is re-earned. Once it is re-earned, it is important to give that freedom again. Love and freedom go hand in hand. Love and control do not.

When your partner is angry and won't talk to you

First, recognize your partner's right to be angry. Your partner has just as much right to his (or her) feelings as you have to yours. He doesn't have a right to abuse you by demeaning you, physically hurting you, or otherwise controlling your behavior. But, note that his simply being angry is not abuse. Just because you don't like it doesn't make it abuse.

Secondly, recognize that just because he is angry does not mean that you have done something wrong. You may have (such as one of those needy behaviors), but you may also have done something right. For example, if you have used a boundary such as walking away or hanging up when he is verbally abusive, he will be angry, but you will have done the right thing. If you use other people's feelings to determine when you have done a bad thing or a good thing, you will become confused. It is the same principle with parenting. When you do the right things in raising your children, sometimes they will be upset about it. If you use their anger as a guide for what to do or what not to do, you would raise selfish, controlling, undisciplined children. The same goes for partners. If you use his anger as a guide to what to do or not to do, then you may turn him into a selfish, controlling, and undisciplined partner—even if he didn't start out that way. The way that you are affects the way that he is (and vice versa).

Thirdly, just because he (or she) is angry does not mean that you need to have a talk about it. If he wants to talk, then do so after he is calm and you are calm, even if that is not until the next day. Don't get into the habit of talking to your partner when either one of you is upset. And, if one of you starts to get really upset, you have talked about it enough for that day. Get back to having a good time together and talk about it another day or not at all. Contrary to what most self-help books say, most of the time talking about problems with your partner will make them worse. Although it may help sometimes, it is not worth doing if most of the time it does harm to your relationship. You must make a change from what works some of the time to what works most of the time if you want to have long term success and a lasting relationship.

When your partner is verbally abusive

Needy people have a few different ways of responding to this situation, none of which are helpful. If your partner called you a bad name, gave you the finger, or compared you to something really bad (like a pile of dog poop), how would you handle that?

If your first reaction is to tell him (or her) that you don't like that and you don't want him to do it again, you actually would be losing respect and making his behavior worse. First of all, he already knows you don't like it. Secondly, even if he apologizes, he will do it again when he is upset with you because he knows you don't like it, and he knows that you will put up with it. Unfortunately, people will continue to treat you badly as long as you put up with their behavior—even if you criticize them for it. Criticizing only tips off other people what to do when they are feeling upset with you.

If your tendency is to also become verbally abusive with your partner, then you will be justifying your partner's behavior.

Since you are doing it, you will not have any right to do anything about your partner's behavior without being a hypocrite. This is why when I coach people who have difficult spouses, the first thing we work on is how they treat their spouses. Before they can successfully use boundaries with their spouse's behavior, they must have their own behavior under control (for a sustained period of time). If there is anything your partner is doing that you don't like, first ask yourself if you are doing anything your partner does not like. Make sure that behavior is actually the best thing to do for your relationship or else stop doing it.

Do you remember the story of the three bitches I told you in chapter one? You must act quickly, decisively, and effectively by removing yourself from verbal abuse situations. Your partner fearing your effective reaction is what is known as respect. It simply is not possible to have a good relationship without respect. You must earn it with your behavior rather than by trying to command your partner to change or by trying to criticize your partner into changing.

When your partner is financially abusive

The basic definition of financial abuse is when someone misuses your money or assets, or hides them from you when you have a right to them. To really understand financial abuse in relationships, we need to expound on this definition. After all, what does it mean, "your money"? Is that only what *you* earn or bring with you into the relationship, or does it include money that your partner makes that should be shared with you?

Many needy people don't recognize abuse even when it is happening to them. That may be because they are from families where the abuse was even more severe than the abuse they are receiving. Or it may be because it is too threatening to perceive as abuse. Our minds have an amazing ability to filter out things that we believe are dangerous to think or believe. After all, abuse is totally unacceptable in this culture. And, if you see it, then you have to do something about it, right? And if you do something about it, your partner might leave you. And that would be worse than whatever your partner is doing to you, right? At least that is the way a needy person thinks. And that is why there are so many women (and men) staying in relationships where they are being abused emotionally, sexually, physically, and/or financially.

Abuse violates your basic rights as a human being—whether or not you are in a relationship with another person. So, if a stranger hits you, it is assault and battery. That doesn't change if you have a relationship with that person. If it is your boyfriend or husband, it is no different and no more acceptable than if it were coming from a stranger. And if your partner is a woman, her violence to you is no more acceptable than if it were coming from a man. That's because your fundamental human rights do not change simply because you are in a relationship.

If a stranger took money that you earned and spent it on himself, what would you call that? I'm hoping you would call it stealing and would realize it is a crime. But, what if your spouse takes your money and spends it on himself or herself? Is that stealing? Well, it is unless it is owed to him or her by fairness or responsibility. When you are in a relationship with another person, you have a certain responsibility to take care of that person and he or she has a certain responsibility to take care of you. In Western cultures, that responsibility is *equal* when it comes to money. You would quickly find this out if you went to a lawyer about having a divorce. Men are not more financially responsible than women are.

Now, what if one of you makes more money than the other? Does this mean that the one making more money gets to have more spending money? No. He or she may need to pay a larger percentage of the bills, but the remainder of the income would belong to both of you (in a committed relationship that is). This is part of what it means to be committed to someone. If a partner will not commit his or her money, time, love, or any other thing, then you do not have a committed relationship. Partially committed is NOT committed.

Financial abuse comes in when your spouse won't pay his or her fair share of the bills and/or won't split the extra spending money with you. How do you know how much is his or her fair share? To calculate this, you need to know the total combined income for both of you. You also need to know the total combined reasonable expenses for your marriage.

Let's take an example:

He earns $50,000/year after taxes

She earns $25,000/year after taxes

Their total annual expenses are $65,000

For this example, the couple earn a total of $75,000 per year. Their total expenses are $65,000 per year (they calculate this by adding together all expenses (e.g. food, clothes, childcare, insurance, retirement savings, healthcare, etc.). So, in their case there would be $10,000 extra per year. Half of that ($5000) would be hers and half of that ($5000) would be his. I calculated this for a year, but you could do it for one week, two weeks, or a month if you like. A year is better because it takes into account unusual payments such as auto and home insurance premiums. The main thing I want you to see is that the income you both have belongs to both of you.

Now you ask me, what if one of you is doing more work than the other, such as labor, child care, or home care? Doesn't that count toward the finances? The answer is "no." Even if one partner does twice as much work as the other, each partner is entitled to half of the income after deducting for expenses. This is because we do not *earn* income, love, attention, sexual favors or any other thing from our committed partners. We are One with our partners, so everything belongs to us equally.

Abuse is generally considered to be abuse when it is doing you harm and not just when it hurts your feelings. If you don't have the money that you need for the daily necessities of living, and/or you do not have the money necessary for mental relaxation in proportion to what your partner has, and you are not voluntarily giving your partner the funds, then it is abuse. If you don't need as much money as your partner and you voluntarily give your partner more than you have, that is not abuse. Your partner didn't do it to you. You did it for your partner. There is a world of difference. And, by the way, when you give your partner money, it does not mean that he or she owes you something in return. For something to truly be a gift, the other person does not have to pay you for it.

Now, what does a secure person do when she is being financially abused? Does she complain about it? No. Does she criticize her husband for it? No. Does she argue with him about it? Again, no. She first points out to him the discrepancy and tells him that she loves him, but cannot stay in a relationship where there is not financial fairness. They can work it out together, or they can meet with an attorney to discuss what is legally fair, or he can leave (or she will), but she will not continue to live in an unfair situation.

As a result, he may initially be angry, but she will earn his respect and stop the abuse (or the relationship will be over and the courts will enforce financial fairness anyhow). Because of that, their relationship can continue to grow and prosper soon after that. A woman who allows herself to be abused—financially or otherwise, will lose her husband's respect and his love. She will end up resenting sacrificing her time and money for him when in the end he rejects her anyhow. Likewise, a man who participates in his own abuse will in the end find himself to blame.

Needy people allow abuse because in the short term it is easier. But in the long term they lose the respect of their partners, their children, and themselves. In the end, they are more lonely than they would have been if they took the time and effort required to stop the abuse.

When your partner is physically abusive

Physical abuse is easier for most people to define. But, many needy people still have a hard time doing that. Physical abuse is generally considered to be unwanted physical force that causes you injury, pain, or impairment. I say "unwanted" to rule out people who are into S&M behavior as well as people who are in violent sports such as kickboxing. If you are doing kickboxing and someone kicks you, that is not physical abuse. Intent may help determine abuse, but regret does not. If someone intentionally hurts you, but then later regrets it, it is still abuse. If someone unintentionally hurts you, it is called an accident.

If someone hits you for the first time, you are hardly to be blamed for it, regardless of what the other person says to justify it. No one deserves to be hit, although it may be necessary in a self-defense situation. If you have cheated on your partner, stolen his money, insulted his manhood, or any other thing, it does not justify his hitting you. There is nothing you can do that will justify his hitting you, unless he needs to do that in self defense to prevent a great physical harm to himself. Even in the case of self defense, his physical actions would need to be limited to the amount of force necessary to just prevent the harm. Knocking someone out with a frying pan when he tries to slap you would be excessive force and you could go to jail for that. Knocking someone out with a frying pan when he is trying to shoot or strangle you would be justified.

Now, let's consider what often happens with needy people. Their partners hit them. They cry and threaten to break off their relationships in one way or another. Their partners (the abusers) sincerely apologize and promise to never do it again. The needy partners forgive their abusive partners. Then, at another time, the abusive partners hit again, the needy partners make threats to leave, the abusive partners apologize and the cycle continues indefinitely. In such a situation of continuing abuse, who is responsible for the abuse continuing? They both are. The first time someone abuses you, you may not have been able to do anything about it. But, if someone is repeatedly abusing you, you are continuing to allow it to happen. You are not responsible for his hitting you. But, you are responsible for not putting an end to this cycle.

So, what is the needy part in the above description? The needy part is *the threat to break off the relationship.* Needy people threaten others. It is an attempt to control other people.

Almost all of the behaviors that needy people do are designed to control their partners, but actually add to problems instead. Threats don't work because other people learn to respond to the threats rather than to control themselves. They do the behavior until they are threatened. Then, they stop temporarily. Then they again do the behavior until they are threatened again, and so on. This is stimulus control, it is not self control. You can see the same kind of thing on the highway when everyone slows down temporarily when they see a police car (the stimulus that controls them). Once they have passed a short distance, they speed up again.

This same kind of behavior happens with some poor parenting. You may have heard a parent say something like, "If you do that one more time, you are going into time out." What does the child learn from this? He (or she) learns that he can do whatever he wants until he hears this threat. Instead of learning to monitor his behavior, he monitors for the threat. So, his behavior never improves. He always acts out at least once, because that's how many times he can (sometimes more) before he hears his parent's threat.

It works the same with abuse. How many times can he hit you if you use threats? The answer is as many times as he wants, as long as he stops each time he experiences the threat of your leaving.

What would a secure person do rather than threaten? Do you know the answer already? As soon as it was safe, she would leave without threatening to leave and without discussion. If she was inclined to continue the relationship, she would require that her husband or boyfriend get help for his problem and also re-earn her trust over a period of *months* before she would commit to him again. And, if he were unwilling to do that, she would end the relationship. A secure woman will not consider staying in a relationship where she is going to live with the threat of abuse looming over her head.

Believe me, I am no fan of divorce. But, I am no fan of abusive relationships, either. If you are not willing to do what it takes to end the abuse and/or he is unwilling to work on the issues behind his abuse and earn your trust again, do not bother contacting a coach for help. If you are so needy as to allow yourself to be battered, you will need some serious counseling. In fact, it is better to work with a counselor than a coach when it comes to domestic violence. This is because a local counselor will be aware of other local agencies that you may need to access for you or your partner in the process of working on your relationship.

One definition of neediness is allowing harm to come to your relationship in the long term, in order to have short term peace or connection. *Security* is doing whatever it takes in the short term, no matter how upset your partner may become, in order to have long term peace and connection. Please note that with managing an abusive partner, as with other secure behaviors, there is no attempt to control your partner. Instead, you control yourself through proper boundaries like removing yourself from the dangerous situation, involving the police if necessary for your protection, and requiring that trust be rebuilt before re-committing. None of this is controlling the other person. He (or she) is free to do what is necessary to save your relationship—or not. You are not putting pressure on him to do it. It remains his choice. This is the really scary part for the needy person because the needy person always fears that her (or his) partner will choose not to earn her trust again. And, that's why so many needy women put up with abuse. They would rather destroy all hopes of love and intimacy with their partners than face the possibility of their partners abandoning them.

One of the most useful questions that I ask women in this or similar situations is, "If you had an adult daughter who was in a relationship like yours, where the exact same things were happening, what would be your advice to her?" Always, my clients are able to tell me the secure thing they would want their daughters to do. That is what they also must do for themselves.

When your partner sexually abuses you

Can you be sexually abused if you are in a committed relationship with someone? Yes, you can. Abuse has to do with violating your basic rights as a human being. If you are forced or coerced into sexual activity, it is abuse and it is a crime. Just like with physical abuse, unless you consent and without coercion, it is abuse.

Just because you don't have enjoyable sex doesn't mean you are being abused, however. If you consent to sex with your partner and he or she does not satisfy you emotionally or physically, that is not abuse. This is because you consented to the sex.

If you are being sexually abused, your response should be the same as if you were being physically abused. You leave the relationship and seek shelter and safety. You involve other people who can help, like counselors and law enforcement. And, if you want to reconcile, you require your partner to get treatment and earn your trust and respect over a number of months before you consider (no guarantees) recommitting to him or her.

All that applies to physical abuse applies here, too. So, if you are being sexually abused, be sure to read that section as well.

When your partner blames you for his or her behavior

It no longer surprises me that needy people blame themselves for their partners' behaviors. Since needy people believe that everything their partners do or don't do is related to them, it is natural for them to blame themselves. Before you do that too, be sure you are not overlooking some key facts.

First, you need to realize that your partner was no angel before he (or she) met you. He may have seemed like an angel when you were first dating because he was on his best behavior in "pursuit mode." After this initial period, when he was sure that he had you securely, his tendency would be to slide back to his previous behaviors. What you see now may be nothing new for him. How he is now may be the same as he was before you met him.

Secondly, any bad behaviors that he blames on relationship stress are a result of his poor coping skills and are not a result of how you have contributed to the stress. Whether he is yelling at you, slapping you, withdrawing for long periods of time, or refusing to talk to you, you didn't cause any of that. As long as he has other choices than to mistreat you, you are not to blame for his choice to mistreat you. And, he always has other choices. For example, he could talk things out with you, he could go to counseling with you, or he could break up with you. The presence of just one good alternative means that he is responsible for any bad choices he makes. He had the freedom and ability to make the more healthy choice. His not taking it was not your fault.

Thirdly, he may blame you simply as a way to justify his behavior—even if you have done nothing to contribute to his stress. Many men and women, for example, blame their partners for petty behaviors in order to justify their thrill seeking with an affair partner, their use of drugs or alcohol, their lack of commitment, and so forth.

Stress from family members and friends

Does your family want you to stop being needy? It's highly unlikely. Your neediness most likely developed in response to conditions in your family when you were young. You adapted in order to match them. Your becoming a secure person will make you mismatch them. You will also mismatch your friends, unless you happen to have some secure friends.

Your family and friends may encourage you to do things which are needy, such as to criticize your partner for the way he or she is treating you. If you tell them that you learned that it is needy to criticize people, they will discredit that idea, because it goes against their idea. They will tell you to stop being a doormat and to stand up for yourself. But, if you criticize your family or stand up to them, you will find that they think *that* is a needy behavior. They would tell you that it is no good to treat them that way and that you will endanger your relationship with them if you do so. It's kind of an emotional double standard that people have. It's ok to criticize, argue, and so on with your partner, but not ok to do that with your family or friends. You need to see the hypocrisy and faulty reasoning in this. If it does not work with your family and friends, it is not going to work with your partner either.

I recommend you not ask your family or friends for advice. If your family needs to know what is going on, tell them in statement form rather than question form.

Secure statement:

"I have decided to get a babysitter so I can go out once in a while instead of waiting until my partner is available to stay home while I go out."

Contrasted with an insecure statement:

"I was thinking that maybe I should get a babysitter so I can go out once in a while instead of waiting until my partner is available to stay home while I go out."

"I have decided," are very secure words. Are they hard for you to say? Many people would have a hard time saying this to family or friends because they would be afraid their family or friends might not like them (leading to rejection) if they said the wrong thing. So they learn to couch their words in passive and noncommittal ways. Secure people make the best decisions they can and then take responsibility for them. Such people are powerful and attractive.

Does your mother want you to call her every day, no matter how busy you are? *Decide* to call her three times a week, or two times, or even one.

Secure statement to your mother:

You: "Mother, I have decided that I will call you on Wednesday and Saturday of each week rather than every day."

Your mother: "Oh, why's that?"
You: "Because that's what I have decided."

One of the things you will be working on in becoming more secure is giving fewer explanations. Secure people sometimes need to explain their behaviors and decisions, but most of the time they don't need to. Explaining actually leads to arguing, which is another needy behavior (needing other people to see things your way). For example:

Insecure talk with your mother:

You: "Mother, I have decided that I will call you on Wednesday and Saturday of each week rather than every day."
Your mother: "Oh, why's that?"
You: "Because I have too many things to do and I get behind in my work."
Mother: "So, other things are more important to do than talk to your own mother?"
You: "Of course not. But, I'm so tired at the end of the day, I feel really tired when I have to talk to you."
Mother: "Oh, so I make you tired? That's a fine thing to say to your own mother. Well, you don't have to call me at all. You can just free up all your time for your more important things and forget me altogether."
You: "Of course I don't want to do that. Look, I can call you every day, I guess."
Mother: "Only if you really want to."

Don't take my word for it. Try it both ways—with explaining and without. See which way gives you better results.

Summary

There is a lot more to overcoming neediness than learning a few techniques for handling everyday situations. But, if you don't know how to handle everyday situations, they will gradually make you needy again. This chapter has offered you guiding principles for how to deal with a variety of situations with your partner.

The key features for managing any kind of conflict and preserving your relationship are to have a balance of loving behavior and boundaries. Neither one on its own is enough to sustain a relationship. Needy people usually err by swinging from one extreme to the other—being all too loving for all too long and losing respect, or being all too tough for all too long until their partners don't care anymore. To be effective in improving your relationships, you have to be loving enough that people care when you use tough boundaries.

These principles are true for every kind of relationship you have. Overcoming neediness may require you to interact in different ways not only with your partner, but also with your parents, siblings, friends, and coworkers. Because none of these people are likely to encourage you to change into a more secure person, you will need to have a secure person on your side. If you have no such person in your life, then it will be best for you to work with a counselor or coach until you can make such friends. It is unrealistic to believe that you will be able to remain secure when you are constantly surrounded by insecure people.

Giving up neediness, like giving up any unhealthy behavior, may require you to cut ties with people who are codependent for your neediness. Healthy living and loving requires having very good boundaries with people who are toxic. When you do that, some of them will break off relations with you and some of them will become more secure to match you. If you are in a relationship now, and your partner cares about you, becoming secure will actually help him or her to become more secure too.

♥11♥

HOW TO HELP A NEEDY PARTNER

You've done a good job in overcoming your neediness. But, it's quite possible that you have a needy partner. You may have never realized that before. But now that you are secure, you can see many of the same needy behaviors in your partner that you used to have. It's tempting just to try to convince your partner that he or she is needy, but your partner is not likely to believe that. Would you have believed that before you started working on your neediness? Or would you have believed that was some excuse that your partner was using to blame you?

You can use this chapter to help a needy partner. You can also give this chapter to your partner so that he or she knows how to help you. I will cover here the necessary steps for making a relationship work with a needy partner.

Stop being codependent for your partner's neediness

Your needy partner believes that the solution to your having a good relationship is for you to do what he or she wants. But, just like an alcoholic who wants you to buy her drinks so that she can stay calm, doing whatever needy people want is a codependent behavior. This is especially true when your partner seeks reassurance or to stop you from enjoying yourself. Far from solving problems, it will create more and more because it will make you more and more resentful as you give up your happiness in order to try to make your partner happy. In the long run, you would end up disengaging and possibly leaving your needy partner because your relationship would be no fun anymore and it would be too much work for you with too little in return.

There is a very difficult transition that your needy partner has to go through. She (or he) has to make the transition from needing you to loving you. And these are far from being the same thing. If she loved you, she would be most concerned about your happiness, your success, and what you need. She would have loving behavior toward you and would be hoping that you would return that love. She would not be trying to force it from you by nagging, complaining, arguing, interrogating, over explaining, or criticizing you. She would not be jealous of you or try to keep you from doing things which help you to enjoy your life. If she were really secure and loving, she wouldn't do any of these things.

A secure person doesn't need to control and badger and complain, even if his or her partner is doing something terribly wrong like cheating, lying, or being verbally abusive. A secure person simply would not put up with these things. She (or he) would leave you. If she gave you a second chance, it would not be until you had changed, earned her trust, and won her heart again. If she were secure, you would respect her and when you made decisions, you would think about how it's going to affect her.

If you are a secure person, you would much rather have a partner who would leave you if you did such terrible things than a partner who would nag and complain and control until you had no love left to give.

So how do you stop being codependent for these needy behaviors without making your partner upset? The answer is that you can't. There is no painless way to heal damage, whether it is physical, psychological, or relational. No matter what you do, your partner is going to become upset. Doing healthy things will make him or her upset for a little while but will end the continuous cycle of needy behaviors which erode your relationship.

Go for long term results

Let me give you an example that's a little different from neediness so you can see better how this works. Suppose you know an anxious person who worries a lot. She comes to you, worried about something and you reassure her. Your reassurance makes her feel better. But, your reassurance doesn't truly take away her anxieties because a little while later she is anxious about something else. And who will she go to with her anxiety? She will go to you. If you reassure her again, she will again feel better for a little while, but will then start to worry about something again. You won't truly be helping her to *overcome* her anxieties. You will just be giving her a short term fix. Your reassuring her will actually help her to continue to have an anxiety problem.

For her, this anxiety problem is something like having a rash from poison ivy. It feels good when she scratches it, but she soon itches again. Scratching doesn't make the rash go away and may actually spread it—making it worse. To truly heal, she has to stop scratching and use some ointment or antihistamine. Most of the needy behaviors of your partner are designed to get you to scratch her (or his) itch—to make her feel better. But because she soon feels insecure again, and because she knows that you reassuring her makes her feel better, she becomes more and more insecure. She becomes addicted to your reassurance. She will even come to believe that it is your job to reassure her, and that if you don't, then you are not being loving.

Her insecurity is not caused by anything that you do—it was there even before you met her. But, what you do or don't do maintains her insecure behaviors. If you are "scratching her itch," then you are maintaining the very behaviors that you are probably becoming very tired of dealing with. Being *codependent* means doing something that maintains another person's problem. You will have to stop being codependent before she will learn to deal with her insecurities in a different way. One of the behaviors where we can see this itch-scratch pattern illustrated is when she accuses you of not loving her:

YOUR PARTNER: *"You don't love me anymore. That's why you want to spend all of your time going out with your friends."*

This is an accusation and criticism at the same time. Depending on how many times you have heard it, it will probably either make you feel like reassuring her or defending yourself:

YOU: *"That's not true. You know I love you very much."*
    Or
YOU: *"I only go out with my friends once in a while. You and I go out every week."*

Regardless of which one of these you choose to say, the effect will be the same—to reassure her. To calm her fears. To sooth her nerves. Even if you get heated and shout, it will still reassure her. You are putting so much energy into convincing her that she believes you must care very much about the relationship.

To stop being codependent in this situation, you must stop reassuring her *at the time that she says these things.* In other words, it is important to emphasize your love to your partner, but not at the time when she is trying to force it from you. So, what do you say when she is trying to force it from you?—the truth:

YOUR PARTNER: *"You don't love me anymore. That's why you want to spend all of your time going out with your friends."*

YOU: *"Sometimes I don't feel like I love you."*

HOW TO HELP A NEEDY PARTNER

This is likely to shock her, but is sincere and has the effect of heightening her insecurity instead of soothing it. She may have a fit, or she may ask you about it. If she has a fit, let her. Don't try to sooth her or participate in an argument. She would just be trying to force you to say that you don't mean it and that you really do love her all the time. If she asks you about it, just be honest. And tell her that sometimes you feel controlled by her and at those times you don't feel like you love her. This is a much kinder thing to do to her than to be patient until the day when you can't take it anymore and decide to leave her.

Maybe you can see now how to answer the other accusation:

YOUR PARTNER: "You would rather be with your friends than me."
YOU: "Yes. Sometimes I would."

There is no reason to deny the obvious. If you like going out with your friends, without her, at least sometimes, then admit it. It would certainly not make any sense to insist that you don't prefer to be with your friends sometimes if that is what you are doing. Don't add any reassuring statements at this time.

However, you must express your love to your partner at other times and show her that you enjoy being with her. Just never do it when she is trying to force it from you. If you don't express your love and desire for her at other times, then it will make her feel even more insecure and will result in even more extreme behaviors.

Dealing with her criticism and her complaints

Your partner's criticism will begin to make you feel like nothing you do is good enough after awhile. So, if you continue to just let it go on unchecked, you will eventually lose all feelings of love for your partner and will long for someone else who will accept you and make you feel loved.

It's important that you understand that your partner is trying to force behaviors from you which will make her (or him) feel more loved and more secure. Remember that she measures the quality of your relationship not by how happy *you* are, but by how happy *she* is. So, in complaining to you about your behavior, she is actually trying to make your relationship better. It's a twisted way of thinking. Maybe you can relate to the following example. Imagine she was going out with her friends and you felt jealous. You might complain to her about her going out or about the friends she keeps. It's not because you want to hurt her, but because you really want her to stay home with you. That would make you feel better about the relationship. If she stayed home for you, you would like the relationship better.

That is what she is trying to do in criticizing your behavior—make the relationship better for her. What she is not thinking about is about how resentful you will become at having to give up things you enjoy and how hurt you feel being criticized. If you made her stay home because of your jealousy, she would also become resentful, because she wouldn't be able to go out with her friends. Of course, if she didn't have friends, she would see no need for you to have them either. Needy people expect empathy, but they are not very good at giving it.

So, how can you respond to her criticism? Do you change what you are doing? Won't that just feed into her critical behavior? Should you defend yourself or criticize back? These are important questions because what you do will determine whether the criticism continues and whether you become resentful to the point that you no longer love her and end up leaving her. I get emails from women (and men) every week who tell me they criticized their partners for years until their partners finally left them. Now, suddenly, they have realized the error of their ways when it is too late. We want to avoid having to put your significant other or spouse in this situation. Being patient is *not* the answer.

When you are criticized, find the truth in the criticism (there is always some truth in criticism although we often don't want to admit it). Admit to the truth without apologies, defensiveness, or blame. Here are some examples:

YOUR PARTNER: *"All you care about is money."*
YOU: *"Money is important to me. I want to make sure we have enough for paying the bills and having fun."*

YOUR PARTNER: *"All you care about is sex."*
YOU: *"I do love sex. It's great."*

YOUR PARTNER: *"You're too lazy to pick up after yourself."*
YOU: *"I do tend to leave things laying around."*

YOUR PARTNER: *"Everywhere we go you are just leering at other women."*
YOU: *"I do enjoy looking at attractive women."*

In these examples, it would be easy for you to become focused on what your partner is saying. But, her (or his) real concerns are not being expressed. You caring about money is *not* her concern. She doesn't feel like you care enough about her. That is her real concern. The same is true for the sex example. Telling you that you are too lazy to pick up after yourself probably does indicate that you are too much of a slob (in which case work on it), or that she is trying to hurt you because she feels hurt for some other thing and is getting a little payback by hurting you. The complaint about you looking at other women is because she is not feeling special enough to you (in which case, your main concern should be whether you are really making her feel like you are attracted to her).

So, you see that for each criticism, there is a legitimate concern on her part that is being expressed, but in a bad way. If you are sure that you are doing your part to make your partner feel loved, important, and attractive, then you can just admit to these things and let your partner be angry about it without entering into any kind of argument over it. Certainly don't try to reassure your partner at this time. Never let your partner force reassurance from you as this just feeds the needy behavior.

If your partner's criticism is valid, just work on changing your behavior without making any promises to change. Promises do more damage than they do good because if you slip up even once, it will bring a strong, negative reaction. If you simply work on changing, then your partner will see the improvement and when you slip up, it won't be breaking any promise and you won't be accused of lying about changing. Remember, just because your partner is needy doesn't mean that you have nothing to work on. None of us is perfect.

Dealing with your partner's arguing

Does your partner argue with you, trying to convince you that you are not a good husband, wife, girlfriend, or boyfriend? If so, what do you think is your best response? Should you argue back, trying to convince him or her that you are actually a good husband, wife, girlfriend, or boyfriend? Should you remain silent and ignore your partner? Should you attack your partner back and tell her (or him) that she is not a good girlfriend or wife? Or, should you do something altogether different from these?

If you argue back, you will be playing into one of the main reasons your partner argues in the first place—to get reassurance from you. Although this will stop your partner's arguing for a little while, you will notice that the same arguments will keep coming up again and again. That's because reassurance doesn't really change someone's mind, or teach them something—it just makes them feel better for a little while. When the anxious feelings come back, they need reassurance again.

If you remain silent and ignore your partner, that will make her escalate her behaviors. She will become more and more angry, possibly even hostile. She will take things to the point where you will no longer be able to ignore them. And, she will have learned in the process that she needs to become more dramatic in order to get the reassurance from you that she needs. Ignoring her starts an escalation of problem behaviors between the two of you that can make things get out of control and will kill your relationship faster than any other thing that you can do. Make sure you don't simply ignore your partner, hoping that his or her bad behaviors will go away. Unfortunately, relationship problems don't just go away when we ignore them. Ignoring relationship problems will create more distance between you and your partner and will also increase your partner's anxiety about the relationship because of the increased distance. The increased anxiety will make your partner behave even more badly, making things worse for you as well.

How about attacking your partner back and telling her that she is not a good girlfriend or wife (or boyfriend or husband)? This does have the benefit of not reassuring her, and so is a better choice than arguing with her. The main problem with attacking your partner is that when you behave this way toward her, you will start to feel much less attracted to her. And, if there is any decency about you at all, you won't want to hurt someone just because they feel insecure and afraid of losing you. Although your partner says things in a bad way, what he or she most fears is losing you. You don't need to hurt him or her for that. You can choose to help your partner with that instead.

The helpful way to deal with your partner's arguing is simply to sincerely agree, without arguing, defending, or blaming. What your partner really needs to do is to deal with reality instead of his or her scary fantasies. Your partner can only do that if you help him or her to see things as they really are. So, for example, if she says that you used to spend more time with her than you do now, and that if you really loved her you would be spending more time with her now, then you can simply admit the reality of this:

"I don't spend as much time with you as I used to."

Notice here, that there are no explanations, no defenses, no arguing, no attacks, and you are not ignoring her. You are simply admitting the truth. Now, what is likely to happen next? Next, she is likely to ask you why you're not spending so much time with her. This is the point where you give an explanation, honestly:

"When we were first dating, I wanted to be with you all the time because our relationship was new and fresh. But, now I miss being with my friends (or doing my hobbies) and so I like to spend more time with them than I used to."

Please note again that there are no arguments here, no attacks, and you are not defending but merely explaining. It is explaining and not defending because it is a response to her question—not in response to her attack. Do not give people explanations in response to attacks. Otherwise, they will force explanations out of you by attacking you.

Your partner may have more questions for you, in which case you keep doing the same thing—answering honestly. This has the benefit of helping your partner to see reality, and also helps you to stay calm and feel confident about what you're doing. The only time you won't feel confident about doing this is if you know that what you are doing is wrong. In that case, you do need to work on changing your behavior.

One thing to understand about the needy person is that she (or he) spends most of her time in her head. She sees a molehill and makes a mountain out of it. She hears a criticism, and can see a divorce or breakup and eternal loneliness in her head. This is why she reacts so strongly to what you consider to be just small things. She is not responding to the reality—she is responding to her imagination. Your being able to be open and honest, and waiting for questions before giving explanations, will help to keep your partner grounded in reality.

Dealing with your partner's interrogations

I define *interrogating* as asking people questions they don't want to answer. It's a really poor relationship skill, because it does not build connections between people. I'm sure that when your partner interrogates you, it makes you kind of irritated and it makes you want to start to avoid him or her. Although this is what it makes you feel like doing, actually doing so would not be helpful. For one, if you start to avoid your partner, you will start to care less about her (or him). Secondly, she will rightly sense that you're caring less about her and are becoming disconnected. This will raise her anxiety level and make her want to interrogate you all the more—perpetuating the problem, creating a downward spiral. You have to learn how to behave in a way which does not create the spiral if your relationship is going to have a chance for success.

Like almost all of the behaviors that a needy person does, her interrogations are meant to force you into reassuring her. So, she may ask where you were, what you did, who you did it with, what you talked about, or any number of variations on that theme.

My recommendation is that you not be secretive with your stuff. Give your partner full access to your cell phone and computer. Let her look at those things to her heart's content and don't lock her out of anything that doesn't have to be secured (for example clients' private information). Be transparent in what you do and that will take care of part of the problem. If you start becoming secretive, she will naturally start to wonder why you're being secretive. And even though it may not be some big reason, it will become one in her mind. If you really have some big secrets that you can't share with her, then maybe you need to consider that you *are* doing something wrong and need to end that or end your relationship.

However, assuming that you're not doing anything wrong and that you are being transparent, how do you deal with these questions that you don't want to answer? For example, you may like to go out and spend time with your friends once in a while and be able to talk about whatever you want to without having to report back to your significant other about it. That's perfectly reasonable. You're not doing anything wrong if you are just talking to your friends and you should be able to talk to your friends about whatever you like as long as you're not betraying your partner's confidence in you.

First, don't fall into the *trap* of answering her question with a question, as in the following exchange:

YOUR PARTNER: "What did you talk about with your friend?"
YOU: "Why do you need to know?"

If you do answer this way, then your partner will sense that you are being evasive and will either say or think something like the following:

YOUR PARTNER: "If it's nothing bad, then you should be to tell me."

And, because you don't want to share with her what you talk about with your friends, she's going to assume it means something bad about your relationship. So, what will you end up doing instead? You will end up lying to her about what you talk about. This is what partners of needy people do—they lie. They do that not to deceive their partners, but in order to calm and reassure their partners. But, because it actually doesn't fix the problem, it creates another problem. Eventually, she (or he) will discover that you are lying to her about things. When you lie to her you dig a deeper hole for yourself and your relationship. Give up lying as it's not necessary and it is destructive. Replace your lies with secure behavior. Consider the following exchange:

YOUR PARTNER: "What did you talk about with your friends?"
YOU: "What I talk about with my friends is between me and them. Just like what I talk about with you is between me and you. I'm not going to change that. If we talk about something that I want to share with you, I will share it with you."

Now, I can guess what you are thinking. You are thinking that if you say this to your partner, he or she's going to be very upset. Well, your partner is going to be very upset if you have been in the habit of revealing what you talk about with your friends in the past. On the other hand, if you're just starting out your relationship, your partner is not likely to be so upset if you say this. He or she will just note it as something about you that is different from the other people he or she has been with. It will not cause problems as you go forward with your partner.

Let me give you an example to illustrate why you don't need to be so concerned about your partner's anger. Suppose you are the parent of a 10-year-old child. Your child has never had a bed time before and you have always allowed her to stay up as late as she wanted. But now, you find that she has been doing poorly in school and in fact is falling asleep in class. In order to try to help her with that, you decide you need to set a bedtime. When you give your daughter a bedtime, she becomes very upset about it and argues and screams and cries. She does whatever she can to get you to give up the idea of giving her a bedtime, especially since she usually texts her friends after 10 PM. Now, does this mean you shouldn't give her a bedtime because it will cause conflict? Or, should you give her the bedtime and be consistent about it until she adjusts to it? Hopefully, you see that the second choice is the right one, even though it causes a lot of conflict at first. This is also the way it is when you start to have healthy boundaries with a needy partner. Your partner won't like it and will become upset. But, if you are consistent, he or she will adjust to it. This will not only make it easier for you, it will make it easier for your partner.

Now there is one caveat. Whenever you set boundaries for someone, you have to be extra sure that you are balancing them with loving behavior. If you had a daughter who had to adjust to a new bedtime, you might want to spend some more time with her on the weekends doing something she would really like to do, to help strengthen your relationship with her. After she gets used to the boundary, you can drop back to your normal level of interaction. Likewise, if you're going to start to use boundaries like this with your significant other, you need to make sure that you're helping him or her to feel loved the rest of the time. This is the time to increase whatever expression of love makes your partner feel most loved.

Dealing with your partner repeatedly talking about relationship problems

Why does your needy partner want to keep talking about your relationship? The reason she (or he) does this is because she believes that repeatedly talking about your relationship will improve it. So, you see, her intention is actually a good one. She doesn't realize that her talking seems more like complaining and criticizing than anything helpful. She also doesn't notice that talking about relationship problems is not actually making your relationship better. Needy people are good at not seeing reality.

For people with damaged relationships, talking about relationships is one of those things that works only one time out of ten. And, when people do things which work one time out of ten, they continue to do them over and over again. This is true even though nine times out of ten they are actually doing more damage. This is similar to the principle of a slot machine. Because slot machines pay off every once in a while, the payoff rewards people for playing. Moreover, each spin brings with it the hope that you might be a winner. Unfortunately, the slot machine rarely pays off as much as you spend. So even though you win a little, you end up losing a lot.

Maybe you have even tried this strategy of talking about your relationship to try to improve your relationship. The idea is something like this, "If I sit my partner down and tell her the kinds of problems that I'm having with this relationship, she will want to work on them to make things better." But, when you actually do this, you find that instead of wanting to work on that problem, she brings up other problems—especially problems that she believes are caused by you. Then what happens? Most likely, you either become angry because she is not sticking to your original point, or you become defensive, or you withdraw from the conversation altogether. It turns out that talking about a relationship is not a very effective way to work on a relationship *unless* it is done in a structured way or under the guidance of a professional. Structure, or a professional's help, will keep the conversation from deteriorating, keep people on track, and keep the conversation going long enough to do some good, without allowing anyone to escape.

One thing you can do when your significant other comes to you is to simply point out reality to her (or him). Stay away from the actual topic that she is bringing up and talk to her about how the last time she brought up problems it made things worse, and the time before that, and the time before that. Tell her, if there is something that she would like you to do, to please just tell you and you will consider it. But you will not have a sit down talk about relationship problems. Nor will you argue with her about it.

If she insists, has a tantrum, or makes a general nuisance of herself, then clear out of there. Do not try to engage her in conversation or reason with her. It's important to notice here that you are not simply withdrawing from the conversation as you may have done before. You have actually given her something to do—to tell you what she wants. Unlike talking about relationship problems, telling people what you want (as opposed to telling them what you *don't* want) turns out to be a really helpful thing to do in a relationship. When people say what they want, it does not require the other person to guess or play games, become defensive, or argue.

For example, maybe your partner would like to talk to you about how you are spending a lot of time going out with your friends and how you don't seem to be spending much time with her. This kind of conversation is likely to lead to an argument and to you wanting to spend even less time with her than you did before she brought this up. On the other hand, if she could say to you that she would like you to take her out once a week, it's going to go much better.

Your role after this is to carefully consider what your partner tells you she (or he) wants. Some of the things that she wants will actually be good for your relationship and will be important for you to do if you want her to continue loving you. Some of the things she tells you she wants will not actually be good to do, because if you did them, you would become more and more resentful—eventually doing harm to your relationship. This would also decrease your feelings of love toward your partner.

You can also be proactive with her—asking her questions that help her to tell you what she wants in different situations. Try to say things in a nice way. For example, if you are going out to dinner together, don't simply ask her what she wants to eat or where she wants to go. Ask her what kind of experience she would like to have with you when you go out. Would she like to have a quiet and romantic dinner? A light and friendly, chatty dinner? Would she like to pretend you're on a first date with her? If you can help her to express her desires this way and you help her to get these simple things, then you will help her to feel loved and special. That will go a long way in eliminating her desire to have those relationship talks with you.

You can set good boundaries with your partner, be a secure man or woman, and live a life that you enjoy as long as you help your partner to enjoy life and feel loved and special. If you only work on enjoying your life, then you will be a selfish person and you will get complaints no matter what kind of partner you are with.

Dealing with your partner's long explanations

This is probably the easiest one to deal with. Insecure people have a tendency to explain everything, even if all you need from them is a simple answer. For example, you might ask something simple like, "Did you take out the trash?" and instead of getting a simple answer, you might get a long, convoluted answer like the following:

"Well, I was going to take out the trash but then I got a telephone call from my sister Becky. She told me that she and her husband are planning a trip to Jamaica but that they are having trouble coordinating their schedules to be able to go. She wanted to know my opinion about what she should do if she's not able to take time off of work to go to Jamaica with her husband. So, that's why I didn't take out the trash."

If your significant other is an explainer, you know how irritating it can be to get such long answers to such simple questions. In fact, you may have gotten to the point (or are getting there) where you are hesitating to ask your partner any questions or even to talk about everyday things with your partner, especially if you are in a hurry. You may be finding it easier and easier just to not talk to your partner. But, the less you talk to her (or him), the more she will want to talk to you.

The reason why explainers explain things in detail is because of habit or insecurity. Often it is both. Just like the other needy behaviors, explaining may help the needy person to feel less needy, but actually does damage to the relationship, slowly and insidiously, creating a worse relationship, which in turn escalates your partner's insecurity.

At some level your partner fears that you are going to attribute wrong motivations to her (or him) if she simply answers your question. For example, if she simply said to you "No, I didn't take out the trash," she may fear that you will think she's lazy, or doesn't care, or is avoidant, or is angry with you. So, in order to prevent you from having such a reaction to her, she gives you an explanation designed to help you understand why she didn't do the thing you've asked her about. Because to her way of thinking, if you understand her reason for not doing something, then you will not be upset about it. This is a fallacy, of course. Even when we understand the reasons people don't do things, we may still be upset about them. After all, everyone has a reason for what they do.

If you avoid asking her questions, or avoid talking to her, just so you don't have to get such long explanations interrupting your conversation every minute, it will make her feel more anxious and insecure. This in turn, will lead her to do even more explaining. You may find that even when you're not saying anything to her, that she is still explaining to you what she is doing or what she is thinking or what she has done. It can drive you crazy. Such "explanations" are not real conversations because they are not enjoyable by both of you. They are monologues. They are *noise*.

What you will need to learn to do is to use a two or three step approach to stop this habit in your partner. First, make sure you're not creating the problem by asking for explanations. If you need to know your partner's reasons for everything, then you have an insecurity problem yourself.

Secondly, when you want a simple answer, just say so before you ask the question. Although it takes a few more seconds to do this, it will prevent your partner from giving a long explanation and actually save you time. Not only that, but you will be helping your partner to learn that nothing bad is going to happen when she just gives you a short answer. It is important, however, that when she gives you such a short answer, you be satisfied with it. You can't expect her to give you explanations when you want them and to not give you explanations when you don't want them. She is not a mind reader. If she has to guess whether you want a long answer or a short one, then she is going to give you long explanations every time rather than upset you part of the time with her short answers. Here is an example of what I'm talking about:

YOU: "I'm going to ask you a question and I just want a short answer without an explanation. Okay?"
YOUR PARTNER: "Okay."
YOU "Did you take out the trash?"
YOUR PARTNER: "No."
YOU: "Thank you for just telling me what I wanted to know. I enjoy talking to you more when I don't hear long explanations."

While this example may seem a little rude, it makes your relationship better, and so it not a bad thing to say. Letting her know what you want is helpful. Notice that in this example you are thanking her for not giving a long explanation. You don't need to do this every time, but it's good to say it once in a while. If you really want your partner to change, you have to be appreciative when she (or he) does. After all, she is taking a risk giving up the old behavior. If she doesn't gain anything from changing, she will revert to the old behavior just because it will benefit her part of the time.

Another thing you can do is to point out to her when she's giving a long explanation. Most people who do this are not aware that they do it. For example, when I teach my needy clients that they shouldn't explain themselves unless they are asked to explain, I catch them when they do it with me and let them know about it. Often, they are surprised to find that they are explaining without even realizing it. For example:

COACH JACK: "Would you be able to schedule again for this time next Monday?"

NEEDY CLIENT: "Oh, next Monday I can't because I have to go to the school to attend a meeting about my son's math grades. The teacher said that if he doesn't bring his grades up, then he may have to repeat the course. . . ."

Of course, all I want to know is if my client is available next Monday or not. Her telling me about her son's math grades is not only not relevant, but slows me down when I need to finish the session. It almost makes me fearful to ask her if she's going to be available next Tuesday, as I may get another explanation about that. So, I need to stop her and point it out:

COACH JACK: "Would you be able to schedule again for this time next Monday?"

NEEDY CLIENT: "Oh, next Monday I can't because..."

COACH JACK (Interrupting in a calm, gentle voice): "Stop. You are explaining to me and I didn't ask you for an explanation."

NEEDY CLIENT: "Wow, I am. I didn't even realize it."

COACH JACK: "Good. Now let's try it again—without the explanation. Would you be able to schedule again for this time next Monday?"

NEEDY CLIENT: "No, I can't."

COACH JACK: "Great answer—direct and to the point. Just what I wanted to know. How about next Tuesday?"
NEEDY CLIENT: That would be fine."
COACH JACK: "Another good answer. Talk to you then."

It's important to be patient with this approach. Remember, your partner is not doing any of these things intentionally. The last thing she wants to do is damage the communication she has with you or the way that you feel about her. But, letting it go on out of kindness is not so kind. It is another example of codependence, since you are playing a role in this destructive behavior.

If you attempt to help her this way for two or three weeks and it doesn't stop, you can start to use a boundary for this behavior. You can simply tell her that whenever she gives you a long explanation, you're going to turn around and walk away in the middle of her explanation. If you do this consistently, it should really help her to break the habit.

And, most importantly, when she gives you the kind of answers that are really good for you, be sure to praise her. It's not an easy thing to become secure, but it's a very valuable thing for both her and you. Don't be afraid to make a big deal out of it. Really helping her to feel good about it is a good investment of your energy and gets you a better relationship in return.

Dealing with your partner's nagging

Secure people don't nag. They ask a couple of times and if you don't follow through, they either let it go, do it themselves, or get someone else to do it. They don't enter into power struggles and they don't create them. But, if you have an insecure partner, you are likely to be nagged. Nagging is one of those things that works okay early in a relationship, somewhat later in a relationship, and very poorly late in a relationship.

You see, one of the problems is that when your relationship is new, you give in to the nagging because you don't want to have problems—even if you think you shouldn't really have to do what your partner wants. But, as this continues and your partner continues to be dissatisfied, you become more and more resentful. Instead of outright saying "no," which would bring an argument, you say you will, but then don't. This helps you to avoid the power struggle, and also helps you to avoid doing something which would make you feel resentful. But, because you don't do it, your partner keeps after you until eventually the stress reaches a point where it is easier for you just to do it. Then you do it. And, once again your partner finds that nagging does work. However, just like all the other needy behaviors, it works at the expense of your relationship. It helps your partner to get a little "fix" while at the same time your marriage or relationship is breaking down.

If you truly want to help your partner, and to save your relationship from needy behaviors like nagging, you're going to need to find something more effective than simple avoidance. From your partner's perspective, the easiest thing for you to do would simply be to follow through the first time you're asked. And actually, your partner has a good point—if you have agreed to do it. So, it's very important that you *only* agree when it is truly right to do so—when agreeing and following through won't cause you to resent your partner more.

How about if your partner asks you to do something that you are not willing to do? If you can give your partner an honest "no" from the beginning, he or she is not likely to continue to nag you. Secure people have no problem saying "yes" or "no" because they are sure of what they want and what they're willing to do. They don't need to lie, they don't need to avoid, they don't need to be intentionally hurtful, and they don't need to please. They do things because they love their partners and because they are the right things to do. When they refuse to do things, it is also because they love their partners and because refusing is the right thing to do. If you are a secure person, then you can follow what Jesus said,

All you need to say is simply "Yes" or "No"; anything beyond this comes from the evil one (Matthew 5:37, NIV).

If you find it hard to do this, then you may want to start at the beginning of this book and learn how to be a more secure person for the sake of your own happiness and the welfare of your relationship.

Loving and praising

There are two very helpful things that you can do to encourage your partner to be more secure and loving toward you.

The first and foremost thing to do is to help her (or him) to feel loved at all times when she is *not* being needy. This means that you need to pay attention to her, treat her nicely, and make her feel special. If you can do this kind of enjoyable work, you will avoid a lot of the unenjoyable work that you will need to do to compensate, or backtrack from having made her feel rejected, neglected, and fearful that you no longer love her.

The other important thing to do is to "catch her" being secure and give her a little extra attention at that time. Don't be afraid to praise her when she is behaving securely. For example, if you go out with your friends and she normally texts you while you are out, but this time she doesn't and instead greets you in a friendly way when you come home, then let her know how much more you looked forward to seeing her because of that. Also, when you do come home from being out, really make her feel like you are glad to see her again. It's important that she know that not texting you actually made you more attracted to her. Or, perhaps you will realize that you didn't follow through with something that you had promised to do and that she didn't nag you at all. Go to her, give her a hug, tell her you're sorry for forgetting and thank her for not nagging you. Tell her how that makes you appreciate her all the more.

Some people think that they shouldn't have to thank someone for doing something which is normal behavior for most people. It's true, that you don't *have to* thank your partner for this. But, it's also true that you don't have to tell her (or him) you love her, or spend time with her, or many other things. You will find that there are many things that you don't have to do in relationships, but if you do them, will make your partner's life and your life more pleasant.

Summary

One thing that I hope you've gotten from this chapter is that although your partner's neediness was not caused by you, you may be codependent for your partner's neediness. That is likely to be one reason you match so well. But, in being codependent, you are also responsible for some of the damage that is being done to your relationship by your partner's needy behaviors. If someone knocks us on the head when we are not looking, we are hardly responsible for it. But if someone keeps knocking us on the head because we are allowing them to do so, then we are also responsible for it.

Up until now, you may not have known the best way to deal with your partner's neediness. You may have thought that you were being kind, nice, or loving by giving in to your partner's complaining or controlling behaviors, unwittingly reinforcing them and bringing your relationship one step closer to ending.

Continuing to "take care" of needy people by giving in to their demands will eventually lead to relational burnout for you. Your love for your partner will disappear and your partner will have a final burst of neediness which will make you want to run from him or her at that time. You don't need to let things get to that point. Your partner is reading this book because he or she doesn't want things to get to that point. Your partner cares enough about your relationship to do something about it. Hopefully, you do as well.

Stopping your codependence for your partner's neediness will not feel like a natural thing. It will, at first, make your partner feel even more anxious and upset. This is unavoidable, but it is the first step in your partner learning to handle his or her fears in a better way than you having to give reassurance. Reassurance is a powerful kind of reward which encourages needy behaviors. If you can be loving, but also firm in your refusal to give in to your partner's neediness, you can keep your relationship strong and greatly decrease stress for both of you.

You will be helping to breathe new life into your relationship. You will also be getting a new and improved partner.

One very important caution for you—change takes time, persistence, and consistency. Not only for your partner, but also for you. Your partner may believe that she (or he) can overcome her neediness in a week just by putting her mind to it, but that is not possible. It's going to take her months of hard work, fighting her impulses to do what she has always done. She will at times be agitated and you may feel like rescuing her. But don't. Just like you can't rescue an alcoholic by giving her a drink, you can't rescue a needy person by reassuring her. She has to make it through this to the point where she doesn't need reassurance from you. She needs to learn to reassure herself and learn to let go of the fear which drives her need for reassurance in the first place.

Becoming secure is no small task and your partner is going to mess up. For you, it's important not to pay too much attention to your partner's messing up, but to pay a whole lot of attention to what your partner is doing better. Letting your partner know what he or she is doing right, and how much you appreciate it, and how much more you love him or her because of it, is perhaps the most important thing you can do.

♥12♥

LIVING A SECURE LIFE

When you overcome neediness, it will give you the edge you have needed for becoming successful in many aspects of your life.   Just becoming secure won't automatically make you successful, however. You will still need to follow good practices to achieve success. This chapter will help you get started with these practices and principles. You will collect more as you continue to grow in knowledge and experience.

Secure and successful people live for today, but with an eye on tomorrow. They periodically look down the road to how they want their work, their relationships, and even their hobbies to be. Then, they behave in a way today that will help them to have the kind of tomorrow they want. They do the same thing the next day, and the next—both enjoying the present and ensuring a good future by working toward something better. Needy people are fear driven; secure people are future driven.

Needy people tend to be fearful about the future and react to every little thing that goes wrong in the day-to-day.   In becoming secure, you need to change your thinking from what you fear to what you want to create. Then, don't worry about the small, bad stuff that happens, but instead keep putting positive effort into your work, your hobbies, and your relationships.   Focus on building a home with a good roof instead of trying to prevent the rain from falling.

By focusing on the principles in this chapter, you will be able to maintain and enjoy the new secure you throughout the rest of your life.

Be the friend and partner you want to have

If you want to have an honest partner, you need to be an honest partner. If you want to have a kind partner, you need to be a kind partner. If you want to have an ambitious partner, you need to be an ambitious partner. You get the idea? Whatever qualities you want in your partner, you need to develop in yourself. Not only is it not the job of others to train you to be the way they are, you also know that secure people won't do that. You are either the way they want you to be, or they will not waste time with you. If you are not an honest person, for example, an honest partner will soon be rid of you (if your partner is secure).

I have made this point strongly earlier in this book by saying that if you want to have a secure partner or secure friends, you need to be secure. This also means that as you make the transition from insecure to secure, you will notice more than ever before that most, if not all of your friends, are needy. They are unlikely to become secure just because you did. You may also notice that your partner is much more needy than you are.

While you don't need to dump your friends or your partner, you will need to behave in a secure way with them. This will result in either their adjusting to that and becoming more secure, or it will result in their rejecting you. This problem is not unique to insecurity, but is common for all major changes in character or lifestyle. An alcoholic who becomes sober may lose all of her drinking buddies. An introvert who becomes an extrovert may lose his less outgoing friends.

It is my recommendation that you use the chapter for helping your partner to become secure, if he or she is insecure, but that you make new friends who are more secure and let the less secure friends slip away. If you don't do that, then the danger is that you will return to being insecure, just so you can connect with your old friends better. Many alcoholics have done the same. If you have new, secure friends, then you won't need the old friends so much, and will be able to better maintain the new you. Without new friends, the new you will start to miss the old you.

So, be the kind of person you want to have as a friend and as a partner and you will end up with friends and a partner that you can enjoy and share your happiness with. And, if you are working to help your partner to be more secure, make sure you don't let his or her behavior become an excuse for you to start being needy again.

See people for who they really are

Needy people have a tendency to misperceive their partners as being better than they actually are, especially at the beginning of a relationship. As a secure person, it will greatly benefit you to begin to see people more accurately and to have accurate expectations of them.

A common problem that needy people have in relationships is idealizing their partners—especially in the beginning. They then expect that standard from their partner at all times and when they don't get it, feel disappointed and take steps (ineffective steps) to shape their partners back into their ideal image. This makes their partners feel unloved, "not good enough," and unaccepted.

Here is a problem that is more obvious with men than with women. When men first date you, they will naturally be on their best behavior. They may listen to you with rapt attention, treat you like a princess, and be very romantic. This goes for most all men. This is not their natural selves. As your relationship goes on and you have contact over an extended period of time, you will notice that some men will change a lot, while others will change less. Whatever they are changing into is how they actually are. It's that behavior—in an established relationship, which should set your expectation, and not the initial behavior. My guess is that you too are on your best behavior early in a relationship.

For these reasons, do not compare men (or women) based on their initial behavior with you. And, do not expect more from them than you are getting after having dated them for a good while. In fact, you may not find out what a person is really like until you have been engaged with him or her for almost a year. As you read in an earlier chapter, I recommend a one year engagement in which you and your fiancé are exclusive and have a fixed date for your marriage.

I have worked with many women, both married and single, who tell me, "This is not how my husband or boyfriend really is. There is something wrong with him that is making him behave this way." When I ask single people how long their boyfriends have been behaving that way, they often say "Since about three months into our relationship." And married women may tell me their husbands have been behaving that way for several years. It becomes part of my job to help them see that their husbands or boyfriends are really the way that they are seeing them right now. They did make a change. They changed from someone they were into someone they are. Even if they really were different before, they are also really how they are now. People change and you need to see them realistically and deal with who they are *now.*

Some men and women see their partners as worse than they actually are. That is also a mistake. We all have our best days and our worst days. How we really are is mainly in the middle of those two things. When you are seeking a partner, consider how he or she is most of the time and expect more of the same in the future. To expect more or less will put a strain on your relationship and also be unfair. To hold your partner to an unrealistically high standard will put stress on your partner to be something he or she is not. To see your partner as worse than he or she is will put your partner in the position of having to prove himself or herself to you, when your partner should just be able to be himself or herself. Don't try to change the people you date. That is a needy behavior. Accept them for who they are and eliminate from your life those who are not a good match for you. It is the best thing you can do for yourself and for them, because someone else is a better match for them, and someone else is a better match for you. There is no need for both of you to miss out on these better matches because you are trying to make a square peg fit into a round hole.

In addition to your partner(s), you need to see other people as they actually are, as well. I do have one caution for you, however. If a lot of people treat you the same way, it may be because of the way you are treating them. For example, if everyone seems to be very serious to you, it may be because you are very serious or tense with them. There are a couple of checks you can do to determine if it is you or them.

First, observe how they are with other people. When women tell me, for example, that their husbands are very closed off and don't like to share, I ask them if their husbands like to share with other people. If they do, then it is something about the relationship that is causing their husbands to close off. If their husbands never open up with anyone, it is likely to be their personality and something to be accepted rather than changed.

The other check is to consider whether the other person has changed with the passage of time. If your partner (or your mother, friend, or anyone else) has always behaved a certain way, it is also more likely to be their personality. Another person's behavior can also be influenced by both your behavior and their personality—accentuating any existing tendencies. Some personalities naturally trigger each other, making people a bad match for each other.

When you find out that people are being who they really are and it is not just the way they behave with you, then you can say to yourself, "That's just the way they are." For example, "He doesn't like to share. That's just the way he is." "She doesn't like to do any activities other than going out to eat. That's just the way she is." Then, stop trying to change that person. Enjoy the aspects of that person that you can enjoy and put up with the rest, or don't be friends with them anymore. There is no requirement that you like everyone or that everyone likes you. In fact, that is not possible. Spend your time with the people you like to be with. Use your thoughts to think about people you enjoy thinking about. Don't torment yourself with other people's bad behaviors.

Take responsibility for your life and happiness

Your life belongs to you. You have just as much right to it as anyone else does to their life. You should not need to sacrifice your life to accommodate others.

Needy people, because of their fear of being abandoned and alone, often seek to commit to others, and commit to do for others, and then expect to get appreciation in exchange for their commitment. But many times they receive much less than they give. Many times they do things for people who really don't care much about them. This takes the joy out of giving and they may start to *demand* the love they were hoping to get. And, they continue to give only in a half-hearted way. This does nothing but push other people away, including partners, friends, and family members.

Second Corinthians teaches us that we should be cheerful givers:

Each of you should give what you have decided in your heart to give, not reluctantly or under compulsion, for God loves a cheerful giver (2 Corinthians 9:7, NIV).

But, what if we are not? What if we are just giving and giving and giving, while being emotionally starved by the ones we are giving to? You need to take a good long look at your life and ask yourself if the things and people you are committed to are really pleasing and fulfilling to you. This goes for your possessions, your relationship with God, and your relationship with other people. You may expect that I am going to say that if they are not pleasing, then you should get rid of them and get someone else or something else. But, that is not what I am going to say. What I am going to say is to examine what is stopping you from committing with your whole heart. Why are you holding back part of yourself? And, who are you really fooling if you only have half-hearted commitments? And, why do you need to fool them anyway?

As a secure person, you no longer have the need to fool people. You can be yourself and accept or decline invitations because it's what you want or don't want. If you are baking cookies for the church bazaar, *decide* that you are doing it because it's important to you or because you enjoy it. Not because it's expected of you or out of obligation. If you are in a relationship, give love and make love because you enjoy it or *want to* give it. Not because you are afraid of what will happen if you don't. If you are a Christian and attending church, decidedly worship with your whole heart. If you want more out of your relationships with people and with God, then you need to put more into them.

At first, you may feel guilty if you start taking your own needs and desires into consideration. But, you will also start to live *genuinely.* Some people will love the new you. Some won't like the new you at all. Those will be the people who have been benefitting from your neediness. And, if you find that you don't like something about the new you, change it. Just change the way you are. It is your life. You no longer need to be the result of programming that was put into you by your parents, teachers, or anyone else.

Where do you want to go, what do you want to do, and who do you want to be? I often tell my clients that changing from needy to secure is like a caterpillar changing into a butterfly. Whereas before you could only see the world from a lowly position, now you are free to fly and no longer hide among the leaves for fear of being gobbled up.

If you have been needy all of your life, there is a very good chance that other people have not really experienced your love. You have been too focused on what they expected from you or on what you were trying to get from them. Now that you don't have to do that anymore, is there some way you want to express your love to them—just because—and with no other reason? There is a great joy in giving just because we want to give. And, there is a great joy in loving just because we want to love. There is also a great joy in worshipping just because we want to worship our God. When you can start to feel that, I believe that you can start to understand why God has joy in loving you. He doesn't have to. And, he doesn't need to. He wants to.

There will be many sacrifices in your life that you will make for others, and many things that you will have to do out of necessity or responsibility, but whenever you can, do it because it is what you want to do.

Switch from reactive to proactive

Needy people tend to be short sighted and reactive. The questions they ask themselves emphasize short term results. They overemphasize how other people will feel about them if they do or don't do something. Because of this, they often agree to do things for others that they don't want to do because they don't want to make someone "mad" at them. They also avoid using good boundaries with their partners for the same reason— "My partner will be mad at me if I do that." While no one wants others to be mad at them, it is not the most important consideration.

A much more important consideration is what *long term* effects your behaviors will have on your relationships. If you repeatedly do more for others than you want to, eventually you will become resentful and avoid others, thereby damaging your relationships. If you don't use good boundaries with your partner, he or she will continue to do damage to your relationship to the point where you have grown so far apart that neither of you may want to be together anymore. If you refuse to discipline your kids because they might get upset, you will create little monsters that will grow into big monsters. You will come to regret ever having kids at all and your relationship with them will be very poor. Small, unhealthy habits grow into the roots that split apart otherwise very strong relationships. It is the small, habitual problems that break down loving feelings.

To avoid these situations, you need to start with the end in mind. That is, you need to mentally visualize yourself *years* down the road in every area that is important to you. For example, if you visualized yourself way down the road, say at retirement time, you might have a vision something like this:

I live with my spouse in a small cottage in the country. We enjoy spending time talking and traveling together. We also get together with our friends. We don't need to worry about finances because we can live on our retirement savings.

This may not be your particular vision, but we can use it as an example. Let's pick out some specific aspects:

Live with spouse
Cottage in the country
Talking
Traveling
Getting together with friends
Living on retirement savings

If you already have a great relationship with your spouse, plenty of money in retirement savings, are healthy and have friends, it is reasonable to assume you will have that in retirement. But, for every part of this vision that you don't have already, you will need to work toward it. It won't magically come to you with the passage of time. If you have a poor relationship with your spouse now, it is not going to become magically good when you retire. If you are not putting money into your retirement now, it is not magically going to appear when you retire.

You work on these kinds of things by laying out a timeline from now until the date of your visualized event. Then, on that timeline, you need to put steps leading up to that visualization, so that by the time you arrive there, you will already have those things. By working backwards from your end goals to your present day, you will see what your next step is, and the one after that, and the one after that. If you are willing to do the work required, you can achieve *anything* that is within your control.

The more specific you can be about your goals, the more specific you can be about the steps. For example, if you would like to have a million dollars in your retirement account and you are 20 years from retirement, you can plug that information into an investment calculator and determine how much you should be investing each year. If your goal is to be married with children, you also know that you have a limited window of opportunity for that and can make a timeline, starting at the endpoint and working backwards. For example:

- have a husband and 2 children when I am 35
- have a husband and 1 child when I am 32
- get married when I am 29
- get engaged when I am 28
- date good potential partners with qualities I like
- work on my qualities so that I can attract good potential mates
- determine my standards for potential partners

Having reached the starting point in your timeline, you can then work forward through the steps. Laying out your plan like this, you will realize the importance of each of the steps. If you compromise on any of the steps, every step after that will be further from your end goal. For this example, if you did not determine your standards and stick to them, you wouldn't develop the right qualities, would be less likely to date good partners, and would more likely end up a single parent than to be married with a family.

Using this approach you will see what is important to spend your time on now and what is not. This is one example of a coaching approach, taken from the business world, and applied to your relationships. Coaching approaches are based on applied positive psychology and business models of success. You can learn them on your own and use them to your advantage, or you can get a coach to walk you through them. Whichever way you do it, you need to switch from a "feeling" approach to a strategic approach if you want to have more success in your relationships (or in anything). One of the saddest results of being a needy person is feeling like you have wasted years of your life when you could have been working on what really mattered to you. One of the most exciting things about being a secure person is making your dreams come true.

Increase your failure rate for more success

Too many people attempt to play it safe by not taking reasonable chances. Far from this making them safe, it results in significant loss. If you have a thousand dollars and bury it in a secret place, will it be safe if no one finds it? No, it won't. Because of inflation, your thousand dollars will be worth less and less over time. The longer you keep it buried in the ground, the more you will lose. If you put that money in the bank, you will gain a small amount of interest and will not lose as much, but you would still lose because the bank will not pay you more interest than the inflation rate. If you invest your money, you may lose it all, or you may gain much more than you originally had. Which choice do you make? As it turns out, needy people tend to be like those who bury their money in the ground. They are *risk averse.* That is, they are so afraid of losing what they have that they do things which cause them to lose what they have anyhow. Successful people tend to be moderately risk taking. As a result, they have more failures than most people, but they also have more successes. And, their successes tend to far outweigh their losses.

Let's apply this principle to relationships. A single woman may be so afraid of losing her new boyfriend, that she will immediately make a commitment to him not to date any other man. This assures her that she can hold on to this man temporarily, while guaranteeing that she will find no better man. On the other hand, a single woman who dates many men will also lose some men because of those men's insecurities. Insecure men are also risk averse, so would not be able to tolerate her dating other men. Those insecure men would naturally be eliminated from her social calendar. As a result, she will end up with secure men only and her life partner will turn out to be one of them. She is likely to have a much longer and happier relationship. For the secure woman, it does not matter how many insecure men she loses if she ends up with a good secure man.

Let's examine the same kind of example with a company. A company has a product that people really like. If the company creates many new products, 90% of them or more may fail. But, if only 10% of those products succeeds, more profit will be made than was spent on the 90% that failed. They needed to try many new products to find the few or the one that put them ahead and kept the company growing.

As you work to become secure, you must not be afraid of increasing your failure rate. Two successes out of 10 tries (20% success) is better than 1 success out of two tries (50% success). This is because two successes beat one success, no matter how many failures you have had. Successful people view failure as eliminating bad choices, much like a sculpture eliminates pieces of marble until the statue within is revealed. Thomas Edison, one of the most famous inventors in our history, credited much of his success to his numerous failed designs. For example, he performed more than 9000 experiments to create a new type of storage battery. He considered each failed experiment to be crucial to his ultimate success since it helped him to get closer to a design that worked.[4] In contrast, the approach of a needy person would have been to try one storage battery that worked just a little, over and over again, hoping that it would start working better. Fearing the failures that would be necessary to have success, they never would have success unless it was by some kind of miracle.

I like to read nonfiction. If I buy 10 books and nine of them are lousy, have I wasted my money? Not if that one in 10 helps me in some significant way. As soon as I discover that a book is actually not helpful, I can discard it and move on to the next. I have no obligation to finish it. I want to eliminate from my life all that is unhelpful as quickly as I can. Then I can focus most of my time on helpful things while replacing the unhelpful things with even more. Through this process of finding what does not

---

[4] Dyer, F. and Martin, T (1910). *Edison: His life and inventions.* New York: Harper & Brothers.

work and eliminating it, I achieve more, faster, than those who take something that does not work and try to make it work. You learned in this book how needy people take very needy behaviors like criticizing and arguing and try repeatedly to make them work rather than take a chance on other methods which might fail, but also might work.

When you find that one person you want to spend the rest of your life with, it will not matter to you how many other people you have eliminated, be it 10 or 100. It will only have mattered that you eliminated them so you could end up with the one you want. The same principle is true for making friends, for finding the right job, for living in a place you really like, for finding a type of exercise that is right for you, and so on.

Have standards and keep them

A secure person is a person who can weigh the evidence and make a decision based not on the quickest gain, the easiest choice, what feels the best, or what other people usually do, but according to an internal set of values. Living according to a set of values is in some ways easier, because it gives you a guide for action in many situations. It is also sometimes harder because your values may clash with someone else's values, or may result in your being deprived of something that is tempting you. There is no successful person in the world who doesn't live according to some set of values, which helps him or her to make decisions. Decisions that many times go against the norm.

The Bible tells us that the highest value is love (1 Corinthians 13:13). Although many people would say that love is the most important aspect of their relationship, many people do not use love to guide them when their relationship is having problems. Some people will consistently put the welfare of their partner ahead of their own. But, in strained relationships, many people (especially needy people), will not consider their partners' welfare or happiness. Suddenly their value of love goes out the window and selfishness takes over. They beg, argue, and promise in an effort to stop their partners from doing things they don't like. Why? To make *themselves* happy. Of course, this is obvious to their partners and gives their partners all the more reason to continue to distance or to leave the relationship. A person who really has a value of love will say something more like, "I don't want you to go. But, even more than that, I don't want you to be unhappy. If going is what you truly need, then I love you enough to help you do that." Do you think a comment like that will push someone out the door? It won't. Neediness and selfishness push people away, not loving them. No one leaves relationships because their partners truly care about them.

If you value honesty, there will be times that you will be tempted to lie because telling the truth in those times would cause a bad result for you. You might lose your job or your relationship. But, a truly secure person would not fear that. A truly secure person would find it more dangerous to violate his or her values.

You must have a set of values and never violate your principles, except in order to keep a higher order principle. For example, you may have a value of not stealing. But, you might have another value of saving lives. If you need to steal a boat in order to rescue a drowning person, you would do it. Saving lives outweighs not stealing.

To the secure person, it does not matter how many other people are living without standards. She (or he) will have her own standards and she will live by them. She will be rejected by some, but she will also have opportunities for secure relationships that needy people would never have. She will also have peace of mind.

Have a standard for the people you date, for the friends you have, for the food you eat, for the way you dress, for what you will and will not do on a date or in your relationships. Have a standard for how much time you will work and which obligations and which people take priority in your life. Many of the people that I coach have nearly lost their relationships because, although they had standards for their partners, they did not have standards for themselves. They did not make their partners a priority, but sought their own satisfaction—taking without giving, until they finally discovered that their partners had no more to give to them.

228

Be honest, but don't say everything

Honesty is one mark of a secure person. Insecure and needy people often believe that they need to lie in order to get people to like them more. They worry that if they are honest, people won't like them, that they will be outcast and friendless. With such fears, it is no wonder that so many people lie. So many people lie so often, that you may find it hard to believe that lying is *totally* unnecessary.

The danger in becoming secure is in going to an extreme in the other direction. If lying is bad, then telling the truth must be good—right? Not always. Sometimes it is better to say nothing or to refuse to say something.

Can you imagine if you went around telling people in the shopping mall that they are dressing unfashionably and their hairstyle is out of date? It might be very honest to do so, but it would not be good. Jesus Christ, the greatest person to ever live, never told a lie, but there were also a great many truths that He never said as well. God knows a lot more than we do and He does not feel it His obligation to point everything out to us. Who could bear to hear all the truths that God could tell us about ourselves?

Likewise, it is not necessary to say everything that comes into your mind to your partner. You don't need to point out flaws in your partner or even everything you like about him or her. It is much more important to get along, with simple honesty, saying no more than is necessary to have an enjoyable relationship.

One common question I deal with as a relationship coach is "Should I tell my committed partner how many lovers I have had or other details about past relationships?" My answer to this is "no." Secure people don't need to know, and insecure people get hung up on it. Be firm the first time your partner asks so there doesn't need to be a second time. What you did before your partner committed to you is not your partner's business. And, what your partner did before committing to you, is not your business. There is one very big exception, however. If there is some ongoing repercussions of a past behavior, your partner needs to know about it.

For example, if you had a child with a previous partner, that would be important for your current mate to know because of your ongoing involvement with your child or your financial obligations. The same would be true of any past partners you continue to be involved with, even casually. Likewise, if you have a criminal record that will affect something in the present or future (for example, adopting a child or getting a job), you need to inform your partner about it. You don't need to inform people you don't have a committed relationship with, unless it would be reasonable to expect that it would be an important factor in their dating you.

A single lie can be the seed of destruction in your relationship. It breaks trust and can encourage dishonesty from your partner. On the other hand, "complete" honesty does not make for "complete" relationships. And never ask your partner something that, if answered honestly, would be destructive to your relationship. Do not obligate others to lie to you so that you can feel better. As a secure person, you no longer need them to do that.

Balance your life

Needy people put too much emphasis on their relationships because they are afraid of being rejected. This is similar to other insecurities that people have. For example, people who are afraid of losing their money are very careful about spending and worry constantly about the movements of the stock market or being robbed. They are not able to enjoy their money, because they are always afraid of losing it—no matter how much they have. We could use the same analogy for health, work, or any aspect of a person's life. Overemphasizing the importance of any one thing not only takes away the enjoyment of that thing, it also affects one's general happiness and takes away from the other parts of our lives that deserve attention as well.

One guideline I give to people is to not think about their partner more than two hours a day. The ideal situation is to be fully engaged with your partner when you are together, giving him or her your time and attention, but when you are not together, to be giving time and attention to whatever else you are doing.

Many needy people spend a lot of time thinking about their partners not only for fear of losing them, but also because they have very few other things in their lives of importance. This can be remedied by making personal goals related to work, family, friends, self-care, spiritual beliefs, and finances, as well as your marriage or relationship. Working on a variety of goals will help you to better use your time and will give you other things to think about.

As I said earlier about dating, secure people will have so many good friends and activities in their lives that they will not date someone who would be likely to mess up any of those things. The same principle applies to committed relationships. If you have a balance of career, friends, self-care, finances, and so forth, you will be less afraid of losing your partner, will not have to think about your partner so much, and will not feel so much of a need to constantly be in touch with your partner or check up on your partner. That will protect your relationship as well as make you a happier person.

The best way to make sure you are balanced and secure is to give *equal* importance to each area of your life. See your health as being just as important as your job, but not more important; your job as just as important as your relationship with your partner, but not more important; your relationship with your partner as just as important as your health, but not more important, and so on. Examine each aspect of your life and adjust how much time and thinking you spend on each of those aspects until you get a balance.

The one possible exception to the above is your relationship with God. Because your relationship with God is the only aspect of your life that will survive past your death, it does make sense to overemphasize Him in your life. But, because God wants you to be healthy and to have balance and to depend on Him rather than putting your faith in anything of this world (including your relationship with your significant other), it will actually make you more secure to depend on Him in all that you do. So, it would *not* be healthy to ask yourself in everything that you do,

"Would my partner want me to do or not do this?" but, it would be healthy in all things to ask, "Would God want me to do or not do this?" Since God unselfishly has your welfare at heart and is the ultimate source of wisdom for all of our actions, we can keep Him in mind in all that we do.

Make new friends that fit the new you

Giving up insecure friends is hard. Becoming secure is hard. But, it will make your life so much better to do both of these things. Let me give you an analogy to help you understand this better.

Alcoholics usually fit in best with other alcoholics. Makes sense, right? After all alcoholics have some serious dysfunction in the eyes of people who are not alcoholics. So, in order to get along with non-alcoholics, alcoholics need to hide their alcoholism. But, with their drinking buddies, they don't. They can fit in, feel better about themselves, and feel more normal. But, when an alcoholic works on overcoming her addiction, she has to stop hanging out with her drinking buddies. If she didn't, she would not fit in with them and there would be a tremendous pressure and temptation to start drinking again.

Many people have believed that they could still hang out with their drinking buddies and just not drink, but it doesn't work. It is not acceptable to their buddies. And, after a short while, the person who was trying to be sober starts to rationalize that having just one drink won't hurt. But, once that first one goes down, it is much easier to have a second and a third.

Obviously it is important for the recovering alcoholic to stay away from friends who are active alcoholics. But, how successful is someone going to be trying to give up alcohol if they don't have any friends at all? Eventually, they will miss the socialization because e*veryone needs someone.*

Neediness is not alcoholism, but it is still dysfunctional and not acceptable to secure people who get quite annoyed with it. How would your needy friends feel if you hung out with them, but did not put up with any of their needy behavior and did not agree with them about how they are victims of bad relationships? Either they would reject you, you would reject them, or you would become one of them again. This is why, if you want to stay secure, you must not hang out with insecure friends. It is also why you need to make new, secure friends.

You don't need to be mean to your friends and you don't need to try to explain to them how you don't want to hang out with them because they are needy. What you need to do is to marginalize them. Make excuses not to meet up with them and become much worse at answering their phone calls or texts. They will find someone to replace you in their lives. Everyone needs someone.

When you behave in a secure way, you will be able to make friends with people who you would never have considered to be good friend material. You had judged them from your needy state. Also, they may have protected themselves from you while you were needy—keeping you at arm's length. Give them a chance to get to know the new secure you. You may find that these people who you thought were unkind are actually nice, healthy people, who have a lifestyle closer to what you are aspiring to have as a secure person.

Set yourself up for success

As a secure person, you will want to move away from being reactive to being proactive. Reactive people choose what they will do throughout their day, just as proactive people do. However reactive people are controlled by circumstances. Their partners become angry with them, and so they immediately seek to justify themselves, or to appease their partners. When they make these choices, they see themselves as having no option. "I had to do it because he got angry," "If she didn't accuse me of lying, I wouldn't have had to explain myself," and so forth. A proactive person does not think this way.

A proactive person determines, in advance of other people's behaviors, how she (or he) will live, what she will be like, and what she will achieve in her lifetime. When something happens to her or when her partner, boss, or family member says or does something, *she already has decided* how she will handle it. This

is one of the great benefits of having a strong value system—
becoming *very familiar* with how to behave, and then *deciding* to
behave in accordance with it. I am not just talking about
religious value systems. This applies to any value system that
you believe in. Failing to make a decision to behave in
accordance with a value system explains how so many people
who purport to have a strong value system end up behaving no
differently from anyone else. Having values is not enough. We
must decide to live by them. If you value being financially
sound, but then run up your credit card bills, your value only
makes you feel bad. If you value treating people with love and
respect, but criticize your spouse, your value system just
amounts to self-deception.

The first step in living according to a set of values is to
become more familiar with how to live according to those
values. If you value being financially sound, you need to learn
many things about budgeting, investing, and possibly marketing
(if you run a business). Simply valuing being financially sound
won't help you if you don't learn how to live according to those
values.

Similarly, many people claim to be Christians who are not
familiar with the Bible and so cannot decide to behave in
accordance with Christian values. You must know how to do a
thing before you can do a thing. Likewise, if you value love and
equality in relationships, you must learn how to communicate
well, resolve conflicts in a win-win manner, and how to help
your partner to feel loved. If you do not, then you cannot decide
to be a great partner for your spouse, no matter how much you
value that. You can no more decide to be something you do not
learn to be than you can decide to be an elephant or a kangaroo.
Without knowing how to be the way we want to be, we cannot
be that way.

You can set yourself up for success in being secure by
carefully studying and reviewing the principles in this book, then
deciding that you will live in accordance with those principles.
Then, when your partner does something that you don't like, or
something tempts you to do what your partner would not like,

you will have a clear principle to follow. You will not have a knee-jerk reaction.

For example, if your partner stays out late and does not call you, you will not have a knee-jerk reaction to call and check on him or her. You already will have decided that your partner is an adult and that it is not your job to be your partner's parent. Additionally, you may have decided that you will trust in God to take care of your partner and to take care of you in case anything did happen to your partner. You also will have decided that when your partner comes home, you will not criticize him or her about coming home late, but will instead greet your partner warmly and be glad to see him or her. You also will have decided that if this behavior becomes a pattern, that you still will not criticize, but will instead use good boundaries so that the problem does not endanger your relationship.

Knowing what to do prepares you for most of the decisions necessary for success. This is as true in relationships as it is in any field. I was not born knowing how to be secure and how to help people reconcile their relationships. I learned these things through study, role models, and practice. I failed my early relationships, but became progressively better. I continued to practice until I became so good at these things that I could help many thousands of people have loving relationships. You too can master any skill you are willing to devote the time to study and practice.

Proactive means determining what you want to achieve, learning how to do that, deciding to do what you learned, and persevering until you achieve it. You can decide to make your current relationship a really good one. But, you must learn and practice. If you are not in a relationship, but want to be, you also can learn, decide, and do. Can you do anything or become anything? No. But, you can do or become anything that you have the potential to become.

Reasonably compare yourself to other people who became what you want to be. If you have the same abilities they had *before* they worked to become what you want to become, then there is the same possibility for you to learn and achieve. Reasonable goals based on a reasonable self-assessment will help you to be realistic about what you can achieve and will help motivate you to do whatever it is you need to do. It will set you up for success.

Summary

As a secure person, you will have a more active role in the kind of life you will have from here on out. You will decide on the kinds of friends and future that you want to have, and you will make a plan so that your actions today will lead you to that tomorrow. In order to achieve some of what you want, you will need to give up some of what you have. This is particularly true in terms of needy friendships and codependent patterns of behavior. Once you stop blaming others for the way you have become and see that where you are today is a result of your own choices, you can then be free to see that how you will be tomorrow is also up to you. Everybody has more potential than what they have currently achieved.

While most people will try to keep you average or no better than them, you don't have to be limited by that. If you are taking a class, you can learn more about the subject than what the professor teaches. If you do a job, you can do more than what the job requires and you can do it better. If you have a relationship, you can do more than what your partner expects from you. You can go all-in on your life without fear of failure. Failures just mean that you had the courage to try something new. Don't live life by avoiding and counting your failures. Live life by counting and multiplying your successes. Do what it takes to become secure and create the life that you want to have.

Appendix

If You Would Like Extra Help

You can access many detailed articles and helpful downloads for improving your relationships, free of charge, on my website: coachjackito.com.

Glossary

Agreement: Finding truth in what the other person is saying. Essential for emotional connection.

Affair/cheating: Secretive behavior or unacceptable affectionate behavior with a person other than your partner, according to your partner's standards. There does not have to be sex or in-person contact in order for there to be cheating.

Arguing: Attempting to prove yourself right and/or the other person wrong.

Commitment: A determination to never end the relationship, except by death. There is no such thing as "temporary commitment."

Complaining: Saying what you don't like about anything or anyone.

Criticizing: Saying what you don't like about the person you are talking to.

Dating: Casual, face to face encounters for pleasure, to get to know someone, and to maintain relationships.

Disagreeing: Saying "no" or stating your opinion without trying to prove yourself right or the other person wrong.

Empathy: Sharing and showing the same feeling as another person. Essential for emotional connection.

Infatuation: A strong desire to be emotionally and physically joined with someone based on an idea of that person that does not match how the other person actually is.

Interrogation: Asking people questions they do not want to answer. Even one question can be an interrogation.

Jealousy: Fearfulness provoked by your partner's contact with other people, even when the contact is innocent.

Love: A deep concern for the welfare of another person. Essential for relationships to succeed.

Loving: Doing what is in the best interest of the other person, even if it requires self-sacrifice. Essential for relationships to succeed.

Nagging: Telling or reminding someone more than twice to do something that you want them to do.

Needing: Attempting to coerce or persuade other people to do what is in your best interest, even if it is a sacrifice for them.

Respect: A mindfulness about the capabilities of someone or something. Respect is earned by living according to your values and by having good boundaries. Essential for relationships to succeed.

Security: A feeling of competence and the absence of worry about future events.

Selfish: Doing what brings you pleasure, when it is harmful for your relationship or to another person.

Sympathy: A concern for another person who has a feeling or situation that you don't share. Often includes helping or advising.

About the Author

Dr. Jack Ito ("Coach Jack") is a licensed clinical psychologist who works as a marriage and relationship coach. His specialties are reconciling relationships when one partner does not want to reconcile, and becoming more secure to get the love you want. He has authored books on improving relationships and on helping people get more out of psychotherapy. His methods are both unconventional and practical. Coach Jack believes that the idea that it, "takes two to work on a relationship," makes many people feel stuck and hopeless. Most people divorce, he believes, not because their relationships can't be improved, but because people don't know how to improve them. His teaching is based on the principle, "when we change the way we relate to others, they change the way they relate to us." This principle is empowering and more in line with what the Bible teaches us about our responsibility to love others. Coach Jack believes that approaches which merely promote tolerance and patience with a misbehaving partner are destructive because they result in loss of respect. Therefore, his coaching emphasizes a combination of love and strong boundaries in order build respect and emotional connection.

Books

In his first book, "What to Do When He Won't Change," Coach Jack lays out a systematic and practical approach for women to improve their relationships with husbands who are angry, selfish, unhappy, or withdrawn.

His second book, "Connecting Through Yes!" provides help for men and women to end conflict in their relationships and get to agreement—a necessary step if love is to be preserved.

His third book, "Therapy Beyond All Expectations," helps men and women to transform their "talk therapy" sessions into "action therapy" sessions.

This current volume, "Overcome Neediness and Get the Love You Want," helps men and women to end insecure behaviors in order to have happier, sustainable relationships.

Family Background

Coach Jack's passion for ending conflict and increasing love in relationships stem from his own experiences as a child in a family filled with violence and fear. Terrorized and abused by a father he passionately feared and hated, Coach Jack accepted Jesus Christ as his Savior at age 14. Coach Jack grew in faith, and both his difficult childhood and professional experiences were given meaning helping others to end conflict and restore love. Something that had not been possible for his own family.

For more than 20 years now, Coach Jack has been helping people to both give love and get love in their relationships. At the time of the writing of this book, he lives with his wife in Atlanta, Georgia. Although married, they are very much girlfriend and boyfriend. They have one son in college and one son in medical school.

ALSO BY COACH JACK

What to Do When He Won't Change

Saving Your Marriage or Relationship When He Is Angry, Selfish, Unhappy, or Avoids You

(2011) 249 pages

Has your spouse become an angry, selfish, unhappy, or avoidant person? Does he refuse to go to counseling or work on your relationship? Would you like a way to make things better without having to end your relationship or threaten to?

In *What To Do When He Won't Change*, you will learn the four major motivations that drive men's behavior in relationships. You can then use the down to earth examples and win-win interventions to work with your husband's motivations rather than against him. The result? Faster change with less conflict.

Available at online bookstores in paperback or as a downloadable Kindle eBook from Amazon.com

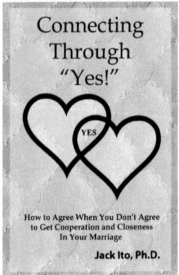

Connecting Through "Yes!"

How to Agree When You Don't Agree to Get Cooperation and Closeness in Your Marriage

(2013) 292 pages

Do you know how to use agreement to transform your biggest areas of marital conflict into closeness, cooperation, and the changes that YOU want in your relationship?

In *Connecting Through "Yes!"* Marriage and Relationship Coach Jack Ito shows you with clear, easy to follow examples, how to positively communicate about the biggest problems that couples face. These are the same techniques his coaching clients use to reconcile marriages, end affairs, deal with addicted spouses, solve problems, end blaming, improve dating, handle money issues, and much more.

Available at online bookstores in paperback or as a downloadable Kindle eBook from Amazon.com

ALSO BY COACH JACK

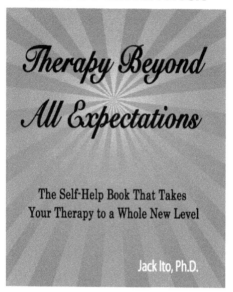

Therapy Beyond All Expectations

The Self-Help Book That Takes Your Therapy to a Whole New Level

(2014) 370 pages

Includes 50 pages of self-help exercises

PSYCHOTHERAPY + SELF-HELP = POWER What do you get when you combine psychotherapy with self-help? An explosion of self understanding and growth, the power to make desired changes and stick with them, and a life that you love. Your therapy hour will keep you on track while your self-help work will help you put your therapy work into practice with the other 167 hours in your week. Featuring more than 50 pages of exercises, insider insights into therapy, and easy to understand explanations to help you make things better, faster.

Available at online bookstores in paperback

245

Index

10 steps for finding a great
   partner, 116
3 important truths, 119
abandonment, 24, 90
abuse, 7, 22, 180, 181
   cycle of, 183
   dealing with, 103
   financial, 19
   not same as anger, 177
   physical, 19, 182
   sexual, 185
   vs. hurt feelings, 181
acceptance, 84
accepting others, 49, 218
accusation example, 194
acting on faith, 40
addiction cycle, 147
advantages of neediness,
   66
affairs, 15, 23, 25, 54
agreement, 45, 84, 103
   doesn't make you a
      doormat, 87
   example, 85
   example with blaming,
      103
anger, 51
   suppressing, 105
answering questions, 88
anxiety problem, 193
anxious attachment, 31
apologizing, 92, 101, 150,
   161
   example, 101, 102
arguing, 45, 83, 198
   dealing with, 199

results of, 83
   vs. refusing, 86
assuming, 50
attachment, 31
avoidance, 93
bad qualities for marriage
   partner, 117
becoming happy, 168
becoming secure
   stages of, 51
behavioral model of
   neediness, 38
being attractive, 168
being careful, 17
being more relaxed, 52
being secretive, 201
being secure
   and responsibility, xvii
   benefits of, 50
being silent
   problem with, 198
being transparent, 201
being yourself, 221
blame, xvii, 10, 21, 167, 186
   example, 102
   responding to, 99
blaming
   example, 100, 101
   used as justification, 187
blindness to reality, 22
boundaries, 43, 163, 185,
   203, 210, 222
   defined, 7
   examples, 8
   in parenting, 9
   protective nature of, 8

vs. threats, 8
boyfriends who won't
    commit, 136
breakup, 3, 15, 24, 26, 38,
    66, 143, 159, 160, 165
breakup message, 165
burn out, 79, 81
caring for dates, 73
cheating, 22, 25, 151
checking up on your
    partner, 43
coaching, 51, 58, 94, 168,
    224
coaching model
    vs. psychological model,
    xvii
codependence
    stopping, 194, 213
codependent, 12, 147, 191,
    193, 213
commitment
    premature, 139
commitment
    encouraging, 134, 136
    premature, 68, 114, 117,
    128, 134, 139
    promoting, 138
communication
    habits, 52
    with uncommitted man,
    137
complaining, 5, 7, 8, 17, 43,
    53
    gender differences in, 80
    not helpful, 82
    when it's good, 82
confidence

relationship to
    competence, xviii
conflict, 161, 171
    reducing, 9
confrontational behavior,
    47
contingency plan, 89, 90
    exercise, 90
controlling behavior, 6, 27,
    65, 115, 148, 149, 192
convincing your partner,
    160
    not to leave, 164
core beliefs of needy
    people, 97
correcting others
    misperceptions, 100
correction criticism, 78, 79
counseling, 168
    for couples, 94
    vs. coaching, 58, 185
criticizing, 78, 174, 178
    example of, 85
cultural and religious
    differences, 127
cycle of neediness, 33
dates
    are not tests, 70
    don't indicate
    commitment, 70
dating, 63, 68, 70
    criteria for, 68
    jealousy in, 68
day to day interactions, 172
deciding, 84
defending oneself, 100
demanding love, 220

denial, 48, 49
depending on God, 231
desperation, 26
diagnosing neediness, 34
disease model, 34
disrespect, 7, 102
divorce, 38, 66, 143, 160
doing what makes sense, 44
don't promise to change, 161
don't chase men, 72
don't date married people, 167
don't punish your partner, 173
don't seek revenge, 169
downward spiral, 42
earning respect, 103
earning trust, 177, 184
effective responding, 53
eliminating relationship talks, 206
emotional distancing, 160
emotional double standard, 187
emotional roller coaster, 115
emotional separation, 160
emotionally disconnected, 161
emotionally unattractive person, 18
encouraging a needy partner, 212
engagement, 127
    importance of one year, 218

exaggerated fears, 33
excessive force vs. justifiable force, 183
exclusive dating, 65, 68
exclusive relationship, 134
explaining, 85, 95, 145
    example of, 95
explanations
    asking for, 99
explosive behavior, 106, 143
faith, 67
faking being secure, 64
falling out of love, 152
family
    as obstacle to becoming secure, 188
fatal attraction, 18
fear
    of abandonment, 16, 32
    of abandonment and isolation, 27
    of isolation and rejection, 11
    self fulfilling nature of, 10
feeling
    anxious, 65
    burned out, 89
    controlled, 147
    hurt, 51
    in love, 160
    less crazy, 30
    like a victim, 13
    like giving up, 51
    not good enough, 6
    stuck, 7, 23
    trapped, 6, 72

feeling better
vs. doing better, 150
feeling burned out, 165
feelings are a lousy guide,
176
fighting, 15
financial abuse, 19, 179
responding to, 182
financial responsibility, 180
finding the right partner,
109, 110, 114
fixing up a man for
marriage, 133
friends
importance of, 155
gender differences, 98
general anxiety problems,
43
get more affection, 59
get respect, 59
getting help, 45
getting space
importance of, 4
give love to get love, 163
giving up childbearing
years, 139
God, xvi
good match vs. bad match,
114
high maintenance woman,
134
hobbies can't replace
friends, 155
honesty in relationships,
229
how to pray, 162
husband's job, 157

Idealization, 2
idealized partners, 48
idealizing your partner, 47
ignoring problems, 199
improving sharing, 54
improving your life, 115
increase your failure rate,
226
increasing security
by helping, 11
by learning self care, 12
independence in
relationships, 50
infatuation phase, 129
infatuation vs. true love, 67
insecure friends, 233
interrogating, 87, 150, 200
dealing with, 201
relationship to anxiety,
201
jealousy, 47, 115, 143
cause of, 143
increases risk of cheating,
152
is an addiction, 147
is not loving, 148
leads to breakup or
divorce, 151
looks like mood swings,
149
origin of, 148
joy
in giving, 221
in loving, 221
in worshipping, 221
learning from results, 44, 45
living genuinely, 221

living together vs. being
married, 156
loneliness, 63, 114
long explanations
dealing with, 206, 208,
209
love, 148
loss of, 102
loving
vs. feeling in love, 169
vs. needing, 227
loving behavior, 163
loving response, 169
loving vs. needing, 80
luck, xvi
lying, 89
problem with, 202
making friends, 115, 155,
217, 233
making personal goals, 231
making promises, 102, 161
making threats
of suicide, 18
to leave, 16
man should be the first to
commit, 140
marital engagement, 69
marriage
idealized view of, 127
marriage counseling, 94
marriage regrets, 19
marrying the wrong person,
66
mature love, 16
and acceptance, 19
maximizing your potential,
35

meeting prospective
partners, 116
men
who won't commit, 135
mind-reading, 50
nagging, 104, 210
dealing with, 211
need for reassurance, 11
neediness
and anxiety, 4
and availability, 75
and controlling behavior,
6
and desperation, 5
and fear of differences, 4
and focus on self, 10
and inability to relax, 12
and inequality in
relationship, 14
and lack of acceptance, 4
and loss of respect, 23
and poor boundaries, 7
and poor social skills, 75
and powerlessness, 14
and premature
commitment, 18
and self torture, 4
as normal, 34
coaching perspective of,
35
connection to trauma, 38
connection with early
loss, 36
identifying, 41
may be learned, 37
origin of, 29
positive aspects of, 1

psychotherapeutic
perspective of, 34
rewarded by anxiety
relief, 18
runs in families, 37
similarity to addictions,
17
test for, 46
usually begins in
childhood, 39
vs. general anxiety, 44
vs. security, 185
who is responsible for, 32
worse as people age, 26
neediness cycle, 25, 27
ending, 192
neediness rejection cycle,
97
needing vs. loving, 156,
163, 192
needy
couples, 15
friends, 216
man vs. needy woman,
72
men vs. women, 26
message example, 71
needy people
are fixers, 84
are initially attractive, 14
attract predators, 118
with needy partners, 63,
168
with secure partners, 15,
64
needy person - caretaker
relationship, 23

needy women cheat
themselves, 133
negative spiral, 201
no contact, 167
no such thing as partial
commitment, 180
non-acceptance, 49
not good enough, 147, 217
oneness relationship, 157
pain
connection to empathy,
xvii
partner
accepting differences of,
51
avoids talking to you, 98
being valuable for, 109
burn out, 24
differences, 4
entitled to be happy, 149
feels burdened, 13
fixing a, 110
importance of matching,
114
is an adult, 175
is responsible for his
behaviors, 187
keeping secrets, 13
needs space, 11, 26
withdrawal, 92
partner's
anger, 203
reaction to jealousy, 145
right to be angry, 177
partnering vs. parenting,
104
partners

being attracted to bad
  ones, 20
disrespectful behavior
  from, 78
not a cure for loneliness,
  114
not a cure for
  unhappiness, 115
not interested in
  listening, 97
real problem of keeping a
  bad one, 21
seeing realistically, 19
think differently, 49
toxic, 18
why they lie, 202
partner's
  defensiveness, 79
  secrecy, 24
personal excellence vs.
  wellness, 35
physical abuse, 19, 182
  responding to, 184
planning a second date, 73
plateaus in progress, 57
player, 64
positive, loving
  environment, 150
post traumatic stress, 38
power of deciding, 188
power struggle, 105
practicing social skills, 77
praise good behavior, 210
predators, 118
pretending to be secure, 75
proactive, 235
productive discussion, 104

professional help
  vs. self help, xv
progress
  signs of, 47
promising
  problem with, 198
promoting sharing, 97
proposing to a man, 137
psychotherapist, 46
psychotherapy, 58
purposes of dating, 73
pursuit mode, 186
questioning, 43
rationalizations, 20
reactive neediness, 39
reactive vs. proactive, 222,
  233
realistic expectations, 217
  importance of, 47
realistic fear, 33
reasons are no excuse, 207
reassurance, 147, 150, 151,
  152, 157
  problem with, 5, 193,
  198
reassurance addiction, 147,
  193
reassurance criticism, 78
  example, 78
reassurance seeking, 5, 43,
  78, 79, 81, 87, 172, 191
reassuring, 150
rebuilding relationships, 17,
  170
reconciling, 24, 164, 166
rejection-avoidance, 96
rejection-result, 96

relationally "grown up", 36
relationally attractive, 114
relationship breaking issue,
    173
relationship bubble, 64
relationship burnout, 7
relationship coach, xiii, xiv,
    46
    vs. counselor, xiv
relationship crisis, 159, 168
relationship cycles, 53
relationship killing issues,
    64
relationship shuffling, 25
repeated explanations, 98
repeatedly defending, 101
resentment, 115
respect, 134, 179
    losing, 173
responding to criticism, 196
responding to financial
    abuse, 182
responding to physical
    abuse, 184
responding to questions, 86
responding to sexual abuse,
    186
responding to verbal abuse,
    178
restraining needy
    behaviors, 51
restraint required in dating,
    70
revenge
    problem with, 179
risk averse, 225
role models, 54, 55, 56

roller coaster relationships,
    17, 105
secretive behavior, 88
secure answer
    example of, 97
secure attachment, 31
secure message example,
    71
secure parenting, 10
secure partners
    attracting, 118
secure person with secure
    partner, 64, 153
secure relationships, 3
seeing people accurately,
    217
self blame, 186
self care, 50
self reassurance, 173
self-assurance, 13
self-esteem, xviii, 22
    increasing, 51
selfish partner, 48
selfishness, 7
self-protection
    vs. protecting the
        relationship, 100
self-upgrade, 162
set yourself up for success,
    234
sexual abuse, 185
    responding to, 186
sharing happiness vs.
    achieving happiness, 167
sharing income and
    expenses, 181
signs